W9-CXT-558

The Cosmos, God and Philosophy

American University Studies

Series V
Philosophy

Vol. 49

PETER LANG
New York · Bern · Frankfurt am Main · Paris

Ralph J. Moore
and Brooke N. Moore

The Cosmos,
God and Philosophy

PETER LANG
New York · Bern · Frankfurt am Main · Paris

Library of Congress Cataloging-in-Publication Data

Moore, Ralph J.
    The cosmos, God, and philosophy / Ralph J. Moore
and Brooke N. Moore.
      p. cm. — (American university studies. Series V,
Philosophy ; vol. 49)
      Bibliography: p.
      1. Religion — Philosophy. 2. God — Proof.
3. Cosmology. I. Moore, Brooke Noel. II. Title.
III. Series: American university studies. Series V,
Philosophy ; vol. 49.
BL51.M679   1989   210 — dc19   88-9448
ISBN 0-8204-0610-4   CIP
ISSN 0739-6392

CIP-Titelaufnahme der Deutschen Bibliothek

Moore, Ralph J.:
The cosmos, God and philosophy / Ralph J.
Moore and Brooke N. Moore. — New York;
Bern; Frankfurt am Main; Paris: Lang, 1988.
  (American University Studies: Ser. 5,
  Philosophy; Vol. 49)
  ISBN 0-8204-0610-4

NE: Moore, Brooke N.:; American University
Studies / 05

Dedicated to the memory of Dorothy Noll Moore
Our Beloved Wife and Mother
Long Departed from Us

Contents

Contents

Preface

This book came to be out of our curiosity as to what should be thought about God and the existence of the universe now that the general picture of the cosmos is so fundamentally and vastly different from that accepted before this century.

There had, of course, in the sixteenth and seventeenth centuries been a previous revolution in the scientific view of the cosmos, in which among other things the earth was dethroned as the center and most important part of the universe, and the universe was conceived as working according to Newtonian mechanics. Thereafter in the nineteenth century revolutionary biological and geological ideas were born and thrived.

Thought about God and about the ultimate cause, explanation and nature of all that there is was profoundly affected by these prior revolutionary changes in the general scientific depiction of that totality. However, there continued to be found empirical justification in the new views of the cosmos for the Judeo-Christian-Mohammedan philosophical belief in the God-Creator. Other religions generally continued their preoccupation with deity or something like it, taking little note of these revolutionary changes in the Western portrayal of the physical universe.

We pursued our curiosity concerning the impact of the twentieth century changed view of the cosmos on philosophical thought about God and the beginning, continuance and nature of the universe by writing this book, intended not only for interested theologians, scientists and philosophers, but for all persons interested in its subject. In Part One we present a general portrayal of the cosmos, that accords with what scientists say about it, and then, guided by this picture, we discuss in Part Two traditional argument concerning the God-Creator hypothesis, noting other possible hypotheses as to the origin, continuance and nature of the universe. Attention in this second part of the book is largely focussed on the Christian view of the Judeo-Christian-Mohammedan God.

The first part of the book, the portrayal of the universe, has been written and it is hoped will be read, with the question always in the back of the mind—what does the existence and evolution and nature of the universe mean with respect to God and alternative ultimate explanations of being and reality.

One of us is a professor of philosophy and the other, his father, is a retired attorney and author and editor of many legal publications. The father approaches the subject from the viewpoint of a jury or a judge trying a case without a jury, and also with the Blaise Pascal outlook that whether or not there is a God or something else basic to everything is necessarily a betting matter, which is something that a verdict of a jury or a finding of fact by a trial court also is in some cases. The son approaches the subject with intent to address it objectively and logically and to govern his personal view of deity accordingly.

Neither of us thinks immortality of human beings is at all likely. Neither thinks ethical living is dependent on belief in God or in immortality of the human soul, though both recognize that this is a difficult issue and that many feel assured of the goodness of their conduct, and so have joy of life in that goodness, only on the assumption that their conduct accords with what they believe is divine proscription. In short, neither of us is predisposed to accept *a priori* proofs of God that assume as a premise that the human soul is immortal or that the reality of ethical values requires the existence of God.

Readers should be aware that we are not scientists. There is always a danger when laymen attempt to state and explain technical matters that what they say will be misleading or incorrect. Nevertheless, it is important for all who are interested in the origin, evolution and nature of the cosmos or in the relationship that these subjects have to the question of God's existence to try to understand the scientific depiction of the universe. We have tried to relate our understanding of that to others in the belief that they may find what we say helpful to them in their efforts to understand it. We hope that errors, whether scientific, philosophical or otherwise, are minimal in what we have written. For all such errors we are fully responsible.

Introduction

Paul said that "Because that which may be known of God is manifest in them; for God hath shewed it unto them. For the invisible things of him from the creation of the world are clearly seen, being understood by the things that are made, even his eternal power and Godhead; so that they are without excuse." (*Romans*, 1: 19,20.)

Newton agreed that we know God "only by his most wise and excellent contrivances of things, and final causes," and he affirmed that "to discourse" of God "from the appearance of things, does certainly belong to natural philosophy." (*Mathematical Principles of Natural Philosophy*, Book III, General Scholium.) These "appearances of things" indicated to Newton that "there is a Being incorporeal, living, intelligent, omnipresent, who in infinite space (as it were in his sensory) sees the things themselves intimately, and thoroughly perceives them, and comprehends them wholly by their immediate presence to himself." According to Newton, because we apprehend only the appearances or images of things, "every true step made in this philosophy brings us not immediately to the knowledge of the First Cause." Nevertheless, he held, each true step brings us nearer to this knowledge, "and on that account is to be highly valued." (*Optics*, Book III.)

The quest by reason, through the appearance of things, for God or for the probability or improbability or the possibility or impossibility of his existence, and the quest by reason, through appearances, for the origin and functioning of the universe, cannot honestly stop with Newton and Newtonian physics and astronomy. Must not every Christian or other believer who is aware, though perhaps only vaguely, of spacetime curvature, the Big Bang and the expanding universe; of the infinity or finitude of the universe being unknown though dependent on whether it is open or closed; of the hundreds of billions of galaxies, each containing tens or hundreds of billions of stars; of the sun and other stars being thermonuclear powerhouse supplying light and energy to the galaxies and to the universe; of the fundamental constituents, forces and functioning of matter-energy; of neutron stars, black holes, pulsars and quasars; and of all that is known and of all that still is mysterious about the universe, the atom and particles—must not this believer, if he or she is a truly thinking person, seek to relate his or her theology, that originated and matured before the twentieth century, to the scientific cosmology of this century?

Must not religious philosophers, be they theists, atheists or agnostics, also construct their religious philosophy, not only on the thought of bygone centuries, but also on twentieth century cosmology? Indeed, must not all thinking persons, concerned with whether or not there is a God and with how the universe came to be and is as it is, inform their opinion in the matter with what in this century has become known about the universe and matter-energy?

This book endeavors to do precisely this, what every believer, philosopher or person who thinks about God being or not being and about the origin and nature of the universe must do—that is, relate his or her thinking, not only to the theology and religious philosophy of the past and of today, but also to contemporary scientific cosmology.

Thus, the book adheres to the Pauline and Newtonian prescription, to look for God in his works—that is, it must be added, if he exists. The book inquires, not only into the possible existence of God, but also into the possible origin and ultimate reality otherwise of the universe, through a layman's look at things in the universe as they are depicted by modern science. It also relates this inquiry to what has been thought about God in relationship to the universe both before Paul and after Paul and Newton.

Accordingly, in this book we endeavor (1) to present a comprehensive depiction of the universe, guided by modern science; (2) to set forth classical and modern concepts of God and proofs and arguments as to his existence and creation and sustenance of the universe; and (3) to relate the former discussion to the latter.

The cosmos has an interiority that primarily is the concern of physics and an exteriority that primarily is the concern of astronomy. The interiority may also be viewed as the microscopic or the subatomic part of the cosmos, and correspondingly its exteriority may be viewed as the macroworld or its supra-atomic part. The book presents a general picture both of the interiority and of the exteriority of the cosmos.

Inevitably, in discussing God and the cosmos in the light of modern cosmology, we consider terrestrial life and its origin, development, functioning and role in the universe, including humanity's responsibility for the survival and destiny of that life, including its own.

The book is not a sociological study of how modern cosmology has in fact affected what people think or believe religiously. It is interested instead in the philosophical impact of modern cosmology on thought, religious and otherwise, about God and on rival hypotheses as to how the universe came to be, continues, and is what it is.

In short, the book is a tying together of thought about God and modern cosmology, from a critical philosophical perspective.

PART ONE

THE COSMOS

1

Searching the Cosmos for God and Truth

In this part of the book we offer a general portrayal of the universe, guided by contemporary cosmology.

By "cosmology" we mean "scientific cosmology," the scientific view of the origin, evolution, structure, composition and functioning of the physical universe and all its parts, including people and their brains and biological structures. Often cosmology is viewed as a branch of philosophy that considers, among other things, the meaning and nature of the more fundamental and universal concepts in terms of which we think about the physical world, including (for example) causation, particularity, change, succession, number, order, force and law. What distinguishes scientific from philosophical cosmology is that the former primarily is concerned with descriptions, explanations and theories of the universe that are based on observation and experimentation. It essentially is empirical inquiry. Thus, when we use "cosmology" as meaning scientific cosmology we refer to the scientific view of the cosmos based on scientific empirical inquiry.

This first part of the book, as readers will promptly observe, is largely descriptive. It is indeed our intent to describe the universe generally but with enough detail to make the general picture meaningful. We are metaphysical and epistemological realists. That is, we believe that a universe of physical objects and processes exists outside the mind, and that knowledge of this universe is possible. Given these premises, we turn to the physical sciences for the most comprehensive, detailed and coherent account of the universe, and present in this section our understanding of the universe as portrayed by cosmology.

Western religious doctrine since Galileo has found itself frequently in conflict with scientific findings, which in time it largely has accepted, though reluctantly and slowly. This eventual acceptance, however, has been mostly in religious belief concerning the nature and structure of matter, the universe, the earth and animal and plant life, and, perhaps to a lesser extent, the possible origin and evolution of the universe, earth and its inhabitants.

In neither the West nor in the East has science much affected basic concepts and proof of, and belief in, God or an immaterial reality that created or explains and governs human beings and the cosmos and the destiny of both. This is not to say that science has not caused much religious defection, against which religions have had to contend.

Science, also, certainly has not destroyed, though it has somewhat diminished, belief in human immortality.

Nor have fringe religious and quasi-religious organizations, arising in recent times in recoil from perceived abuses in established religions and science, departed from basic concepts of a God that created and sustains people and the universe. Many of these fringe organizations disdain scientific truth and instead embrace pseudoscience and superstition, and blindly follow (and enrich) leaders who pretend to be God or his disciples or to be founts of revelation of religious and secular wisdom. Usually, however, these groups, like established religions, envision God or an immaterial reality as causing or explaining everything, as offering a better way of life and as rewarding those who comply with prescribed ways of behavior and belief with heaven, nirvana, or the like.

Established religions, as well as these new societies, not only continue to believe in a deity that somehow differs from the ordinary stuff of which the universe and our bodies are constituted, but also generally continue to believe in a soul and a spirit-world or something similar that also somehow differs from ordinary matter and from our bodies.

It is with philosophical justification for this essential core of religious belief in a deity, which core is old and has survived scientific enlightment, that we are concerned in Part Two. But here in Part One our intent is to offer a general description of the universe, guided by what science now has to say about it. This description will frequently employ metaphor. Thus, in our basic metaphor we treat the universe as a four-dimensional loom of spacetime on which the expanding four-dimensional fabric of matter and of radiation is being woven by the basic interactions of particles: the gravitational, the electromagnetic, the strong and the weak.

As we look out into the universe we do not see it as it is now. Instead, we now see it as it was when the light or other electromagnetic radiation that we receive left its source. With the aid of telescopes and other receptors for this natural communication, especially with the help of the cosmic red shift, we can take a voyage of the senses and intellect outward in space and backward in time, perhaps to the inception of the universe in the Big Bang. Thus, in the first chapters of this part of the book we discuss the red shift (cosmology's analogue to Jacob's ladder), distancepast markers and the Big Bang.

Next we describe the loom of spacetime and the fabric of matter and of radiation being woven upon it. Then in several chapters we are concerned with the atom and the subatomic world. In following chapters we portray the macroworld of galaxies, stars, the sun, planets, nebulue and other astronomical objects. In the last chapter of Part One we discuss earth, humanity and life and intelligence on earth, and possibly elsewhere in the universe. Throughout Part One we comment now and then on what our cosmic portrayal evidences or means as to God or something else as the ultimate explanation of the cosmos.

2

The Red-Shift Ladder

Jacob's ladder, seen by him in a dream, reached up to heaven from the earth. The red-shift ladder is one on which we mentally can climb down into distancepast to the origin of the universe in the Big Bang. Most scientists agree that probably the universe began in, and is, the Big Bang, about which modern cosmology has much to say.

We refer to "distancepast" by the one word, because doing so is consistent with referring to spacetime by one word, as is done by Einstein and modern cosmologists in conceiving of spacetime as a continuity. It is correct, of course, to speak of distance and the past separately, and often it is necessary to do so. "Distancepast" emphasizes that when we look away from us, at stars or galaxies, at the sun or moon, at houses across the street or at our fingers, we observe them all both at a distance and in the past. This, of course, is because we observe them by light, which, though speedy, takes time to travel from them to us. So, we also refer to things as "pastdistant" or "distantpast."

"Spacetime" and "distancepast" also describe the gap between events, conceived as points in spacetime or in distancepast. The word "events," of course, also has other connotations, such as an automobile accident, a human birth or a political election. Events, in these other connotations, are comprised by the "weaving" of matter on points on the "loom of spacetime," as discussed in subsequent chapters.

We speak of climbing "down" rather than "up" the red-shift ladder into the distancepast toward the origin of the universe even though telescopes are pointed up toward the sky. We do so because toward the beginning of the Big Bang (the universe) is more aptly called "down" rather than "up". If we had a ladder by which we could reach the center of the earth, we would speak of going "down" that ladder. The universe may be likened to a ball insofar as it is an unfurling of matter, radiation and spacetime from the origin or source of the Big Bang and insofar as the origin or source is analogous to the center of a ball. Thus, we think of climbing (mentally) down into the distancepast to the origin of the universe. Parenthetically, the comparison of the universe to a ball is imperfect and most misleading because, as we shall see, unlike a ball, the universe has neither external surface nor center. Nor is there any outside, or anything outside, the universe.

How much of the distancepast will we be able to observe, when and if we have instrumentation to observe it back to the beginning of the Big Bang? We can never observe that part of the distancepast, the light from which has already passed the earth unless we have done so as it reached the earth.

Telescopy, optical, radio and other, enables us to observe down into the distancepast, but it is what is called "the red shift" that most importantly helps us to orient ourselves in the great distancepast and mentally to climb down into it toward the beginning of the Big Bang, knowing where we are as we go, with reference both to the beginning of the Big Bang and to where we physically are now. In short, by the red shift we know how far down in the great distancepast observed galaxies, quasars, stars or other objects are from us and how far they are up in distancepast from the beginning of the Big Bang.

Thus, we view the red shift as in effect a ladder by which mentally we can descend to the inception of the universe in the Big Bang. Indeed, we mentally can go up and down this ladder to the beginning of the cosmic explosion (and perhaps to God?) much as the angels in Jacob's dream went down and up the ladder reaching from the earth to heaven. But what is the red shift?

The red shift is the shift of lines and the continuous spread of the spectrum of light and of all other electromagnetic radiation toward the red end of the spectrum. The red shift is caused by the lengthening of the wavelength of the light or other radiation, which in turn results, in regard to what is known as the "Doppler effect," from relative motion or regression of the source of light or radiation from the observer.

A blue shift toward the blue end of the spectrum is due to the shortening of the wavelength of light or other radiation caused, in regard to the Doppler effect, by relative motion of the source toward the observer.

The red and blue shifts of light and other radiation, insofar as they are Doppler effects, are due to relative motion of the source and the observer in spacetime. There are, however, two other kinds of red and blue shifts of light and other radiation, *not involving* relative motion. These are called the "gravitational" and "cosmological" (or "cosmic") shifts.

Decrease of gravitational force on light as it leaves the earth or another astronomical body causes a lengthening of the wavelength of the light and hence a red shift in its spectrum. This shift is a gravitational and not a Doppler effect.

Expansion or contraction of space (and thus of the universe) directly affects the wavelength of light or other radiation, without regard to relative motion, and this causes respectively a red or blue shift. This is a cosmic and *not* a Doppler effect. As light or other radiation passes through expanding or contracting spacetime, its wavelength respectively stretches or shrinks. While the universe expands generally, in certain regions and localities, as near a galactic or stellar black hole, it is contracting.

Red and blue shifts of astronomical objects generally are due to a composite of Doppler, gravitational and cosmic effects. A Doppler blue shift (caused by relative motion of the object and earth toward each other) may be greater than a red shift caused, jointly or severally, by cosmic expansion and by decrease of gravitational force; and the net composite shift will then be blue. For example, light from the Andromeda galaxy M31 has a blue shift.

The farther away that the source of light or other radiation is from us, the less its red shift is Doppler, due to relative motion from us, and the more it is cosmic due to expansion of the universe.

Edwin Hubble, Milton Humason and other astronomers, in discovering that far-distant galaxies are receding from us and from each other with increasing velocities and that the universe is expanding, used the red shift, assuming it to be wholly Doppler, which it is not as is now realized by astronomers. To assume that the red shift of any light or other radiation from anywhere in spacetime is due wholly to a Doppler effect results in a false mental picture of the universe, one in which galaxies are hurtling through space with velocities approaching the speed of light, though in truth they are relatively fixed in spacetime; in which the universe expands at a constant rate from its beginning, for all time and everywhere, which is not true; in which space terminates abruptly at the surface of a sphere, beyond which the velocity of expansion would exceed the speed of light, though in truth the universe has no external surface; and in which we live at the center of that sphere, though in truth anywhere in the universe is as central as anywhere else in it as discussed in Chapter 5.

The red shift of light or other radiation from an astronomical object enables us to determine approximately how fast it is receding from us and how much its speed is accelerating, and to determine also how far it is from us, and how far it is from the beginning of the Big Bang, in the distancepast. Thus, the red shift is like a ruler down into the distancepast. It is also like a ladder that is ruled by its rungs so as to make it a ruler. On it mentally, we know how far we are in lightyears from its top (the present) and from its bottom (the beginning of the Big Bang), and we know how fast we are climbing down and the acceleration or deceleration of the speed of our descent.

This correlation of the red shift to the distancepast and to the recessional speed and acceleration or deceleration of astronomical objects has been determined by observation and comparison of them and by the utilization of various distancepast markers discussed in the ensuing chapter.

It has been determined by observation that the red shift is proportional to the recessional velocities of galaxies; the faster that they recede, the greater is their red shift. Accordingly, recessional velocities of galaxies and quasars can be determined by their red shifts in comparison with the known red shifts and known velocities of other galaxies, whose red shifts and velocities have been determined as noted by other means. The recessional velocities of quasars likewise can be determined by their red shifts and comparison with known red shifts and known velocities of some galaxies. The recessional velocities of quasars is enormous, in many instances being more than ninety percent of the speed of light.

The distancepast, as well as the recessional velocities, of galaxies and quasars can be ascertained by the red shift of their light and other radiation, though with some uncertainty which increases with distancepast. This ascertainment of distancepast of galaxies and quasars is possible because their recessional velocities multiplied by the Hubble constant (or term) is proportional to their distancepast from us.

The Hubble constant is a measure of the rate of expansion of the universe. Because its precise value is undetermined, the nearness of galaxies and quasars in calculable only approximately. Accordingly, we are somewhat uncertain, when we mentally are far down on the red-shift ladder, as to just how far we are from our physical "now" and how far we are from the beginning of the Big Bang. The uncertainty, as said, increases with the increase of distancepast.

Therefore, subject to some uncertainty as to great distancepast, the red shift is, as noted before, a ruler measuring the depth of the distancepast as well as a ruled ladder into it, on which we mentally can descend and ascend. That is, it is a measure of distancepast from us to observed galaxies and quasars, and of their recessional speed and acceleration. Also, the red shift, subject to that uncertainty, is a calendar of the universe in lightyears and years ago.

The red shift is expressed as the ratio between the increase of wavelength and the wavelength of light or other electromagnetic radiation when it was emitted by an object in the distancepast. In other words, it is expressed as the increase divided by the original wavelength. Thus, for example, it may be expressed as .1, 1, 2, 3, and so forth. How is the wavelength of the light or radiation at the time it was emitted determined? The light or radiation tells us what kinds of atoms emitted it, and that tells us what the wavelength was at the time of emission. It is assumed that atoms are the same everywhere in the universe. This is an instance of starlight language which tells us very much about the universe, as is more fully discussed in Chapter 16.

At the bottom of the red-shift ladder, where the explosion of the universe began, shall we find God, and also theologians and believers already there, welcoming us? Or shall we find evidence on our descent and at the bottom of the ladder, tending to corroborate, or to refute, traditional proofs of the existence of God and of his creation of the universe? We think that anything optically observed or mentally ascertained on optical and mental descent into the distancepast or at the beginning of the universe in the Big Bang will be, as evidence for or against God's existence and divine creation, a matter for subjective appraisal, though some will regard it as objective proof. Our personal views are stated in concluding chapters.

3

Distancepast Markers and Rulers

Distancepast markers and rulers, in addition to the red shift, have been found and are used by science.

When we look down into the distancepast even with the most powerful telescopes, the stars and galaxies outside the Local Group appear only as points of light. Until there was some knowledge of how far in the distancepast these points of light were, not much could be known as to what they were. When, however, some knowledge of their distancepast was acquired, that knowledge together with knowledge of their apparent brightness and of the spectra of their light and knowledge of the inside of the atom were used to calculate and determine their intrinsic brightness, size, mass, composition, temperature, color, spin, motions and many other of their physical properties and conditions. Furthermore, knowledge of their distancepast and the red shift of their spectra led to the realization that there were hundreds of billions of galaxies outside the Milky Way and that the universe was far, far vaster than had been thought, that it was expanding and that it probably originated in the Big Bang.

What are some of these distancepast markers and rulers? The determination of distancepast of the moon, sun, and planets was comparatively easy, and of the nearest stars not very difficult; but the determination of distancepast of the farther stars, galaxies and quasars has been most difficult, the difficulty enlarging with increasing distancepast. Various techniques have been used in making these determinations, and certain useful distancepast markers have been established.

Distancepast of the sun, moon and planets

Parallax

This is demonstrated by looking at one's finger at arm's length, first with one eye and then with the other closed. The finger shifts against the background, the displacement, i.e., the difference in direction of the two lines of observation, constituting an angle.

Distancepast to the moon, sun and planets has been determined by their parallax, i.e., their angular displacement against the background of the stars, when viewed simultaneously from two different places on the surface of the earth. Knowledge of the parallax and of the distance between the two places (a base line) makes the determination trigometrically easy.

The base line in lightyears or lightminutes gives a spacetime determination. In miles it gives a spacetime determination subject to inherent error due to ignoring the travel time of light.

Diurnal parallax

The parallax of the moon, sun or a planet, when viewed from the opposite ends of a base line established by the earth's spin, is a diurnal parallax.

Determination by laser beam and radar

More accurate determination than by diurnal parallax, indeed extremely accurate determination, of the moon's distancepast has been made by laser beam reflection from reflectors left on the moon in manned and unmanned flight. Similarly, extremely accurate determination of the distancepast of the planets has been made by radar, i.e., by bouncing radio waves from them, which return to earth. Venus usually has been used for this purpose because, of all the planets, it is most suitable therefor, as it makes a closer approach than the others to the earth and has a large surface. Its distancepast, thus determined with great precision, makes the distancepast of the sun and of the other planets calculable with near-perfect precision, because the relative distancepasts of the sun and planets are known almost exactly by calculations based on their orbits and the law of gravitation. Radar cannot be used directly in determining the distancepast of the sun.

Distancepast determination of the closer stars— heliocentric parallax

The diurnal parallax of the stars is either indiscernible or too neglible to be of any use in ascertaining their distancepast. However, to determine the distancepast of the nearer stars, heliocentric parallax can be used.

The base line provided by the diameter of the earth's orbit is $185\frac{1}{2}$ million miles (or $1\frac{2}{3}$ lightminutes), which is two AU (astronomical units), or twice the average distance between the earth and the sun. Heliocentric parallax (one-half the angle of displacement of the star as viewed from opposite ends of the orbital diameter) and the orbital radius (equivalent of one AU) are employed in a simple trigometric determination of the star's distancepast.

Heliocentric stellar parallax can be used accurately only for stellar distancepast of not more than three hundred lightyears, and for only about eight thousand stars.

Distancepast determination of stars 300–33,000 lightyears away

Mean or statistical parallax

Beyond 300 lightyears and up to 1500 lightyears, the distancepast of stars can be determined by mean or statistical parallax. This is the parallax that a group of stars, whose distancepast is approximately the same, and whose proper motion (across the line of sight) averages zero, has because of their apparent motion in the opposite direction to the direction of the sun's proper motion (in which the observer participates). Because of the sun's proper motion there is a displacement of the selected group of stars against the background of the other stars. An analogous parallax is that of low hills or buildings against a mountainous background as an observer travels by them in an automobile or a train. They seem to move slowly in the direction opposite to that of the observer.

Within a year the displacement of the stars in the selected group is appreciable and can be used with the known distance that the sun has travelled in proper motion as a base line for triangular determination of the distancepast of stars in the group. One mode of selection of the group is to take stars of the same spectral class and of the same magnitude in one section of the sky. These will have approximately the same distancepast from the earth. Star classes and magnitudes are discussed in Chapter 16.

A group of stars whose distancepast has been determined in this manner (or any other manner, for that matter) can be used as a distancepast marker and as a standard candle for determining the distancepast of other stars of the same intrinsic brightness by their apparent brightness.

Moving cluster method

The Hyades, an open cluster of stars, is moving away from us with a velocity determinable by its red shift. Because of this it has a measurable change of apparent angular size with time. By its velocity and change of apparent angular size in a given time its distancepast has been calculated by the equation: r = vta/a' − a, where r is distancepast, t the time interval, a' is one half the angular size at the first observation and a is one half the angular size at the second observation. The distancepast is 140 lightyears.

The Hyades, its distancepast determined, is a standard candle by which distancepast to all open clusters, not too faint for measurement of the properties of their Main Sequence stars, is ascertainable. Main Sequence stars are discussed in Chapter 16. The distancepast ascertainment is made thus.

H-R diagrams, which are explained in Chapter 16, are constructed for open clusters whose distancepast is unknown. Matching these diagrams with H-R diagrams for the Hyades or other open clusters whose distancepast already has been determined shows (1) the apparent brightness along the Main Sequence of the cluster whose distancepast is being determined and (2) the intrinsic brightness along the Main Sequence of the Hyades or other standard-candle cluster; and upon this data the distancepast of the former is calculable by the inverse square law of light, discussed subsequently. Basic to the calculation is the assumption that all open clusters have just about the same Main Sequence.

The distancepast of open clusters is determinable in this manner up to 2,600 lightyears.

Spectroscopic parallax

The distancepast of stars as far away as 33,000 lightyears can be determined by what is called their "spectroscopic parallax" or the "spectroscopic distance method." It is based on the simple principle that the distancepast of a farther star can be determined by comparing its apparent brightness with the apparent brightness of a nearer star whose intrinsic brightness is the same as that of the farther star. Similarly, if two candles are equally bright in fact (inherently), but one appears brighter than the other, the latter obviously is farther away.

The rule is that the brightness of either a candle or a star, or of anything, apparently diminishes with the square of the distance. This is the inverse square law for light, which relates apparent to intrinsic brightness by the equation: m − M = 5 log d − 5, where m is apparent magnitude, M absolute magnitude and d distancepast in parsecs or lightyears.

In order to discover the distancepast of a star on this simple principle by the spectroscopic method or, in effect, by its spectroscopic parallax, an H-R diagram based on many stars is used. First the spectral type or luminosity class of the star are determined from its spectrum. Then by reference to the H-R diagram the intrinsic brightness (absolute magnitude) of the star is ascertained. The apparent brightness is found photometrically. On the apparent and intrinsic brightness the distancepast in parsecs or lightyears is calculated.

From 33,000 to 13 million lightyears

Variable stars

The determination of the distancepast of certain variable stars, discussed in Chapter 16, by the relation of the period of the variability of their light to their apparent and intrinsic brightness has been one of the most important means of establishing them as distancepast markers by which (1) the distancepast of other stars and galaxies can be determined and (2) scaling the universe has been possible.

The fact that apparent brightness of certain variable stars is proportional to the length of the period of their variability was established by Henrietta Leavitt as the result of her examination over many years of photographs of stars in the Magellenic Clouds, in which she discovered over two thousand variable stars. The variable stars in which she found the relationships were those with short periods between a few days and a few weeks, which came to be known as Cepheids because their light curves (showing light variations during a certain period) resembled those of the star Delta Cephei.

Because these variables in the Magellenic Clouds are all approximately at the same distancepast from the earth, it was concluded that their intrinsic brightness as well as their apparent brightness is proportional to the length of their light variation period. The longer their period, the brighter they look and the brighter they really are.

It happens that many Cepheids in our galaxy are close enough so that their distancepast has been determined by geocentric, statistical or spectroscopic parallax. Accordingly, a scale of their intrinsic brightness to the length of their periods was constructed. This scale is used to determine the intrinsic brightness of more distantpast Cepheids in galaxies out to thirteen million lightyears.

Both the apparent and the intrinsic brightness of the more distant Cepheids being ascertained, their distancepast is calculable by the inverse square law of light, discussed above.

RR Lyrae and other kinds of variables are similarly used for distancepast determination. RR Lyrae are found throughout the Milky Way and so constitute distancepast markers and standard candles throughout the galaxy. They are older (Population II) stars and occur with frequency in globular clusters and for that reason sometimes are called "cluster variables." Population II stars and globular clusters are discussed in Chapter 16.

In the Milky Way variables abound along the spiral arms and in the globular clusters, and occur throughout our galaxy. Harlow Shapley in 1916–17, observing variables, which he thought were Cepheids but which turned out to be RR Lyrae, in the globular clusters, which ring our galaxy and occur elsewhere in it, and using the luminosity-period relationship of variables, calculated the distancepast of the globular clusters. From their distancepast he inferred that the Milky Way is ten times larger than had been thought, though later he reduced that appraisal to conform with the then current consensus of opinion as to the galaxy's size.

From the concentration of the globular clusters in one part of the sky in the direction of Sagittarius and from the apparent ringing of the galaxy by the globulars, Shapley thought it obvious and announced that the sun is not the center of the galaxy. He dethroned it. If the sun were the center, the globular clusters would appear more evenly distributed. It has now definitely been established that the center of the galaxy is in the direction of Sagittarius.

Cepheid variables can be used in determining distancepast and as standard candles as far out (as deep down in the distancepast) as thirteen million lightyears, a vast advance from 33,000 lightyears, the maximum distancepast practically determinable by spectroscopic parallax. They can be observed in the great Andromeda galaxy, which is 2.2 million lightyears away, and in galaxies beyond it to a distancepast of thirteen million lightyears, but beyond that distancepast variables are presently unobservable.

Beyond visible cepheids

Distancepast determination becomes increasingly difficult beyond thirteen million lightyears away. Nevertheless, there are objects luminous enough to be optically observable out to many billion lightyears away, whose distancepast is ascertainable by relating their apparent brightness or their apparent angular size to the apparent brightness or the apparent angular size of other objects of equal intrinsic brightness or equal intrinsic angular size, close enough to have had by some means their distancepast in lightyears and its relationship to their apparent brightness or to their apparent angular size established. The means by which these properties of the other objects may have been established may have been their heliocentric, statistical or spectroscopic parallax or may have been the agency of variable stars.

The principles involved are simple. The farther away an object or another object of the same luminosity is from an observer, the dimmer it will appear to him, as previously discussed. Likewise, the farther away an object or another object of the same linear size is from the observer, the smaller its apparent angular size will appear to him. The apparent angular size is inversely proportional to the distancepast.

Thus, if object A and object B are equally bright in fact, that is, intrinsically, and A is one thousand lightyears away but B appears to be $\frac{1}{100}$ as bright as A, then B is ten thousand times as far away as A. Or, if A and B are of the same angular size and A is one thousand lightyears away but appears to have twice the angular size of B, then B is two thousand lightyears away.

Farther objects whose distancepast in lightyears is established by comparison of their apparent brightness with the apparent brightness of nearer objects intrinsically as bright as they themselves are can themselves be used as standard candles for the measurement, in the same or some other way, of the distancepast of other objects of still greater distancepast. Likewise, far away objects whose distancepastin lightyears is established by comparison of their apparent angular size with the apparent angular size of nearer objects of equal linear size can themselves be used as standard rulers for still more distantpast objects.

Beyond 200 million lightyears, except for ScI galaxies and supernovae discussed in Chapter 16, only the red shift can provide an approximation of the distancepast of observed objects: galaxies, protogalaxies and quasars. It can do this in lightyears by being calibrated with standard candles or standard rulers whose distancepast in lightyears has been established in some mode. The red shift ladder overlaps all distancepast markers and rulers since it reaches from the earth to the most distant light or radiation observable. In practice it generally is used to determine distancepast only beyond where that can be more accurately determined in other ways.

Quasars are the most distantpast of observable objects, but their approximate distancepast can be established only by the red shift in their spectra. Reasons for this, among others, are the wide dispersion of the wavelengths and the irregular variability of their light. Quasars are discussed in Chapter 16.

Novae and supernovae

On the basis of the velocity of expansion and the increase of size over a period of years of the diffusion of gas and debris expelled in a nova or supernovae explosion, the distancepast of the exploding stars can be measured out to $32\frac{1}{2}$ lightyears in the case of novae and out to thirteen billion lightyears in the case of supernovae. Accordingly, novae, insofar as they are observable, can be used as determiners of the distancepast of stars in our galaxy and of the distancepast of other galaxies in which they occur, and they occur regularly in all galaxies. The same is true of supernovae, except that they occur very infrequently, their occurrence in the Milky Way, for example, being only once in every two hundred years. Nova and supernovae are discussed in Chapter 16.

Query

Is it divinely or naturally providential, or has it been inevitable because of the original mix of the Big Bang, or is it merely by chance, that the universe has constituents, forces, processes and laws by which the distancepast from us of all things observed can be ascertained by us with considerable accuracy; and that the mind of the human being has evolved out of star dust, so that it can make these tremendous determinations and construct for itself its amazingly true picture of the geography of the Milky Way and of the universe?

4

The Little Bomb and the Big Bang

The "Little Bomb" is our name for the dimensionless singularity or almost dimensionless something from which, in the opinion of most astronomers, the Big Bang came. In this singularity or minuteness all the matter and energy in our enormous physical universe, with its trillions of stars and intergalactic clouds, all its radiation and all its macroscopic and microscopic things, were jampacked together and held by the crush of gravity in a state of protomatter-energy or "ylem," as George Gamow has named the original infinitely dense stuff of the universe.

What was the Little Bomb like? It was like a black hole, and even more like a white hole. Black holes, discussed in a later chapter probably exist and are the result of self-gravitational collapse of giant stars. White holes are the opposite of black holes; they are singularities spewing out matter-energy. There is no evidence that they exist, but the Little Bomb is certainly what a white hole would be like.

Some scientists refrain from calling the Little Bomb a dimensionless singularity. Instead, they refer to it as a "dense mass," "infinite density," an "infinite dense state," "a very dense and hot state," "a small, unbelievably dense ball," or the like. If it existed, it was the initial item, the original state. It was that which exploded in the Big Bang, the explosion with which our universe began, and with which spacetime and matter-energy came into being.

The Big Bang is still exploding and is our expanding universe. The Milky Way is a minute fragment of spacetime and of matter-energy, riding the blast and being carried farther and farther apart from most of the other galaxies. Our solar system, in turn, is only a speck in the Milky Way, and our earth hardly a speck in the solar system.

However, the term, "Big Bang," is a half-misnomer and is most misleading. The "explosion" was not outward into space, and it had no duration in external time, because all space and time were and are within it. One should not visualize it as like a dynamite or atomic explosion, blasting matter, radiation and shock waves out into the atmosphere or into space. Indeed, one should refrain entirely from visualizing it from an external viewpoint. We can look into distancepast, using optical, radio and other radiation telescopes in any direction, as any direction is toward the source, and unmistakably see that the explosion is continuing or, in other words, that the universe is expanding. But it is a continuing explosion without an external surface or edge and without an exterior.

What caused the Little Bomb to explode into the Big Bang? What overcame the crushing grip of gravity, with such tremendous force that spacetime, carrying matter-energy, is expanding with so much velocity that there may be insufficient mass-energy in the explosion to give gravity enough strength finally to stop the expansion and cause spacetime with matter-energy to collapse back into a dimensionless or almost dimensionless minuteness? No one knows why the Little Bomb went off, and many astronomers believe that it is impossible to know, even by traces (as apparently there are none), what transpired in the Big Bang before 10^{-43} seconds after zero time (when it began).

Did the Big Bang really occur? Most astronomers and physicists think that it did. Indeed, theoretical and observational evidence confirm this beyond a reasonable doubt.

Einstein's theory of general relativity predicts and observational evidence establishes clearly that the universe is expanding. That necessarily implies that previously it was smaller, denser and hotter, and that, if the expansion has continued long enough, the universe was at one time a dimensionless singularity or an almost dimensionless minuteness, that is, in either case, a Little Bomb. The observational evidence indicates beyond a reasonable doubt that the expansion has continued that long. The observational evidence further requires the conclusion, beyond a reasonable doubt, that the expansion like that of an explosion was tremendously rapid as it began and has been steadily slowing down since then.

Einstein did not at first perceive, and he long resisted, the prediction of his general relativity equations that the universe was expanding. He abhorred the implication that the universe might have had a beginning. He finally admitted, after there was no doubt that the universe is expanding, that his theory of general relativity predicted it, and shortly before his death he conceded that the universe had a beginning.

After Einstein's equations were published in 1917, William de Sitter, a Dutch astronomer, Alexander Friedmann, a Russian mathematician and Georges Lemaitre, a Belgian priest and astronomer, respectively at different times announced solutions to Einstein's general relativity equations, indicating that the universe is expanding. Vesto Melvin

Slipher, an American astronomer, in 1913 observed, incidentally to another quest, that some nearby galaxies were receding from us at enormous speeds, up to two million miles per hour.

Lemaitre probably is the first who thought of an explosion-beginning of the universe, though he called the beginning the "primeval atom," which he thought contained all the matter of the universe and exploded, dispersing the matter into space in outward-moving galaxies. Until the late 1940's the explosion theory had some acceptance, but it encountered difficulty in that the Hubble constant, the measure of expansion of the universe, resulted in its apparently being younger than the estimated age of the solar system. From the late 1940's until 1965 the steady-state theory of an everlasting universe expanding because of slow but continuous accretion of hydrogen out of nothing had wide acceptance.

The explosion theory, nevertheless, stayed alive, and in 1952 and thereafter revised estimates that distances of galaxies were much greater than previously thought, so that the original value assigned the Hubble constant was reduced, indicated that the age of the universe is sufficient to be consistent with the explosion theory.

Even while the steady-state theory was becoming widely accepted, George Gamow and his associates, Ralph Alpher and Robert Herman, as well as others, continued investigation of the explosion theory, calling the Little Bomb the "Big Squeeze." About this time the name, "Big Bang," for the explosion took over. Gamow and his associates predicted that radiation from the hot Big Bang must have survived until now, cooled between five and fifty degrees Kelvin. Their prediction was forgotten, but over a decade later J.E. Peebles made the same prediction and maintained that the radiation might be detectable.

Then, in 1965 Arno Penzias and Robert Wilson of Bell Telephone Laboratories, while working on a communication satellite project, discovered a radio-receptive radiation always coming from everywhere in the sky with a wavelength of seven centimeters, indicative of a temperature of three degrees Kelvin. They had discovered the predicted left-over radiation of the early stage of the Big Bang! For their discovery they were awarded in 1978 the Nobel Prize in physics. Because of this discovery and of evidence of recession of galaxies from each other most astronomers and physicists now think that most probably there was Big-Bang birth of the universe, fifteen to twenty billion years ago. They do not know, and many of them think that it never can be known, how that birth occurred, whether from a Little Bomb or Big Squeeze or the like, or from nothing or from a God-Creator if there be one.

The discovery of the background radiation was the death-knell for the steady-state theory for most scientists, because they thought that theory could not explain the phenomenon.

Evidence of the probability of the Big Bang birth of the universe includes the background radiation; the expansion of the universe from the distancepast for as far as it can be telescopically observed; the gradual deceleration of the expansion; the totally different structure and much greater density and heat of the universe in the distancepast; the correspondence of the observed quantity of helium in our galaxy today with its formation in a Big Bang; and the observed ratio of deuterium to hydrogen in our galaxy.

How long will the Big Bang continue? That is, how long will the universe expand? The answer depends on which is stronger: the gravity of the universe or the initial force of the Big Bang. It's a question of the velocity of the expansion, determined by the initial blasting force, whatever it was, equalling or surpassing the escape velocity necessary to overcome the gravity exerted by all matter-energy in the universe. Presently, it appears that there is far too little matter-energy in the universe to stop and reverse its expansion. Accordingly, the expansion seemingly will continue forever, that is, the universe appears to be open and infinite. If so, the galaxies, forever flying apart, will become slag and cinders as all stars completely die.

Recently, however, more and more matter-energy, previously hidden, unknown or unsuspected, is being discovered or suspected to be in intergalactic space, in the haloes of galaxies and of stars and elsewhere. The total matter-energy in nutrinos and black holes is unknown, at least with any certainty. Possibly, therefore, there may be enough matter-energy in the universe to exert enough gravitational force upon the expansion to halt and reverse it, so that the universe will contract back into a singularity or minuteness, like the Little Bomb from which it exploded. If this is the case, the universe is finite and closed.

The Little Bomb singularity or minuteness, out of which the Big Bang came, may have been, if the present universe collapses back into a singularity or minuteness, the singularity or minuteness into which a previous universe collapsed; and there may be a succession of universes, expanding and contracting from singularity or minuteness to singularity or minuteness without beginning or end. That this is the case is held by the oscillating universe theory. However, there is no trace whatsoever, that has been found, and probably there will never be, of a universe that preceded our own. Any such trace would have been destroyed in the infinite heat of the first instant of the Big Bang.

How do the Little Bomb and the Big Bang affect traditional concepts and proof of the Christian-Jewish-Mohammedan God? Although the second half of this book is devoted to this question and related questions, it is obvious that the Big Bang theory agrees with the Biblical account of creation insofar as they both signify that the universe had a beginning.

Is the scientist, when and if he successfully climbs down the distance-past ladder to reach the Little Bomb, to there find God, together with theologians of recent and past ages gathered about it, at a safe distance, waiting for it to explode into the Big Bang?

Theologians and others, who believe in the God-Creator or who are persuaded that probably or possibly he exists, should have no difficulty in regarding scientific creation as God's mode of creation, conforming very well with the Biblical account of it.

However, some scientists—perhaps many—dislike the idea of the religious creation of the universe. The idea upsets them, perhaps, because in their life-long work and professional milieu they have come to regard causality ad infinitum as the natural order of the universe. Even when they have religious faith or persuasion, some rebel against accepting the Big Bang as creation *ex nihilo*. Instead, they go no further than to think of the Little Bomb, Big Squeeze or the like, out of which the Big Bang came, as something fantastically small, dense and hot, but not necessarily dimensionless. Most scientists accept that it is now impossible to know what happened before 10^{-43} seconds after the commencement of the Big Bang.

Some scientists and philosophers, however, are challenged or persuaded by realization of the Big Bang to re-examine the possibility of the God-Creator, though few, one suspects, would endow him with many, if any, human attributes. Most attributes they might imagine he possibly possesses probably would be by way of analogy to human intellectual rather than emotional characteristics. This challenge and persuasion would not be limited to some scientists and philosophers, of course, but would be shared by other people, perhaps many. However, to the philosophical issues we shall return in Part Two.

5

The Loom of Spacetime

Spacetime can be viewed as a loom upon which the fabric of matter and of radiation is being woven. It is a four-dimensional loom, and the fabric being woven upon it is also four-dimensional. The fourth dimension is time. The weaving of the fabric actually is "in" or "within" the loom, but we shall continue to say that it is "on" or "upon" the loom, as is the case with respect to an ordinary loom.

This metephor of a loom and of the fabric being woven upon it should not be taken too literally. Nor should it be overworked or forced. It is helpful in conceptualizing the relationship of spacetime with matter and radiation. For this purpose it is used much in this and the next chapter, and from time to time elsewhere in the book. By "radiation" in this context is meant light and other electromagnetic radiation.

Spacetime as a continuum

The loom of spacetime began with the Big Bang. Neither space nor time can, and they do not, exist separately, though it is justifiable to think of them as separate for both practical and theoretical purposes, as we do. Space could not have existed before time began, and it can only exist as time passes. Time cannot exist as the duration of nothing except meaninglessly as nothing. There is no absolute space, and there is no absolute time. Even apart from the fact that they began with the Big Bang, space and time cannot exist separately, and they cannot exist without matter and radiation, the fabric being woven upon the loom of spacetime. The extension of nothing is nothing. The duration of nothing is nothing.

Expansion of spacetime

The loom of spacetime, as said, came into being with the Big Bang and was at first either dimensionless or most minute. Since its coming to be, it has been expanding in every direction except one, which is the past;

and remember that the past began with it. The same is true of the fabric of matter and of radiation as it is being woven upon the loom. The expanding loom and the expanding fabric on it constitute the expanding Big Bang, which is the expanding universe.

The expansion has overall uniformity subject to some deceleration and subject to regional and local variations due to variant distributions of mass, causing variant curvatures of spacetime and, hence, variant accumulations of gravitational force.

Galaxies do not expand, and neighboring galaxies do not necessarily pull apart, since their gravity keeps them together, but in general galaxies are continually pulled farther and farther apart from one another, being carried by expanding spacetime.

The loom has been expanding globularly though without globular surface, edge or limit. In an ordinary globe something that starts at the center or elsewhere in the globe's interior and that moves straight outward will eventually reach the globular surface and pass beyond it into space or whatever surrounds the globe. But in the interior of the loom of spacetime a thing cannot move in a straight line, because spacetime curves. Nor can the moving thing reach or pass the surface of the spacetime loom, because spacetime has no external surface. Further, however closely to straight a thing manages to move, it will, if it continues far enough, return to its starting point if the universe is finite and long-lasting enough; or it will curve away forever, if the universe is infinite.

The arrow of spacetime

We think of the arrow of time as one-dimensional, pointing to the future. But it also points from the past. However, this conception of time is too narrow, because the arrow actually points outward in all directions from the beginning of the Big Bang and toward its outward globular expansion. It also points, not necessarily along a straight line, but along the curvature of spacetime. Only if that curvature is zero, does it point along a straight line, as discussed later. Curiously, outward from the earth in any direction is not only downward toward the beginning of the Big Bang, but it is backward in time toward that event from which the arrow of time points; and this is true of every place in spacetime. More appropriately, the arrow is the "arrow of spacetime," since it points in the one direction of expanding spacetime.

What constitutes spacetime

The substance of the loom of spacetime is neither nothing nor matter; nor is it energy, the other form of matter. It is the structure of the loom, the relationship of its parts. Is it more? It is not ether, as once thought, i.e. something like water, gas or other matter. Leastwise, it has no dragging or breaking effect, so far observable, upon light, particles, the earth or any material thing moving through it, as the air has on an airplane or water on a boat. This was shown by the Michelson-Morely experiments in 1887, which demonstrated that light travels equally fast in all directions, including the direction in which the earth moves. Nevertheless, space, time and spacetime are all mutable, as though space were ether, as discussed subsequently.

Center of spacetime

Does the loom of spacetime have a center? Or is it without a center as well as without an external surface, edge or limit? The answer is that it has a center, but only in the sense that if one could look down far enough from any point in spacetime in any direction and could see far enough (about twenty billion lightyears), he would observe the beginning of the Big Bang. The "center" of "globular" spacetime, then, is the beginning of spacetime. This center, however, no longer exists from the human perspective because the past no longer exists from that perspective. From the perspective of the present at any point in spacetime (there is no universal present or now), that point is central in space to all points in space just as any point on the surface of an expanding balloon is central to all points on the surface of the balloon. That is, there is no one center, and every point (event) in spacetime is a center of spacetime and of the universe.

Curvature of spacetime

Spacetime curves, its curvature being caused by mass and resulting in gravity, according to the general theory of relativity, as discussed in Chapter 12. Does space, as one ingredient of spacetime, curve? It must curve if spacetime is a single continuum as it must be.

Abstractly, space can be thought of as flat like a Euclidian plane, spherical like the surface of a sphere, or hyperbolic like the central region of a saddle. In flat space straight lines can be parallel to each other and never meet. In spherical space there are no parallels to a straight line, and at any two points opposite each other on the sphere all geodesics between them meet. In hyperbolic space there are many parallels (in the sense of never meeting) to a straight line, curving toward and then away from it with a constant curvature.

Each of the three kinds of space involves a different congruent geometry (invarient under translations and rotations), differing as to triangles, angles, relationship of circumference and diameter, and in other respects. Whether the space ingredient of spacetime, and, hence, the curvature of spacetime is overall flat, spherical or hyperbolic depends on the total mass-energy in the universe. If it is enough, it will reverse the expansion of the universe,and spacetime is spherical and closed. If it is not enough to have that effect, space as an ingredient of spacetime, and, hence, spacetime, either is flat with zero curvature or hyperbolic with negative curvature, depending on the total mass-energy in the universe; and the universe is open and will expand forever.

At present it is not known whether or not there is enough mass-energy in the universe to make spacetime overall spherical, so that the expansion of the universe will be reversed. But it seems that probably there is not enough mass-energy in the universe to have that effect.

Events in spacetime

Events on the loom of spacetime are like points in space or instants in time. Indeed, an event in spacetime is constituted by the coincidence of a point in space and an instant in time.

An event in spacetime, like a point in space, is dimensionless, and like an instant in time it is without duration. The fabric of matter is being woven by attachment to events on the spacetime loom, in patterns of galaxies, stars, planets, rocks, living beings, molecules, atoms, leptons, quarks, photons and all macroscopic and microscopic material things. The weaving uses only a small portion of the infinite number of events on the loom. The unused events constitute empty space on the loom. Because most events on the loom are unused in the weaving, the sky is mostly black, and in it we see the patterns of matter illuminated by light and other electromagnetic radiation.

Worldlines

The shortest line between any two events is a geodesic in spacetime. The line of events encountered by any particle, light ray, person, star or any material thing from its beginning to its end is called a "worldline." (A worldline is thus a line through spacetime, not merely space.) The straighter a thing's worldline, the longer is its route through spacetime. A twin who travelled about the earth or in space would have a worldline less straight than a twin who stayed at home most of his life, and so the world line of the traveler would be closer to a geodesic. Consequently, the traveler would be following a shorter spacetime route than his stay-at-home twin, and when he returned home he would find his twin older than he. This twin paradox is further developed later.

Speed of light

The unobstructed speed of light and of all other electromagnetic radiation is 186,282.397 miles per second. It is the same for all observers without regard to their different speeds in the same direction as light or other radiation. For example, two spaceships are travelling from the earth, one at one fifth and one at one third the speed of light. A light beam from the earth will pass each of them at 186,282.397 miles per second. The speed of light or of other radiation is unaffected by wavelength. It is universally represented by "c."

The speed of light and other electromagnetic radiation is slowed down during its passage through glass, air or other matter.

Constancy of the speed of light implies the mutability of spacetime, as we shall see.

Mutability of spacetime

Not only does spacetime curve, but it is mutable. It is not constant, inelastic or invariant as absolute space and absolute time were long conceived to be. Both time and space, and hence spacetime, expand and contract locally, here and there, in accordance with the amount of mass and, hence, of gravity locally present, and in accordance also with the velocity and acceleration of material things in reference to one another and with reference to the speed of light.

Both special relativity, explained by Albert Einstein in 1905, and general relativity explained by him in 1915, disclose the mutability of spacetime. It is our intent not to expound these theories, but to picture the loom of spacetime as elucidated by them, in appraising the universe, as Paul would have us do, as evidently the work of God, or, as we want to do also, as the work of matter-energy itself or as the work of chance. Some exposition of both the special and the general theories of relativity must accompany our depiction of spacetime as revealed by them.

It is apparent at once, from the constancy of the speed of light, that spacetime contracts or expands in accordance with the velocity of two observers of each other with respect to each other. For if the same light that passes both does so at the same velocity, as each measures it according to himself (his own frame of reference), then obviously the light is constant and it is spacetime that is not. The same is true as between any particle or object in motion relative to the "fixed" stars. Spacetime is mutable between the particle or object and them.

Space and time are also mutable in the sense that observers in different frames of reference so view them and can't agree as to when or where two events in spacetime occur, though they can agree as to "where-when" they occur, as will be explained.

Mutability in accordance with special relativity

The special theory of relativity holds that there is no standard of measurement of time or of space that is universally the same or valid. The reason is the invariance of the speed of light. When the speed of light is taken into consideration, as it must be, in relating the measurement of time and space by one observer to that of another in uniform relative motion, it results in disagreement as to their measurements, slight where measurements are astronomically small, but tremendous otherwise.

Because observers in relative motion cannot agree on the time and location of an observed occurrence or on the interval in time or space between any two observed occurrences, they cannot agree as to any simultaneity or order in occurrence, although they can agree on the happening and the order of causality of occurrences. Each observer is as correct in his frame of reference as any other observer is in his, as to the time and place of an occurrence or as to the interval in time or space between any two occurrences, though they are in disagreement with each other. Accordingly, there is no universal sameness of time or of space or universal present. Our spacetime loom is mutable throughout, and it has no pervasive nowness.

While observers in relative motion cannot agree on the intervals in time or in space between any two physical happenings, they can agree as to the interval in spacetime between any two observed physical things or happenings. This spacetime interval is a constant like the speed of light and is expressed by τ (Tau), which is defined by the equation: $\tau = T^2 - \frac{1}{c^2} R^2$, where T and R respectively are the time and the space intervals between the two things or happenings.

Mutability in accordance with general relativity

Under the general theory of relativity gravity is an effect of spacetime curvature responsive to mass, as discussed more fully in Chapter 12. Varying mass from place to place in spacetime causes varying curvature of space and, hence, varying gravity.

Time also varies according to the strength of gravity. Clocks run more slowly no matter what kind of clock, the innerworkings of atoms and cells are slower, hearts beat more slowly, and organisms live longer, the nearer they are to a center of gravity, e.g., of the earth, of any planet, of a galaxy or of any region of spacetime. The converse also is true. Things speed up the farther they are from a center of gravity.

What is true of gravity is also true of acceleration, more acceleration being equivalent of more gravity and less acceleration being equivalent of less gravity, in affecting spacetime constancy. Thus acceleration speeds up, and deceleration slows down, things just as gravity does. But this equivalence pertains only locally, i.e., where inhomogeneities in regions of spacetime, due to mass, are relatively small.

The twin paradox

This paradox is much used in illustrating the mutability of spacetime. A twin traveling in a spaceship from earth at a substantial fraction of the speed of light to a far distantfuture place, e.g., a quasar now observed in the distancepast, at a distance and in a time measured by him, by clocks and by his velocity, and by astronomical sightings, would judge his total time and distance travelled to be T and D. But his twin who stayed behind and watched the spaceship until its return, using like clocks and sightings, would judge the time of the trip to be 2T and its distance to be 2D, and both would be right. This result is a consequence of space shrinkage under special relativity.

The travelling twin on his return would find that the twin who stayed on earth had aged much more than he by many years or decades, or had died centuries or millennia ago, notwithstanding his trip by his reckoning was only half as long in time and distance as reckoned on earth. The travelling twin's clock had run more slowly just as he aged more slowly during the flight. The cells of his body and the molecules and atoms in his cells had aged more slowly—as had everything else in and on his spaceship—than they would have on earth.

The travelling twin's slower aging and the slower running of his clock would be in response not only to his immense velocity but also in response to acceleration in beginning his flight and in beginning his return flight, and also in response to the lessening of gravity as he moved away from the earth. There would be a reciprocal faster running of his clock and increase of aging due to deceleration and increased gravitational force when they occurred, but the net result, depending on an explanation too subtle and lengthy to be stated here, would be a great diminution of time of the trip and of his aging.

Interaction of the loom and the fabric

The loom of spacetime and the fabric of matter being woven upon it profoundly affect each other. The loom tells the fabric where to be woven upon it; and the fabric tells the loom how to curve and how much and where to do so, and how to stretch or shrink variously throughout it, though the loom continually expands, spreading apart the galactic patterns on the fabric.

Spacetime as static from "outside" view of it

The loom of space is in one sense static. All space and all time are included in it. The weaving of the fabric of matter upon it is complete. There is no motion in it according to some imaginary external time and space, but there is no external time or space. Nevertheless, the time and space from our viewpoint within the loom are still fluid in that, when we observe spacetime, we see time moving into the future and space extending, and expanding with matter and radiation, in all directions.

Spacetime and God

How are we to relate traditional concepts of God to spacetime as envisaged by modern cosmology? Obviously, since spacetime began with the Big Bang and is part of it, we face the question whether or not with the Big Bang it had a natural or supernatural cause or no cause at all. In addition, we have the question whether or not the loom of spacetime and the weaving of the fabric of matter and of radiation upon it are evidence of design indicative of a divine weaver.

As for the concept of God as eternal in time, this concept obviously is inconsistent with the idea of time commencing with the Big Bang. However, the concept of the eternity of God as non-temporal, entertained generally by the Fathers of the Roman Catholic Church and officially by the Church today, and also held by many theologians and philosophers outside the Church, is consistent with time originating with the Big Bang. The idea of an eternal atemporal God is also consistent with the oscillating and steady-state theories of the universe.

The omnipresence that is frequently attributed to a temporal God would be restricted to expanding spacetime that has no edge or surface. But this restriction would presumably not apply to a non-temporal eternal God.

On the whole, the traditional concept of God with respect to space and time are broad and elastic enough to be reconciled with our modern view of spacetime as originating with the Big Bang, being a single continuum, continually expanding and being curved and mutable. The Bible conceived of the world of earth and the firmament as being created in an abyss. The Bible did not conceive of the abyss being created with the world as is now thought by many to be the case.

Subsequent thought came to regard the abyss as absolute unlimited space in absolute unlimited time, in which God acted in creating and sustaining in it the world as an island of small dimensions. While viewed as small in absolute space and absolute time, the world was regarded as vast compared to man. Now, what was then thought to be the world is known to be less than a speck in the universe. So God wrought infinitely more than he was thought to have wrought when he created, if he did, the world in an abyss. But the abyss, if it is space and time, is not absolute, as it was created or came to be with matter and radiation in it, according to the Einsteinian view.

Certainly, the relationship of God, if he exists, with spacetime according to the Einsteinian view of it is much different from what would be his relationship with absolute space and absolute time if they exist. With this observation we leave readers to think for themselves what effect, if any, the prevailing Einsteinian view of spacetime has on their thoughts as to a God-Creator. In the next Chapter we depict generally the weaving of the fabric of matter and of radiation on the loom of spacetime.

6

The Fabric of Matter and of Radiation

On the expanding four-dimensional loom of spacetime the expanding four-dimensional fabric of matter and of radiation is being woven by four basic interactions of leptons, quarks and photons, the most elementary particles so far as is now known. Perhaps gravitons, theoretically the force-carrying particles of the gravitational force, should also be included as elementary particles. It may turn out that leptons and quarks are constituted of still more elementary particles, pointlike, stringlike or formless, or perhaps of nothing but energy like photons. Physicists, philosophers and others can only theorize or speculate about it. Perhaps leptons, quarks, photons and gravitons are all ultimately comprised of the same thing. Our best guess, and that of many physicists, is that this is true and will be found out in time, at least as to all these entities but gravitons.

To return to our metaphor, the fabric is affixed to the loom at points of joinder of space and time, which we have called "events" which theoretically must be infinite in number because they are extensionless. Is the fabric affixed to all of them? If so, it has been done in such a manner that light, that part of the electromagnetic spectrum to which the eye is sensitive, does not come from most of them, so that the sky is dark to the eye and its telescopic aids.

Joseph's coat was of many colors, and the fabric of matter and of radiation not only is of many colors to the human eye, but also is made of a few elementary particles (perhaps even of only one) woven into many kinds of materials and kinds of radiation.

Remember that from our human perspective, that is, within and as part of the fabric, the fabric is being woven and is expanding. From "outside" the loom of spacetime, however (though there is no outside of it to Einstein's followers), an observer, perhaps the Creator, would not use the progressive tense to describe the weaving of the fabric, unless he has his own time, as there is no human time outside the loom. We do not have two times. If there is no time outside spacetime, and if he exists, the loom and fabric and all their continuing expansion, though infinite, is to him complete, still and eternal, beyond and without continual temporal or spatial extending or expanding.

To repeat our previous caution, the metaphor of a four-dimensional loom and fabric should not be taken too literally and should not be belabored. But from time to time we will resort to it as aid to visualizing the cosmos.

In this and following chapters we shall be following the probe of science into the interior of matter and radiation. When we do this, it should be remembered always that we are probing into the distance-past, near and far, even to the distancepast of the quasars and of the explosion of the Little Bomb in the Big Bang. For some distancepast from us the fabric was much as it is about us in our private "now," but in the great distancepast it was different. For eons after the start of time in the Big Bang there was only radiation, and after matter came into being it took eons for it to gather into galaxies and stars.

Some basic definitions

"Particles," in the broad sense, means the constituents of matter, composite or elementary, and includes molecules, atoms and subatomic particles. We use the word in this broad sense only when the context indicates that usage. Otherwise, we use "particles" and "subatomic particles" synonomously to refer to particles in the atom and to those not in it that are the same as those in it or like those in it in that they are leptons, hadrons or quarks; and to refer also to neutrinos, photons and gravitons. That is, we use these terms synonomously to refer to leptons (which include electrons), hadrons (which include protons and neutrons), quarks (which are the constituents of hadrons), neutrinos, photons and gravitons. To clarify the picture, protons and neutrons are called "nucleons" because they comprise the atomic nucleus. They exist outside as well as inside the atom, although neutrons in a free state have a half-life of only twelve to fifteen minutes, which means that it will take that time for half of a large sample of them to decay.

We use "subatomic" as a noun as well as an adjective to refer both to the inside of the atom and to its constituent particles, and also to refer to particles outside the atom that are elementary or composite on no higher level than the particles in it, and further to refer to photons, the quanta of light and of other electromagnetic radiation. The subatomic can also aptly be referred to as the "microworld."

We use "supra-atomic" or "the supra-atomic" to refer to the "macroworld," above the level of the atom and atomic structure.

The subatomic can be viewed as the interiority of the fabric of matter and of radiation, and the supra-atomic as their exteriority.

Photons are, as said, the quanta or packets of energy in light and in other electromagnetic radiation and are massless. They are sometimes particulate and sometimes wavelike in behavior. Physicists no longer ask themselves whether and to what extent they are particles or are waves, and regard that question as meaningless. Instead, they ask themselves what photons are and do. They are or are not particles or matter depending on how "particles" and "matter" are defined. We prefer to include them as "particles."

"Matter" we define as particles in aggregation or singly. "Radiation" we define as energy emitted, and as the emission itself, from matter or particles and in particles or waves, or physically caused and transmitted through a material medium. We use "mass" to mean that property of matter that causes spacetime curvature and gravitation, and will reverse expansion of the universe if there is enough matter in it. Some physicists may take exception to these definitions, but we base them on what physicists say and what is important to communicate.

Levels of matter

Internally, the fabric of matter is constituted, on a first level, of molecules, atoms and free particles. A molecule can be a single atom, or it is plural atoms chemically bound together. Molecules are irreducible without the particular substance constituted by them losing its identity; e.g., water ceasing to be water.

On a lower level, matter is constituted by nucleons and electrons, both within and outside the atom, and by other particles outside the atom. On a still lower level all matter is constituted by quarks and leptons.

There may be a fourth and final level constituted by constituents of quarks and leptons. There may be a common basic particle out of which both quarks and leptons are constituted. The search for their constituents, if they should be composite, is under way, and theory may determine their existence and new accelerators detect them.

The states of matter

There are four states of matter in the universe, the three main ones on earth being solids, liquids and gas.

In solids, molecules, which are comprised of atoms, are fixed or almost fixed in relation to each other, so that solids have particular shapes and volumes and do not flow; nor are they easily compressed.

In gasses, molecules move freely and even randomly and are relatively far apart from one another, so that gas expands unless restrained or compressed, and has no inherent fixed shape or volume.

Liquids have specific volumes and densities and flow because their molecules or atoms, though close together, are free to move past one another. They follow gravity and stay within containers until the containers overflow.

Under extremely high temperature and pressure, as in the sun and stars, matter becomes a plasma in which electrons are separated from atoms so that the plasma is composed of electrons and bare nuclei. The atoms become electrically charged and are called "ions." At still higher temperature even the nuclei can break up to form nucleons.

Radiation can also be considered a state of matter insofar as it is particulate, at least if its particles have mass.

Antimatter

Antimatter is matter and not something else. It is composed of antiparticles. A single antiparticle is antimatter, just as a single particle is matter, at least where the antiparticle and particle have mass. If "matter" is defined broadly enough to include photons, "antimatter" must be similarly defined. Photons are the antiparticles of themselves.

Theoretically, for every particle there is an antiparticle, and for many particles their antiparticles have been detected. A particle and its antiparticle have the same mass and spin but opposite electric charge, opposite baryon number (a quantum number of baryons, which include protons and neutrons) and other opposite properties.

Particles and their antiparticles annihilate each other when they meet. That is, they are instantly converted into pions and other particles that within microseconds change into gamma rays, neutrinos, electrons and other particles.

Particles and their antiparticles sometimes are created or emerge in pairs, instantly annihilating each other as they do. They are then called "virtual" particles, meaning that they almost but not quite are particles. This is very strongly believed by eminent physicists to happen with great frequency in what is a vacuum according to classical physics. Indeed "perfect" vacuums are thought to seethe with virtual particle-antiparticle pairs emerging and almost instantly annihilating each other.

This phenomenon is involved in a theory of the theoretical physicist, S. W. Hawkins, as to how particles escape from a black hole. (See Chapter 18). It also is the basis of some theorizing as to how the universe originated out of a vacuum.

The antiparticle of the electron is the positron, not only the first antiparticle but also the first other than ordinary particle discovered. Its discovery was in 1932 by Carl Anderson in balloon observation, using a cloud chamber, of a cosmic ray collision with a particle in the earth's atmosphere. In 1955 antiprotons and antineutrons were produced in an accelerator built for this discovery. Antineutrinos, also first found in the 1950's, are discussed in Chapter 10.

Photons and pions (or π mesons), both having neutral electric charge, are their own antiparticles.

On earth and in our solar system, antiparticles are not produced naturally in any significance, and this seems to be true throughout our entire galaxy, the Milky Way. There may however, be galaxies or regions of the universe that are antimatter, made primarily of antiatoms constituted by positrons in quantum states about nuclei comprised of antiprotons and antineutrons. Light and other electromagnetic radiation from them, if they should exist, would be the same as light and radiation emitted in our galaxy and region of the universe, and by matter and particles anywhere. Thus, it is impossible to discover their existence through their light or other electromagnetic radiation. Efforts, so far unsuccessful, have been made to detect them from cosmic radiation which it is thought would be emitted by border areas between matter and antimatter regions.

It is very probable that in early stages of the universe particles and their antiparticles extensively annihilated each other, though for some unknown reason enough particles were left over to constitute our material universe. If antiparticles had survived instead, an antimatter universe would have been woven on the four-dimensional loom of spacetime.

Radiation

Much is said elsewhere in this and following chapters about light and electromagnetic radiation and need not be repeated here. "Light" is sometimes used to refer to all electromagnetic radiation. For clarity, while it may be cumbersome and tiresome, we repeatedly use the phrase "light and other electromagnetic radiation." The phrase means both the radiating and the energy emitted, which are both particulate and wavelike.

As said above, physicists now ask what radiation is, and they ask whether in a particular phenomenon it is particulate or wavelike; they no longer ask whether *per se* it is particulate or wavelike. It is a disturbance caused by oscillation or acceleration of an electric charge propagating outward, in electric and magnetic fields, embodied in packets of energy (quanta), to infinity and exhibiting both particulate and wavelike behavior.

The frequency range of the waves (quanta) is related to the wavelength by the equation: the frequency times the wavelength is equal to the speed of light. That speed in a vacuum is 186,282.397 miles or 229,792.458 kilometers per second, and the same at all wavelengths.

The ranges of both wavelength and frequency are enormous. The spectrum (array) of the frequency and the wavelength from short wavelength and high frequency to long wavelength and low frequency are gamma rays, X-rays, ultraviolet radiation, visable, infrared, micro and radio waves.

Wavelength of ordinary waves (water, air, etc.) is from crest to crest; in electromagnetic waves it is from the end of one cycle to the end of the next. Frequency is the number of waves per time unit.

The Weaver

The concept of God, belief in him and arguments for his existence developed over the millennia, when knowledge of the microworld as well as of the macroworld was utterly meager, as it has been until the lifetime of some of us now living. Nevertheless, there had long been a prevalent belief, going back at least to classical Greece, that the fabric of the universe was made of the same stuff everywhere. There was much controversy as to whether the fabric is particulate or continuous, as to who the Weaver is, and as to many other questions pertaining to it. The words, "elements" and "atoms," and many more we now use in talking about matter and the universe have come from long ago.

We now know vastly more about the fabric of matter and of radiation. We know that it is being woven out of leptons, quarks and photons through four fundamental interactions on the expanding four-dimensional loom of spacetime. The weaving most probably is fundamentally the same throughout our spacetime cosmos, though its exteriority has changed with expanding spacetime, from being all radiation to being radiation and matter.

Neither uncertainly about the appearance, birth and lifetime of particular particles nor about their location, momentum or other behavior impairs or diminishes the completely systematic weaving of the four-dimensional fabric of the material universe. *En masse* the microworld as well as the macroworld is orderly and is predictable through theoretical and experimental investigation, although much of both is unknown, and much perhaps is unfathomable.

Whether or not God plays dice with particles, such as individual particles in the microworld, the end result appears to be an orderly cosmos, as though designed and woven by a divine weaver.

Relentless search for understanding the cosmos, and theoretical and experimental development of classical and quantum mechanics and of special and general relativity, all aided by amazing modern instrumentation for probing the interiority of matter and of radiation and for observing their spread to the far reaches of distancepast (microscopy, telescopy and spectroscopy) have given us, even those of us who are not scientists and must rely on what we are told by the scientists, a considerable understanding of how the fabric of the material universe is woven out of a few kinds of basic particles by a few kinds of interaction, though several other kinds of particles are utilized in the weaving process.

When we look about us at our fruitful earth, its sheltering atmosphere and its teeming life, do we see God through his works, as Paul said we would? We can explain them quite well but not completely through science. If we, however, look deeply, as we now can, into matter and radiation, and, if we look as closely as we now can at them throughout most of the distancepast, do we see manifested, as Paul did in things of this earth, a divine Weaver?

Then again there may be no need, though desire may remain with many, to invoke a divine Weaver as the ultimate explanation of reality. Perhaps that explanation is the eternity of matter and radiation. Perhaps it is chance in a nothingness. The long inquiry into why and how will continue as long as humanity does, be the searchers motivated by religious zeal (not necessarily a particular adherence) or otherwise.

Readers, who choose to do so, may keep these questions as to the Weaver in mind as we proceed in the next several chapters to portray a lay view of the interiority of matter and radiation and thereafter a lay view of their externality in the distancepast. We shall refer to them time and again, and in Part Two consider philosophy as to God in light of our portrayal of the cosmos.

7

The Subatomic

The subatomic, or the interiority of matter and of radiation, differs in many startling basic ways from the supra-atomic, its exteriority. We live in the supra-atomic through our senses, aided by telescopic and other instrumentation, and it all tends to make sense to us despite hard-to-fathom external aspects of realities like gravity, black holes and the speed of light. When, however, we probe into matter and radiation we find an interiority most unfamiliar and alien to our way of thinking. Physicists, who accomplished that penetration by subtle indirect means, tried at first to accommodate what they inferred from their observation to their familiarity with, and their way of thinking about, the exteriority of things. Anyone naturally is inclined to do that when he or she is introduced to the world within the atom or below its level of structure, just as we all try to accommodate our first experience with a vastly different culture to our familiarity with, and way of thinking about, our own.

It didn't work for physicists when they tried to fit the new world of the subatomic into their preconceptions based on their knowledge of the old world of the supra-atomic, and they had to develop quantum mechanics, in order to understand the new world and sensibly to organize their rapidly developing knowledge of it.

Quantum mechanics and knowledge of the atom developed somewhat together and reached young maturity in the first third of this century. Also, in the first two decades of this century special and general relativity came, through the genius of Einstein, to be understood and has to be taken into account in both classical and quantum mechanics. In the supra-atomic, relativity becomes important practically as well as theoretically as distances, time, distancepast and mass become considerable, as will be manifested in later chapters discussing the supra-atomic, that is, the externality of matter and of radiation.

In the subatomic, special relativity has required that quantum mechanics be divided into (1) nonrelativistic quantum mechanics relating to particles with velocities that do not approach the speed of light and, accordingly, are not created or destroyed and (2) relativistic quantum mechanics relating to particles that move with or near the speed of light and, accordingly, are created or destroyed. (See discussion of extraordinary particles, Chapter 10.)

So far, gravity and, hence, general relativity have had minor roles as to the subatomic, because gravity has only negligible effect on subatomic particles, an effect which generally may be ignored. However, gravitational force is taken into account in unified field theory in which, in accordance sometimes with a highly mathematical theory called "supergravity", it is sought to find a unified field for the gravitational, electromagnetic, strong and weak forces (see next chapter), and a common truly elementary particle of which both leptons and quarks are constituted.

While it is unnecessary and inappropriate to explain classical or quantum mechanics or the special or general theories of relativity, it is within our endeavor to depict generally the interiority of matter and of radiation according to modern physics. That general depiction is best accomplished by noting significant differences between the subatomic and the supra-atomic, that is, between the interiority and the exteriority of matter and of radiation or, in other words, between what we look at and what we look into in the universe. The differences are astonishing. Certainly, how the subatomic differs from the supra-atomic would be most amazing to scientists, and more so to ordinary people, of the nineteenth century. How then does the subatomic differ strikingly from the supra-atomic?

Quantizing

The first important difference to be mentioned, from which quantum mechanics derives its name, is that in the subatomic (and also in regard to atoms and molecules) energy and various physical quantities are quantized; that is, they can change in value only in definite amounts called quanta, and not in just any amount. This is true, for example, of the energy of particles, the distance of orbiting electrons from the atomic nucleus (see next chapter) and the period and direction of the spin of a particle (see Chapter 10). In the supra-atomic, on the other hand, changes in permissible value of things is continuous: an automobile can go at any speed up to its maximum speed capacity; orbits of planets and other satellites can be at any distance from the center of mass they orbit, depending on their mass and velocity; and one can be at any point on the surface of the earth if he has means to get there.

A brief early history of the quantizing of the subatomic clarifies what it means. The history begins with Max Karl Ernst Ludwig Planck (1858–1947) and black-body radiation, which had been partially explained by physicists before he more fully explained it by the theory that the radiation consists of packets, analogous to matter being comprised of atoms. He called the packets quanta, each being a quantum, the singular being the Latin word for "how much." Einstein in 1905 verified that light and other electromagnetic radiation are, indeed, particulate as well as wavelike, since the particulate essence (waves also are of the essence) explains the photoelectric effect, i.e. light or other electromagnetic radiation beamed on the surface of a solid causes it to emit electrons.

Planck had theorized that radiation can be absorbed by matter only in quanta and not continuously as a sponge can soak up water or a container can be filled, up to the capacity of the sponge or container. The absorption of energy was as though a container could be filled or drunk from only an ounce at a time.

Planck had further theorized that electromagnetic quanta differ in energy according to wavelength and, hence, according to color of light. The shorter the wavelength, the more energetic are the constituent quanta; i.e., the energy is inversely proportional to the wavelength. He said further that the energy equals the frequency of the wave times the constant, known now as Planck's constant.

The Planck constant

The constant in this equation between energy and frequency is expressed by h. Often used is $\hbar$, which equals $\frac{h}{2\pi}$. The value of h is approximately 6.63×10^{-34} Joule-second, a hard-to-imagine small number.

The Planck constant is the fundamental constant of quantum mechanics and appears again and again in expressing permissible specific values in quantized quantities. Not only does Planck's equation fully explain black-body radiation, but it has been vitally instrumental in explaining atoms, their electrons and neutrons and other particles.

Quantizing numbers and states

Quantizing in the subatomic entails quantum numbers and quantum states. Quantum numbers are integer (or integral) numbers, i.e., 1, 2, 3, etc., and noninteger numbers, e.g., $\frac{1}{2}$, 1, $\frac{3}{2}$, etc., which express the values of quantized physical quantities, e.g., energy, angular momentum, spin. A unique set of quantum numbers describes the quantum state of an atom, electron or other particle. A ground state is the particle's lowest energy state. An excited state is one with greater energy than the ground state.

Particle-wave duality

Perhaps the most fundamental difference between the subatomic and the supra-atomic is that in the subatomic there is a particle-wave duality. The duality was first discovered in light and other electro-magnetic radiation. Realization in 1897 through the work of J. J. Thomson that cathode rays were material particles electrically stripped from atoms had been preceded by H. A. Lorentz's postulation in 1896 that electric charge is in discrete units rather than continuous. The particle-wavelike character of photons was definitively established by Einstein's explanation of the photoelectric effect, as discussed previously.

In 1923 it was shown by Louis Victor de Broglie that particles like electrons should be particle-wavelike just as photons are, and in 1925 Erwin Schrödinger showed that the wavelike character of electrons better explains, than does their particulate character, the interiority of the atom, as discussed in Chapter 9. Schrödinger's wave equation is as important in nonrelativistic quantum mechanics as Newton's laws of motion are in classical mechanics. That all particles are wavelike as well as particulate is now fully accepted and is fundamental in quantum mechanics, which is sometimes called "wave mechanics." The fact is basic to the modern view of what matter is and how it and electromagnetic radiation interact.

Complimentarity

The particle-wave duality of particles results in another peculiarity of the subatomic. Some of its phenomena can be better or only understood by regarding particles as solid points of mass, and other of its phenomena can be better or only understood by regarding them as waves. Consequently, experimentation may fail or belie theory or predictions based on the wavelike character of particles, when the theory or prediction should be based on their particulate character, and the converse likewise is true. This peculiarity of the subatomic is one instance of what is known in quantum mechanics as the principle of complementarity.

Illustratively, the particulate rather than the wave character of photons better explains the photoelectric effect as above noted. Likewise, the particulate character of electrons explains why their velocity cannot equal that of light. On the other hand, their wave character explains the interiority of the atom. See Chapter 9. Also, the wave character of electrons is most apparent in the interference of electron waves with each other, creating a wave whose amplitude is the sum of the amplitudes of the interferring waves; this interference and its result are the same as the interference of light waves with each other and the result of that interference.

Uncertainty

Another peculiarity of the subatomic, arising from the wave-particle duality of light and other electromagnetic radiation, is the Heisenberg uncertainty principle, one of the most important and known principles of quantum mechanics. This principle is that it is impossible simultaneously to measure both the location and the momentum of a subatomic particle, because light or other electromagnetic radiation has to be beamed on it in order to measure it and observe the measurement, and the light, being particulate with energy, exerts enough force on it to make it immediately and drastically change its location, momentum and direction. This is different, of course from the effect of light or radio waves beamed on an object in the supra-atomic, such as a ball or grain of sand; the location and momentum of the object is unaffected or, at the most, unnoticeably affected.

The principle precisely is that the product of the uncertainty as to a particle's position times the uncertainty as to its momentum must always be greater than the order of Planck's constant, discussed above. It is an exceedingly small number.

It should be carefully noted that the uncertainty principle neither asserts that a particle has a location or has momentum nor that, if it has, one or the other cannot be precisely measured. It asserts only that both cannot be precisely measured at the same time. However, as either is more precisely measured, the other becomes less precisely measurable.

Is the uncertainty principle a law of nature as well as an unavoidable limitation on measurement? That is, is the uncertainty indeterminateness? There is a difference conceptually between immeasurability and indeterminateness. Does location become more indeterminate as momentum becomes more determinate, and vice versa, irrespective of immeasureability without disturbance?

If a means could be contrived of measuring simultaneously location and momentum of a particle without disturbing it, would the principle still hold as to indeterminateness of both and as to increasing indeterminateness of one resulting from increasing determinateness of the other? Physicists think, it seems, that the physics of any new non-disturbing measurement of particles would still verify the principle, at least as an indeterminacy as distinguished from an uncertainty principle. One realizes, of course, that "uncertainty" and "indeterminancy" can be used synonomously in a context excluding any relevancy of measurability

The principle as one of indeterminacy irrespective of measureability seems to have positive physical effects, such as to permit particles to tunnel through a barrier impassable by them according to classical mechanics and, hence, to escape black holes, and also to endow "perfect" vacuums with prolific creativity of virtual particle-antiparticle pairs as discussed in the preceding chapter and in Chapter 10 and 18. Most nonphysicists cannot be other than agnostic as to whether or not the uncertainty principle is an ultimate law of nature or, as some would say, of God.

Uncertainty as to the subatomic is broader than that as to the location and momentum of a particle. It cannot be known when or where a particle will appear or come into being, how long it will live or even that it is. Facts cannot be stated about it as they can about particular planets or about things on earth.

The reason for the uncertainty of the subatomic may well lie in its very nature and not merely in the extreme difficulty, if not impossibility, of observing, detecting or measuring what is so minute that it is almost dimensionless or nothing. Individual subatomic particles seem to be so random in behavior that many physicists conclude that God *does* play dice with them, contrary to Einstein's assertion that he does not. In either case the study of atomic particles is a study of how God, nature or chance has created and maintains the universe.

Uncertainty as to individual subatomic particles pertains also to groups of them. If, however, enough of them or large enough groups of them are observed, which is possible by various means, a basis is provided for probability and prediction, according to statistical study and mathematical laws of probability, as to their individual birth, lifetime and death; their motion, spin, location, and other behavior and properties; their relations and interactions *inter sese*; their responsiveness to the electromagnetic, strong, weak and gravitational forces; and their group structure and dynamics.

Exclusion principle

Still another peculiarity of the subatomic is manifested in the Pauli exclusion principle, which, as enunciated by Wolfgang Pauli in 1925, is that no two electrons in an atom can have the same quantum numbers, i.e. be in the same quantum state at the same time. Subsequently, it was found that the principle is applicable to protons and neutrons and to all particles with nonintegral spin, e.g., baryons and leptons. It is not applicable to particles with integral spin, e.g., photons and mesons. Nor is it applicable to the one electron in a hydrogen atom. Its role is central in many subatomic phenomena and in the periodic table of the elements, which we shall not discuss.

8

Basic Interactions and Forces

The basic interactions by which elementary and composite particles and bodies and assemblages of matter are being woven into the fabric of matter and radiation are four: the gravitational, the electromagnetic, the strong and the weak. The forces involved in these interactions are called "the fundamental forces of nature" and are respectively the gravitational, the electromagnetic, the strong and the weak. The interactions involve "force" because they cause changes and stabilization in motion, momentum and direction of particles, in their energy and in their kinds, through the intervention of other particles called "carrier particles".

The interventions are caused by attractions and repulsions, seemingly not ultimately understood. They occur when particles are sufficiently close to each other, the necessary proximity varying with the kind of particles. They can occur as a result of particle collisions in nature and in laboratories and particle accelerators.

The term "charge" has long been used in regard to the electromagnetic force as attractive between like and repulsive between unlike manifestations of the force, the manifestations by experience being only two and opposite to each other, respectively by convention called "positive" and "negative." In regard to the "color" force, the manifestation of the strong force in the bonding of quarks into nucleons and other hadrons, analogous "charge" terminology is used (See Chapter 10.)

The four forces of nature manifest themselves in the supra-atomic in the formation of atoms, molecules, cells and larger bodies and aggregations of matter, including play marbles, animals, planets, galaxies, and gaseous nebulae, that is, in the macroscopic patterns of matter being woven upon the loom of spacetime.

These basic interactions of particles may all be manifestations of the same fundamental interaction; some physicists are actively seeking that single basic interaction, concomitant with their search for a single basic constituent of both leptons and quarks and with their search for a single unified field of particle interactions.

For about a century it has been realized that the electromagnetic interaction is one and not two interactions. Now identity of the electromagnetic and the weak interactions as the electroweak interaction seems to be close to ascertainment. An identity of the electroweak and the strong force, to be called the "electronuclear" force, is also being sought, theoretically and to some extent experimentally. Finding it seems far away.

The questions of ultimately how and why the weaving of matter and of radiation began and continues through the basic interactions remain unknown. Is it God-caused, self-caused or without explanation? It may be that in time physicists will understand from better knowledge of the Big Bang why the weaving continues, though the explanation of why the Little Bomb exploded in the Big Bang may never be known by mortal beings.

Strength of interactions

The short-range forces, the strong and the weak, occur only in the nucleus of the atom. The gravitational and electromagnetic are long-range forces that occur within the atom and out of it, with ranges throughout the universe. But within the atom gravitational force is so negligible that it generally is ignored in subatomic investigation.

The strong force is immensely by far the strongest of the four forces within its range of 10^{-13} of a centimeter, equal to the diameter of a proton. If its strength at this distance is represented by 1, then at this distance the comparative strengths of the weak, electromagnetic and gravitational forces are respectively 10^{-13}, 10^{-2} and 10^{-38}. So at this distance the weak force is far, far weaker than the strong; the electromagnetic is far, far weaker than the strong but far, far stronger than the weak; and the gravitational is many times feebler even than the weak. The range of the weak force is only 10^{-16} of a centimeter.

The gravitational interaction

The reach of the gravitational force and that of electromagnetic force are long-range and, indeed, said to be infinite. That is, their ranges are throughout the universe and are infinite if it is.

The gravitational and electromagnetic forces, in their effects outside the atom, that is, in the macroworld, are encountered in everyday experience and have long been known. The gravitational undoubtedly has been the longest experienced, and by the time of Sir Isaac Newton it was well enough understood, or through his genius became well enough understood, to be described by him in 1687 by his statement of the law of universal gravitation, according to which its attraction between any two particles or aggregate masses is proportional to their respective totals of mass and inversely proportional to the square of the distance between them.

In 1915 a more radical understanding of the gravitational force was enunciated by Albert Einstein in his theory of general relativity, according to which the force results from, or its manifestation can better be described as, the curvature of space by mass. Now, however, it is thought by many physicists, that the force is effected by force-carrying particles called "gravitons," operative in gravitational fields.

Far less is known about the basic relationship, if any, of the gravitational to the other basic forces of nature than is known of the interrelationships of the others. The gravitational force in its cosmic effect is discussed in a subsequent chapter and necessarily is treated in many connections throughout this book.

Electromagnetic interactions

We now know that light and other electromagnetic radiation, electricity and magnetism are ultimately caused by the electromagnetic interaction of electrons and quarks, or, in other words, by the electromagnetic force. The quarks act in the process as constituents of the nuclei of charged atoms or ions, i.e., atoms with more or less than their normal number of electrons.

At one time there was no thought that light, electricity and magnetism were related, but by 1820 it had become known that electric currents produced magnetism, and between 1830 and 1864 the relationships *inter sese* of electric charge and current (the flow of charge), electric fields, magnetic fields and electromagnetic fields had become understood through the work of Michael Faraday in the 1830's, James Clerk Maxwell in the 1860's, and others.

Electromagnetic phenomena, insofar as they occur in space, were thought to utilize the medium of the ether, a substance permeating all space, until the Michelson-Morley experiment in 1887 and Einstein's theory of special relativity in 1905 put an end to the notion of the ether. The experiment showed no change in the speed of light in any direction and, hence, no drag on light or on the earth as light on the earth moves through space. One aspect of the theory is that light in a vacuum moves at the same speed irrespective of the speed of the source or the observer.

Light or other electromagnetic radiation is energy carried by waves outward in all directions, and it is also the waves themselves, in an electromagnetic field generated by the oscillation or acceleration of an electric charge. The field is "electromagnetic" because it has both an electric field vector (direction) and a magnetic field vector (see discussion of fields, below). The radiation is also particulate in nature, having photons as constituents.

More is said about electromagnetic radiation at many places throughout this book.

Strong interaction

Simply stated, the strong interaction is that which holds protons and neutrons together in atomic nuclei, and, in its role as the color force, holds quarks together in protons and neutrons and other hadrons. It holds atoms and hadrons together against the repulsive electromagnetic force, because it is about one hundred times stronger than the electromagnetic force. Why repulsions between protons didn't blow up atomic nuclei was a mystery, leading to the theoretical surmise by Hidecki Yukawa in 1938 of a restraining strong interaction between protons mediated by force-carrying particles called "mesons." Within fifteen years thereafter the theory was verified by experimentation.

It should also be noted here that the exclusion principle, according to which no two electrons having identical sets of quantum numbers can simultaneously occupy an atom, exerts a barrier to penetration of atoms and contributes to the solidity of solid matter.

Weak interaction

This interaction has been much studied by particle physicists and in many ways it is better known than the strong force. Its relationship to the electromagnetic force and probable identification with it in an electroweak force in the near future was noted above. It works through intermediary force-carrying particles, as subsequently discussed.

The weak interaction has important roles in nuclear and atomic decay, natural radioactivity, neutrino emissions and interactions; and in nuclear burning in the stars, in the conversion in that burning of one element into a heavier one and in the production through that burning and conversion in giant stars of the heavy elements. These latter are dispersed, when those stars explode in supernovae, into space and thereafter are gathered and incorporated in star systems, in planets like the earth and in our human bodies. Through the weak interaction, also, neutrons, which have one "up" and two "down" quarks, are converted into protons, which have two up and one down quark, and in the process (beta decay) an electron and an antineutrino are emitted. (See Chapter 10).

Force-carrying particles

The four basic interactions occur through the exchange of force-carrying particles between the interacting particles. Each kind of interaction is mediated by a particular kind of force-carrying particles: the gravitational by gravitons; the electromagnetic by photons; the strong by gluons; and the weak by weak sector bosons, of which there are three, the W^+, the W^- and Z°. These are also called "weakons."

Gravitons have never been observed or detected, and their existence is speculative. Photons and weakons have been observed directly.

Theoretically, gluons are confined inside nucleons and other hadrons and cannot be observed in isolation, but it is not inconceiveable that in the future they might be observed, despite present theory. They are confined because, like quarks, they have color charge of their own and so bind to quarks in the hadrons. In this respect they differ from photons, which are their own force-carrying particles and which are neutral in electric charge.

The force-carrying particles have only an extremely transitory existence, so minimal that they hardly exist at all and have been called "virtual" particles as distinguished from real particles. We have noted that particle-antiparticle pairs emerging from a vacuum and instantly annihilating each other also are called "virtual" particles. (See Chapter 6.) The existence of force-carrying particles would violate conservation of energy except that they "pay back" the energy they borrow before its taking can be detected as in paying back a bank account before an overdraft on it can be detected.

The force-carrying particles exist only long enough to be emitted by one particle and to be absorbed by another in their interaction (exchange of force).

The tendency now among physicists is to refer to force-carrying particles without the qualification "virtual." This may be due to the fact that most of them have been experimentally detected.

Physicists think that the four basic interactions of particles through force-carrying particles is required by the invariance of a law of nature, that of preservation of symmetry, analogous to that of conservation of energy or of electric or color charge. The mediating particle must exist to preserve symmetry, meaning mathematical symmetry envisaged by "guage theories" used in quantum theory as to particle interactions. Further explanation of this law of symmetry would be necessarily difficult and is unnecessary here. However, predictions under gauge theories of behavior of the electromagnetic, strong and weak forces have been remarkably successful.

Fields

The basic interactions of particles (or the fundamental forces of nature) have fields, i.e., the extent of their influence in space or, more accurately in spacetime, though it is usually said "in space." Another way of stating this is that fields are embodied in force-carrying particles.

Thus, there are gravitational, electromagnetic, weak and strong fields. An electromagnetic field results from the interaction of electric and magnetic fields, which are regions in space in which the effect of an electric charge or a magnetic force can be felt or observed. Electroweak interactions or forces, which probably exist, have, if they do, electroweak fields, the extent in space in which their influences can be felt or observed.

The existence of electric, magnetic and electromagnetic fields were described by Maxwell in the 1860's. It was thought that they were fields of lines of force between charges in the ether, until the notion of the ether was abandoned in 1905; thereafter, they were conceived as regions of lines of force between charges in empty space. Somehow action at a distance between charges in empty space occurred, but how? The answer partially came in the realization that developed over the last forty years, that lines of force involved in the fields are embodied in force-carrying particles. Analogously, lines of force involved in weak and strong fields are embodied in force-carrying particles of the weak and strong forces. The same is presumed to be true of the gravitational field and its force, though the concept of field in this regard needs reconciliation with Einstein's conception of gravity as activated by the curvature of space, a matter discussed in Chapter 12.

"Lines of force" are not real. They are imaginary, conceived or drawn to represent force in a field.

The force carrying particles were sought and predicted through quantum theory as to fields of the forces and determined to exist by detection of photons and weakons. Quantum theory is that the fields are quantized, i.e. operative through quanta or discrete parcels of energy.

The quanta have been determined to be the force-carrying particles. The quanta of the gravitational force have been predicted to be gravitons.

Action at a distance

How action occurs at a distance, as in the case of ocean tides, sunburn and magnetism, has been an age-old puzzle to philosophers, scientists and others. After acquisition of knowledge of electromagnetism, leading in the 1860's to Maxwell's equations, it was thought until 1905 that seeming electromagnetic interaction was by contact through the ether. After the notion of an ether was dropped, it still was thought that the interaction was through space, and so at a distance. During the last forty-five years it has become realized that the interaction is through the exchange of photons, which are packets of energy, or quanta. These are virtual ("almost") particles, but, as said above, in the last few years physicists tend to call them "force-carrying particles," omitting "virtual."

It is now known, as previously discussed, that the weak and strong interactions as well as the electromagnetic, occur through the exchange of force-carrying particles, and it is speculated that this is true, too, of the gravitational force.

Are the basic interactions of particles (of fundamental forces of nature) action at a distance or by contact? The seeming answer appears to be by contact through the emission by one particle of a force-carrying particle and the absorption of the force-carrying particle by a third particle. That is, action is fundamentally between particle A and particle C through A's emission and C's absorption of a force-carrying particle B. Admittedly, "absorption" is somewhat vague. What is the contact we infer from it between C and B?

How and why does the exchange of a force-carrying particle occur, whether it is action by contact or at a distance? The answer to the question, if ever known, may throw light on how the universe is sustained and how the original particles of the Little Bomb interacted to create the Big Bang, the expanding universe. Would the answers have any weight with respect to God or rival hypotheses about the ultimate explanation of reality?

9

The Atom and Ordinary Particles

It is expeditious to consider the atom and its particles in a single chapter since it is difficult to discuss either without discussing the other. By "ordinary particles" we mean those in the atom and like ones outside it. These are electrons, protons, neutrons and quarks. As before said, the protons and neutrons collectively are called "nucleons" because they constitute the atomic nucleus. Protons and neutrons are composed of quarks, to be discussed in Chapter 10.

Our interest is in a general picture of the atom, as essential to our depiction of the cosmos, and a brief historical account of acquisition of knowledge of it will facilitate general understanding of it.

The first idea that ordinary matter of all kinds is made of minute elementary particles usually is attributed to Democritus, the Fifth Century, B. C., Greek philosopher, who also thought that these particles are indivisible and called them "atoms", meaning indivisible. During the centuries between Democritus and Robert Boyle (1627–1691) and John Dalton (1766–1844) some philosophical attention, not insignificant or unimportant, was given to the idea of atoms, but it was relatively infrequent. Giodano Bruno (1548?–1600), who espoused atomism and other disturbing unorthodox scientific ideas, was burned as a heretic for them.

Boyle is credited with introducing the concept of irreducible chemical elements, as basic kinds of matter. Dalton developed the theory that the irreducible elements are indivisible atoms; differences among elements are due to differences among atoms; a molecule is one or more atoms; and chemical compounds are of more than one kind of atom.

The notion that the atom is a structureless, indivisible and elementary universal particle persisted until the beginning of this century. Then it became realized that the atom has particles and structure, contemporaneously with its becoming certain that the atom is real.

Nineteenth Century chemical investigation of the elements after Dalton rested on his atomic theory and chiefly sought determinations of atomic weights of the elements, which largely culminated in 1904 with determinations made very precisely by Theodore William Richards. Since then the determinations have been even more precisely refined.

As noted, during this period it became realized that substances are comprised of small groups of atoms bound together in "molecules;" the word means, derivatively from Latin, bits of matter.

Chemists then were, as they are now, primarily interested in how substances combine with each other, and their observations of the combinations were explained by the assumption that each element (class of substances) contains multiple atoms of one kind. They were not concerned much with what atoms are in themselves. Physicists, however, were so concerned, as they are now.

As early as the eighteenth century it was imagined that gas pressure—its resistance to compression—is due to its being composed of atoms moving in all directions. Brownian motion is named after Robert Brown, a botanist, who in 1827 observed that pollen grains in water have a random wiggly motion. He thought the motion might be due to a germination of the grain. However, it became well known that any microscopic objects in gas or water have Brownian motion and a resulting drift, and it was conjectured that the motion is caused by the impact of moving gas or water molecules on the suspended object.

In papers by Einstein, published between 1905 and 1908, setting forth his molecular-kinetic theory of heat, he attributed Brownian motion to molecular disturbance of the suspended object. He invited experimentation to verify his theory, and this was done by Juan Perrin in 1908.

Was the atom, its reality having been formerly established, elementary or composite? Ascertainment of its composite nature overlapped to some extent ascertainment of its reality.

Discovery of subatomic particles

The first subatomic particles to become known were the electron, the proton and the neutron, the ordinary particles of matter, and the photon, the particle of light and of other electromagnetic radiation. They were discovered and much was learned of them after 1890 and in the early decades of this century, contemporaneously, in part, and hand-in-hand with the development of quantum mechanics. This was before the advent of particle accelerators and detectors. Their discovery was effected through theory and experimentation with cathode rays, radiation from radioactivity, cloud chambers, scintillation counters, Geiger counters and other laboratory equipment. More will be said about these observation methods and devices.

Discovery of the electron

The electron was first discovered through experimentation with cathode tubes and rays, which had begun as early as the mid-nineteenth century. Inside the tubes there was nearly a vacuum, a little rarefied gas remaining. An electric current through the tube from a cathode at one end of the tube to an anode at the other produced a line of glowing gas from near the cathode to the anode. It was debated whether the rays, the lines of glowing gas, were light or particles. In 1897 J. J. Thomson found a way to determine the speed of the rays,which proved to be about one-tenth that of light. So the rays had to be comprised of particles, negatively charged since they were attracted to the positively charged anode. The particles were later called "electrons."

Some knowledge of electrons having been attained, the atom was visualized to be something like a bun with raisins scattered in it. But this picture of it didn't last long.

Means of observation and detection

It will be helpful at this point, to understanding of acquisition of knowledge of the atom and to visualizing it, to digress somewhat to describe the means by which the knowledge developed. Use of the cathode tube to find the electron has been noted above.

By this time there was much known about radiation from radioactive substances though not much about the radioactivity itself. Alpha radiation could be directed at metal foil, and the results observed. Some alpha rays would pass directly through the foil; others would pass through it but scatter angularly as they emerged and others would bounce straight back or angularly from the foil. Much could be inferred from this behavior of the rays as to the inside of the atom.

Scintillators and Geiger counters also were used early in investigation of the atom and particles and are still used for this purpose. Charged particles, such as alpha rays, passing close by atoms strip them of their outer electrons, ionizing them, or cause their electrons, absorbing energy, to jump from a lower to a higher orbit (state). These electrons quickly jump back to the lower orbits, emitting, as they do, photons carrying away the absorbed energy. The photons cause flashes of light. A scintillator is any material that scintillates (flashes light) when its atoms thus or otherwise emit photons. During the early period of atomic and particle investigation observers would sit in the dark, watching and counting the scintillations, from which much could be inferred as to the inside of the atom and its particles. Scintillation is still much used in particle detection and study, but scintillation counters have replaced the watchers in the dark.

A Geiger (more properly a Geiger-Muller) counter is something like a cathode tube in that it is basically a tube or box with only a little rarefied gas in it. A wire (an axial anode) from a battery terminal, positively charged, goes into the tube or box at one end and down its center. Another wire from the battery is attached to the wall of the tube or box or a cathode about it. A voltage through the gas is thus created, but not enough to cause a current.

Charged particle such as alpha rays can enter the tube or box through a window, usually of mica, and when they do they ionize gas atoms they pass, i.e., strip them of electrons. The electrons move toward the positively charged wire anode, and the ionized atoms move to the wall or cathode. If the voltage is high enough, the electrons will accelerate (attain more energy) and ionize more atoms, creating an avalanche of electrons which on reaching the wire anode induces a pulse of current that can be used to activate a counter or cause a click through a sound amplifier. Sophisticated versions of Geiger counters still are much used in detecting and studying particles.

Use of the cloud chamber in demonstrating the existence of the neutron is subsequently discussed.

Discovery of the nucleus

By experimentation with alpha rays Ernest Rutherford (1871–1937) established that the atom must have at its center much of its mass. Only that could explain the way in which alpha particles bounced directly back when they were directed at atoms. Rutherford called the central mass a "nucleus." Earlier, in 1908, he had been awarded the Nobel Prize in chemistry for identification of alpha and beta radiation.

Discovery of the proton

Next Rutherford in continued experimentation with alpha rays established that the mass concentrated in the atom's center must be positively charged since it repelled positively charged particles; so he called it the "proton."

Discovery of the neutron

This came next. Rutherford in 1920 suggested the neutron's existence in order to explain why the mass of the electrons in the atom was more than that of its nucleus. The neutron's existence was confirmed in 1932 by James Chadwick in experimentation with radioactive radiation striking a sheet of berryllium. Resulting radiation from the sheet entering a cloud chamber of hydrogen, helium, oxygen or other gas showed no trace until it struck an atom nor after that, but the atom recoiled from the blow, leaving a trace of its motion in the gas as it did. The particle that radiated from the sheet and entered the cloud chamber had to be neutral in charge; otherwise, its passage in the chamber would have disturbed particles and left a trace.

Chadwick performed the experiment using other metals for sheets, and on the basis of the different velocities of recoil of the atoms in the chamber, their different sizes and other data he calculated that the neutral particle (the neutron) must have the same mass as the proton. Now it is known that the neutron has a little more mass. For his discovery Chadwick received the Nobel Prize.

Orbits and states

Thus, it was learned that the atom has electrons, protons and neutrons, but what did they do in it? Rutherford's experimentation indicated that the electrons moved in orbits about the positively charged nucleus and were equal to it in charge. That fact, if it were true, caused another question. According to electrodynamic theory electrically charged particles orbiting about a body should emit electromagnetic radiation and thereby lose energy, so that eventually they would plunge into the center of the body. In the case of the hydrogen atom it should take less than a second for its one electron to fall into its proton nucleus, but this obviously does not occur.

Niels Bohr in 1913 answered the problem by a theory of permissible orbits. Electrons can move only in orbits at certain distances from the nucleus and not at just any distance from it, and an election moving in its permissible orbit does not lose energy. This seemed to be only an assertion of what obviously is true despite electrodynamic theory. It was explained a decade later by the quantum theory of energy in the subatomic. The permissible orbits result from the quantum nature of energy in a system like the atom.

The Rutherford-Bohr atom was something like the solar planetary system except for the limited permissibility of orbits. But it turned out to be a partially untrue picture. That is because in 1923 Schrödinger showed, as discussed in Chapter 7, the wave character of electrons. It better explains their behavior in atoms than does their particulate character. As waves they exist in permissible energy states about the nucleus. The states are sometimes still called "orbits" or "stationary orbits" by physicists, who use the terminology for convenience only.

The uncertainty (indeterminacy) principle makes precise determination simultaneously of the location and of the momentum or motion of any electron in an atom impossible. The concept of a predictable electron path about the atomic nucleus is erroneous.

An atom is in its ground state when its electrons are in the lowest energy states allowed them by the exclusion principle, and an atom in that state stays in it until its outer electrons are excited into jumping out of it or its inner electrons are excited into jumping into a higher state (orbit). Then it is in an excited state. The excitement can be caused naturally or by human contrivance as by beaming charged particles at atoms or by heating them. Excitement of atoms naturally caused happens frequently on our macroscopic time scale, but infrequently though fairly regularly on the subatomic time scale.

It has been noted above that the electron after jumping into a higher energy state in an atom quickly falls back into the lower state from which it jumped, emitting its excess energy in light as it does. It jumps back in only about $10^{-8\text{th}}$ of a second.

It is interesting that free electrons, including any escaping from atoms, are not subject to quantum energy law. They can have any energy in an unquantized continuity. Not all subatomic quantities are quantized.

Shape of orbits and atoms

Generally the smaller the number of electrons in an atom, the more circular are the electron orbits (states), and that of the single electron in the hydrogen atom is the most circular. As the number of electrons in an atom increases, the orbits spread out somewhat irregularly and the electrons move in a roughly spherically shaped cloud about the nucleus, and the atom assumes the same shape.

Angular momentum

While electron orbits in an atom are better explained as energy states, they still have angular momentum, that is, a tendency to keep orbiting at the same rate (orbits per unit time) until the rate is changed by an external force. The angular momentum is quantized in permissible integral (0, 1, 2, etc.) multiples of $\hbar$. As noted in Chapter 7, $\hbar$ is $\frac{h}{2\pi}$, and *h* symbolizes Planck's constant. The integer is the quantum number of the magnitude of the angular momentum. The projection of the angular momentum also is quantized. Permissible values of the projection are two times the values of the magnitude plus one, e.g., 3, when the quantum number of the magnitude is 1. This means that the projection can be in only three directions, and not just any direction.

The angular momentum of the spin of particles is discussed in the next chapter.

Uncertainty

The atom is subject to the uncertainty principle. Ascertaining momentum of electrons in their orbits (states) increases indeterminacy of their location, and the converse also is true. Both their location and momentum (or motion) at the same time can't be precisely known.

It must be admitted that the general picture of the atom and its particles, given by modern physics, is somewhat fuzzy, especially as to electrons. They are particulate while also being waves. They are quantized in orbits which are better understood as energy states. Their waves spread out in those states, and they move in a cloud about the nucleus. The picture of quarks within protons and neutrons is somewhat different but similarly somewhat fuzzy, the quarks also being both particulate and wavelike and occupying states. (As to quarks generally, see Chapter 10.)

Exclusion

As noted in Chapter 7, under the exclusion principle no two electrons in an atom can have the same set of quantum numbers, that is, be in the same state (occupy the same orbit). Quarks also are subject to the exclusion principle. This principle contributes a measure of certainty to the general picture of the atom and its ingredients.

Number of particles in atoms

How many electrons do different kinds of atoms (different elements) have? They normally have the same number of electrons as protons, and so are neutral in charge. If they lose or gain an electron, they become ions. Ions are either molecules or atoms that gain or lose an electron. Ionization can occur in several ways, including chemical reaction and radiation passing through substances. Negative ionization occurs when a molecule or atom captures an electron.

Atoms in nature have up to ninety protons and ninety electrons, inclusive, and atoms not in nature but produced by nuclear reactors and accelerators, i.e., the "transuranic" atoms, have 91 to 103 protons and the same number of electrons. The proton or atom number of a kind of atom, i.e., of a particular chemical element, expresses the number of protons in that kind of atom (that chemical element).

The number of neutrons in the nuclei of different kinds of atoms (of particular elements) varies. The mass or nucleon number expresses the total number of protons and neutrons in the nucleus of a particular kind of atom (particular element), and is the number nearest in value to the atomic weight, recently renamed "relative atomic mass," of that kind of atom (particular chemical element), which is the average mass (weight) of that kind of atom (particular chemical element), expressed in units of $\frac{1}{12}$ of the mass (weight) of the carbon 12 atom.

Sizes and empty space

To complete this general picture of the atom, something should be said about the size of the atom and of its particles, and as to empty space within it. Large numbers are expressed in powers of ten, e.g., 10^{10} meaning 1 followed by ten zeros and 10^{-10} meaning after a decimal point ten zeros followed by 1. All atoms are about the same size, having a diameter of about 10^{-8} cm. An atomic nucleus has a diameter of about 10^{-12} cm and has 99.975 percent of the total mass of the atom. An electron has about $\frac{1}{3672}$ as much mass as the nucleus has.

A gram of water has 3×10^{22} molecules, and other corporeal substances have about the same number. A molecule has one or more atoms. The human body has as many atoms as the universe has stars, billions upon billions.

The nucleus occupies about $10^{-12\text{th}}$ of the volume of the atom; the cloud of electrons about the nucleus about $10^{-13\text{th}}$. Thus, there is an enormous amount of empty space in the atom, though much of that is occupied by the waves associated with its particles.

The nucleus, on the other hand, has very little empty space comparatively since typically protons and neutrons occupy a considerable part of its volume.

Seeing the atom microscopically

Are atoms too small to be imaged microscopically? Until recently yes, because light waves are too long to be focussed on them. Now with scanning- transmission electron microscopes, isolated heavy atoms, e.g. uranium and lead, have been imaged. The electron wave is much shorter than that of light, being about that of X-rays (which can't be used microscopically); thus much greater resolution can be obtained with electron waves. The scanning electron beam passes over the atom without considerably disturbing or damaging it. By quickly repeated pictures of the same atoms it is possible to infer their motions.

Dust of the earth

When God, nature or chance created humans out of the dust of the earth, he or it did so out of atoms, out of its chemical elements, constituting the dust. The course from primordial radiation, that flooded all spacetime immediately after the Little Bomb exploded, to atoms and then to living cells and terrestrial life, culminating from our viewpoint in human life, is many billions of years old and complicated, most likely beyond fathomability. Is the hand or will of God hidden in the process or revealed by it, or is there other divine revelation as some believe? Is it stupid to even imagine that divine Intelligence would use a process so long and complicated as the evolution of man from the beginning of time to create for Himself associate angels? Or is it a way to forge perfect beings? Should the evidence of what the atom is and how through it human intelligence emerged from the explosion of the Little Bomb go to the jury of the human mind, or the jury of the human heart, on the issue of ultimate reality being God, something else, or sheer meaningless-ness?

10

More as to Particles

To complete our general portrayal of the subatomic, more must be said about particles. Understanding of the ordinary particles of which atoms are constituted is greatly aided by the study of extraordinary particles produced by high-energy particle accelerators. These are also produced by cosmic-ray collisions with other particles. Some of them, as force-carrying particles, mediate the basic interactions of particles, as discussed in Chapter 8. Otherwise, they are uncommon in nature because the high energies necessary to produce them in particle collisions are also uncommon in nature.

Neutrinos and cosmic rays, also discussed in this chapter, are special particles, ordinary in their abundance and extraordinary in their behavior and recent discovery. They are not extremely transient as are the extraordinary particles produced by high-energy particle collisions.

Attention is also given in this chapter to classification of particles, leptons and quarks, spin and natural radioactivity.

Particle accelerators

In the preceding chapter note was taken of methods and devices for exploring the atom and for detection and study of its constituent particles. In the last four decades these methods and devices have been supplemented by high energy particle accelerators for producing and studying extraordinary particles, and nuclear reactors have also been supplementarily employed for that purpose.

The accelerators achieve high velocities, substantially over 90 percent of that of light, which is necessary for particle collisions to produce extraordinary particles. Electrons have been accelerated by accelerators nearly to the speed of light, indeed to 0.999,999,999,86 of it. Beams of neutrinos, which naturally travel nearly at the speed of light because they have nearly no mass, are produced and used. Protons, electrons and ions are most used in accelerator beams.

Extraordinary particles

Of these there are hundreds, often called "exotic" and sometimes a "zoo." They are detected through collisions of high-energy particles with other particles. Particles must have enormous velocities, approaching the speed of light, for their collisions with other particles to result in the creation or release of extraordinary particles. Some cosmic rays, which are mainly protons, have enough energy for their collisions with other particles in space or in the terrestrial atmosphere to produce extraordinary particles. In 1932 Carl Anderson, as previously noted, in observation from a balloon of a cosmic ray collision with another particle detected the positron, the antiparticle of the electron. It was the first extraordinary as well as the first anti-particle discovered.

Are extraordinary particles created or only released in high-energy particle collisions? The mass of the new particles is greater than that of the colliding particles. So the extraordinary particles must be created, at least in part, out of their kinetic (motion) energy. The kinetic energy to create new particles must be enormous, thus high energy accelerators are essential in order to create extraordinary particles in the collisions. This follows from special relativity, which recognizes mass as a form of energy in addition to potential and kinetic energy.

The process involved in high-energy particle collision, annihilation of old and creation of new extraordinary particles, is the converse of that involved in nuclear bombs and nuclear power. Since under special relativity mass is a form of energy and since Einstein's equation is that energy equals mass times the speed of light squared, it follows that little mass is convertible into enormous energy and that enormous energy is convertible into mass, but only very little. The means of conversion has been found in the former respect by nuclear weapons and nuclear reactors and in the latter respect by particle accelerators.

For economic reasons, among others, particles accelerators have been much more used than cosmic-ray observation for discovery and study of extraordinary particles.

The importance of high-energy particles and extraordinary particles lies in probing with the former into the interiority of matter, and with the latter in the classification of all particles and better understanding of both extraordinary and ordinary particles. Also, from the probing and study of its results, and from quantum, symmetry and other theory, and also from probing and theory buttressing each other has come knowledge (1) of the basic interactions of matter, i.e., of the fundamental forces of nature; (2) of force-carrying particles and their partial solving of the age-old puzzle of action at a distance; and (3) of the quark structure of the proton, neutron and other hadrons. In addition, theory and probing by high-energy particles well may lead to knowledge of the interiority of leptons and of quarks, out of which all matter and radiation is constituted, and may lead to finding that both leptons and quarks are comprised of the same ultimate elementary particles, perhaps only packets of energy like the photon.

Classification of particles

It was both necessary and possible to classify the hundreds of different kinds of extraordinary particles into as few main classes with as little subclassification as possible, and to include the ordinary particles in the classification since the desirability of doing that is obvious. Classification facilitates understanding what particles are and what they are not and what they do and don't, can and cannot do, and how they are related. It has facilitated and guided both particle theory and experimentation, and also the statement of natural laws governing particles and the subatomic world. Further, it helps to elucidate the inception of the universe in the Big Bang.

The classification of particles has been on certain bases, such as their responses to the different fundamental interactions and their spin and charges. One main classification is on the basis of their response to the strong interaction or force. Those that respond to that force are called "hadrons," the name being from a Greek word for strong. Most particles fall into this main group, including the two ordinary particles, protons and neutrons.

Particles that respond to the weak force are called "leptons," the name coming from a Greek word meaning fine or slight.

A subclassification of hadrons relates to the outcome of their radioactive decay. If the outcome includes a proton among other stable particles, the hadron is a baryon; otherwise, it is a meson. The proton itself is a baryon.

Another classification is on the basis of speed of decay. Hadrons decaying extremely slowly in about 10^{-10} second are called "strange," and those decaying far, far more rapidly in about 10^{-23} seconds are called "nonstrange." The terminology was adopted because the much slower decay seemed strange to physicists.

Other classifications are on the basis of spin quantum number (see discussion of spin, later) and isotopic spin (or isospin) quantum number, analogus to spin quantum number and measuring a quantum related to electric charge. There is further classification.

Isospin is difficult to understand and need not be understood for the purpose of our general picture of particles. However, the classifying of particles according to baryon number (expressing quanta of conserved quantity restricting how baryons can decay or transform), strangeness and isospin led to the postulation and experimental verification of the quark structure of the proton, neutron and other hadrons. Particles classified according to these three factors resulted in octets of particles; thus, the classification was called the "eightfold way." It was explainable, according to mathematical group theory, by the quark hypothesis that the hadrons were composite rather than elementary particles. The constituents were called "quarks," the name being suggested by a phrase "Three quarks for Muster Mark," in James Joyce's *Finnegans Wake*. This explanation of the eightfold way of classification was suggested in 1964 independently by Murray Gell-Mann and George Zweig.

Originally, it was pictured that hadrons were comprised of three constituents. Now it is known that all baryons are comprised of three quarks, and mesons of a quark and antiquark.

Leptons and quarks

The fabric of matter and of radiation is woven with three elementary particles: quarks, leptons, and photons, and probably with a fourth, gravitons. A general picture, quite exiguous, of the presently accepted quark and lepton structure of matter, in all its forms, avoiding a too technical depiction, is presented in this section.

Both leptons and quarks are truly elementary particles, so far as is now known. They differ fundamentally from each other in that quarks participate in the strong interaction and leptons do not; leptons can and sometimes do exist independently, and quarks do not and probably cannot; and there are other basic differences.

There are six classes of leptons: the electron, the electron neutrino, the muon, the muon neutrino, the tau and the tau neutrino. We need say little about muons and taus, which have mass and exist only for an instant. Each, especially the tau, is far heavier than the electron, which is nearly massless. For each lepton there is an antilepton. Neutrinos are later treated.

Six classes (called "flavors") of quarks, varying in electric charge, spin and mass, have been given the fanciful names of "up, down, charm, strange, top (or truth) and bottom (or beauty)" or "u, d, c, s, t, b."

Quarks also have a "color" charge, differing from but somewhat like their electric charge. The "color charge" is another name for quarks' responsiveness (coupling) to the strong interaction. There are three different colors (kinds of responsiveness), called "red, blue or green."

The "flavor" and "color" nomenclature has nothing to do with taste or with the color of things to the human eye. The prefix "chromo" has also been adapted in the words "chromodynamics" and "chromomagnetism" relative to the theory and coupling power of the color charge.

As a quark may be one of six flavors and one of the three colors, there are eighteen varieties of quarks. Each of these has an antiquark with equal mass but opposite values of electric and color charge. Thus, there are eighteen varieties of antiquarks. Hadrons are combinations out of these thirty six varieties. As said above, baryons have three quarks, and mesons have two: a quark and an antiquark.

Protons have two u quarks and one d quark, and neutrons have one u quark and two d quarks. Both are "white" or neutral in color charge because the three quarks of each are of the three colors, one being red, another blue and another green. This is analogous to the atom and nucleon being neutral in electric charge because in each its components are equal positively and negatively in that charge.

Quarks have a fractional electric charge. Baryon quarks each have one third of the electric charge of the baryon they constitute; and the quark and antiquark in a meson each has one half of the electric charge of the meson.

This simplified picture of quarks is augmented by discussion later of their spin and of their right or left-handedness.

Neutrinos

Neutrinos are as fantastic as reality can be, as much so as the curvature of space and black holes. They come from just about everywhere in the universe, moving as fast or nearly as fast as light through a vacuum and, unlike light, with undeterred speed through every material substance and object, except a black hole, until they are stopped or slowed down by the weak interaction with some particles, which happens rarely.

Neutrinos respond only to the weak force and gravity and are the only elementary particles thus limited. Gravity has negligible effect upon them, but like photons they follow the curvature of space and are sucked into black holes when they get too close to them.

Neutrinos are leptons. They are as massless or nearly as massless as photons. Some theory and experimentation have suggested strongly, however, that they have slight mass, though virtually none, ten to thirteen thousand times less than electrons have. If it is true that they have some mass, a major portion of the mass of the universe may be in them, and in that event the universe may have enough mass and consequently enough gravitational force eventually to reverse its expansion. However, the character of the flux of neutrinos from Supernova 1987 in the large Magellanic Cloud, detected in early 1987, has been considered to be strong evidence that neutrinos have no mass or hardly any, no more than 5 eV to 25 eV, since the flux appears to have travelled to earth at, or nearly at, the speed of light. If this is true, neutrinos have little significance as to reversing the expansion of the universe. Obviously, the number and mass of neutrinos are not enough to have already caused the collapse of the universe back into itself.

How many neutrinos are there then in the universe? It seems that they occupy all of it, moving through it in every direction. There are, indeed, just about as many neutrinos as there are photons, and like photons they are a billion times more numerous than protons and neutrons. The flux of solar neutrinos upon the earth is enough so that one hundred quadrillion of them pass every second through every person on earth. Those now passing through the reader will be farther away than the moon in seconds.

There are three kinds of neutrinos and a corresponding kind of antineutrinos for each of them, each of the six kinds being emitted in a different kind of particle decay. Electron neutrinos and antineutrinos are emitted in beta decay. It is the antineutrino that is emitted with an electron in ordinary beta decay. Muon neutrinos and antineutrinos are emitted in association with muon decay and emission. Tau lepton neutrinos and antineutrinos are emitted in association with tau-lepton decay and emission. Muons and tau leptons are heavy leptons, having mass.

Each kind of neutrino and antineutrino has different behavior and a different role in weak particle interaction and consequently in the structuring and functioning of atoms and particles and of the universe. Neutrinos have left-handed spin and antineutrinos have right-handed spin. Neutrinos and antineutrinos commonly are referred to collectively as neutrinos.

Neutrinos are, it seems, naturally produced through particle interaction and particle decay, in enormous number and in myriad places throughout the universe. They are emitted from nuclear fusion in the center of the sun, to speed through it and out into space; and they are produced similarly by the billions upon billions of other stars in the universe. They are prodigeously emitted in supernovae. They emerge in vast multiplicity from cosmic-ray bombardment of particles in space and in the earth's atmosphere, and from particle collisions and interactions in space, gas and solids and in other events and places.

Neutrinos flood our "present" spacetime from near and far distance-past, even, it is theorized, from the beginning of the Big Bang. There should be and probably is a universal background of neutrinos of two degrees Kelvin produced in the first few moments of the Big Bang, about us in every direction, just as there is a universal background of three-degree Kelvin electromagnetic radiation left over from the Big Bang's inception, which has been detected by radio astronomy and is considered to be almost conclusive evidence of the Big Bang's occurrence.

Occasionally, but very seldom, neutrinos interact weakly with other particles in the earth's atmosphere and interior, and in its waters and solid matter. This happens often enough to make detection possible through predicted and resulting effects of neutrino interactions, causing muon emissions, light, sound waves and other observable phenomena. Consequently, it has been endeavored to detect neutrinos, especially those coming to earth from the sun, by their effects. For the purpose tanks of fluid and sensory equipment have been used in deep mines, the reason for deep underground search being to escape interference with the detection process by cosmic rays and particle interactions above, on and in the earth's surface and crust. Solar neutrinos have been detected, but not nearly as much as expected, and theoretical particle physicists are trying to find out why.

Humanity has been totally unaware of the sea of speeding neutrinos occupying entire spacetime, until very recently. The existence of neutrinos was first postulated by Wolfgang Pauli in 1930 as explanatory of seeming violation in beta decay of the law of energy conservation. The proton into which a neutron changes and the electron emitted in the decay have slightly less mass than the neutron, so there seemed to be a loss of energy since mass equals energy. Pauli reasoned that another undetected small particle must be emitted as well as the electron in the decay. Later this was called the "neutrino" (meaning a tiny neutron) by Enrico Fermi. The existence of neutrinos was experimentally confirmed in 1956.

Neutrinos are produced in nuclear reactors and particle accelerators. Today, neutrinos are routinely produced and used to probe into the innermost constituency, structure and mechanics of matter. They have been most instrumental in determining the quark structure and dynamics of the proton and neutron and of other hadrons.

Increasing knowledge of matter and of neutrinos themselves, resulting from their employment by particle accelerators, enables physicists and astronomers better to know the macrostructure of the universe. They are beginning to decode neutrino language as they have been decoding star-light and other electromagnetic language, so as to understand what it tells us about the weaving of the fabric of matter and of radiation on the loom of spacetime.

What neutrinos add in evidence as to the origin and sustenance of the universe being through nature without God or ultimately through God, and as to his existence, is for one to determine for oneself if desired. Certainly, they seem consistent with the universe being a cosmos rather than a chaos. Determination that there is a background of neutrino radiation from when the Little Bomb exploded would be strong additional evidence that it did. Should neutrinos then be thought to be an ingredient and an instrument employed by a divine Designer in the weaving of the universe?

Cosmic rays

These are like neutrinos in that apparently they pervade the universe, racing through it in all directions, often with speeds approaching that of light and with enormous kinetic energies. Leastwise, they come to the earth from all directions and certainly permeate our galaxy, and those with the highest-energy theoretically can escape it into intergalactic space. Theoretically, also, those with the highest-energy reaching the earth's atmosphere well may come from outside the Milky Way. It has been established that other galaxies, too, have cosmic rays. One can reasonably surmise, accordingly, that they are abundant in most galaxies, at least in those resembling the Milky Way, and that the highest-energy ones course about in intergallactic space. It has been theorized that in the universe they are produced nearly as prodigeously as light and more so than radio waves and X-rays combined.

Cosmic rays were discovered in 1912 by Viktor Hess during balloon ascensions. He ascertained that they increased in number markedly with altitude, evidencing their blockage by the earth's atmosphere. Probably only one in a million primary cosmic rays that reach its atmosphere reach its surface.

Cosmic rays are particles, having, like all particles, waves associated with them. They mostly are atomic nuclei, and most of the nuclei are hydrogen protons stripped of their electrons. (Each hydrogen atom consists of one proton and one electron.) Most of the remainder of the nuclei are helium. The rest range in proton number up to iron, but include even heavier elements such as uranium. The lighter elements, lithium, beryllium, and boron, are included, but are relatively scarce. Their presence is strongly indicative of their creation in cosmic-ray collisions with other particles, since it is unlikely that they, like the heavier elements, could have been created in the nuclear furnace of giant stars. Also included in cosmic ray flux are electrons (one percent of the flux), positrons (antielectrons), neutrinos and gamma rays.

Cosmic rays vary considerably in energy, but the energy of the more energetic ones equal and surpass by far the particle energies produced in particle accelerators. Cosmic rays attain energies of 10^{20} electron volts, and what is considered a cosmic ray includes any particle in or from space with energy of over 10^8 electron volts. Particle accelerators, existing and planned, are capable of endowing particles with energies up to 10^{12} to 10^{15} electron volts. The energy of cosmic radiation is far greater than that of any other radiation naturally produced.

While the energy of cosmic rays can be enormous, their intensity is very low. This is especially true of the highest-energy ones. Their intensity is their number per unit time reaching earth's atmosphere per square space unit. Their intensity is about that of starlight. The highest energy ones are so far apart and infrequent that it is difficult to study them in the atmosphere or in space. Instead, they are studied through the secondary and progeny particles that result when they collide with other particles in the atmosphere.

Most cosmic rays are charged particles and so most reaching earth's atmosphere are diverted by its magnetic field toward its poles, but most of these are transformed by particle collisions into other particles, which in turn collide with still other particles, the process continuing in showers or cascades of particles that reach the surface of the earth. These are studied through their activation of detectors.

Where and how cosmic rays are produced in the Milky Way and in other galaxies and are put into flight through spacetime have long been a mystery that remains largely unsolved. Any mechanism of nature that produces them is perforce a natural particle accelerator of tremendous power.

It is very difficult to pinpoint sources of cosmic ray production in the Milky Way or in the universe. This is because it is most difficult to determine the direction of cosmic rays from somewhere in spacetime to earth, since mostly they are charged particles and, accordingly, are redirected by galactic, solar-system and other magnetic fields. Thus, most do not pursue a direct course from the place of their origin to the earth, that is, according to general relativity, the shortest curved path to that destination.

Gamma rays, however, are neutral in charge, and, consequently, gamma rays produced together with cosmic rays or by cosmic ray collisions follow the shortest route from their place of origin to earth. Observation of the direction from which gamma rays reach earth has revealed one source of cosmic rays, Cygnus X-3, a binary star system, in which one star is a pulsar neutron star that spins rapidly. The spin accelerates protons to high energy, and when some of these collide with atomic nuclei in the companion star, gamma rays are emitted in the same direction as that of cosmic rays also produced in the collisions. Undoubtedly, other specific sources of cosmic rays and of specific ways in which they are produced will be found.

Cosmic rays produced in the Milky Way are trapped within its magnetic field, but the most energetic probably escape it. The same thing must occur in other galaxies. Magnetic fields may enhance the speed and energy of cosmic rays.

After the discovery of cosmic rays in 1912, there was much observation and study of them and of their collisions with atmospheric particles, balloons being used for the purpose, and later ground detectors also being used to study the showers or cascades of secondary and progeny particles, instigated by primary cosmic ray collisions with atmospheric particles.

It is uneconomic to use cosmic ray collisions where accelerator particle collisions fulfill the intended purpose, but otherwise cosmic ray observation and study continue and are considerable and contribute vastly to astrophysical, astronomical and physical knowledge.

Spin

Subatomic particles have spin, i.e., a state of rotation about their axes, but it is quite different from spin in the supra-atomic, as much so as the orbiting of electrons in an atom differ from orbiting planets about the sun.

The spin of a particle has been variously defined. One definition is that spin is the intrinsic angular momentum of a particle which exists even when the particle is at rest. Another is that spin is a property of certain elementary particles to act as though they were spinning about their axes. Still another is that spin is a fundamental property of a particle that describes its state of rotation. Still one more definition is that spin is a kind of angular momentum of some particles that can be pictured as rotation about their axes.

The total angular momentum of a particle includes its orbital momentum and its intrinsic momentum (spin) in its translational motion.

Spin in the subatomic, unlike spin in the supra-atomic, is quantized. Particles can spin only with certain, and not just any, rates, i.e., number of periods per time unit.

Likewise, spin or intrinsic angular momentum of a particle is quantized. Angular momentum is the tendency of the rotation to continue at the same rate until affected by an external force. Allowable quanta of the angular momentum or of change in it are expressed in multiples of $\frac{1}{2}\hbar$, i.e., $-\frac{1}{2}$, 0, $\frac{1}{2}$, 1, $\frac{3}{2}$, 2, etc. This is the spin quantum number of a particle. It was noted in Chapter 7 that quantized (allowable) orbit angular momenta of a particle are expressed in whole integral multiples of $\hbar$, i.e., 0, 1, 2, 3, etc. As said in Chapter 7, $\hbar$ means $\frac{h}{2\pi}$; and h symbolizes Plank's constant.

The direction of the angular momentum of the spin of a particle also is quantized. This means that in regard to an established direction in space the angular momentum can point only in certain directions and not in just any direction. This compulsion governs where a particle is in a magnetic field, since the field has a direction defined by its poles. In the supra-atomic the angular momentum of a spinning object can point in any direction in reference to an established direction.

The direction of the angular momentum is the direction of the spin.

Protons, neutrons, electrons, and neutrinos are among many particles with spin $\frac{1}{2}$. Several mesons have spin 0, though two of them, the phi and the psi, have spin 1. The h-meson has a spin of 4, the highest so far detected, though not necessarily the highest detectable. The photon has spin zero. The graviton is thought to have spin 2. The force-carrier bosons, W^+, W^- and Z^o, carriers of the weak force, have spin 1. Gluons, carriers of the strong force, have spin 1.

The quantizing of the direction of the angular momentum of particles entails that those with spin $\frac{1}{2}$ can point only up or only down with reference to an established direction of up and down. That is, spin $\frac{1}{2}$ particles can spin only in one of two opposite directions. For spin 1 particles, allowable directions are three: up, down and sideway in one direction perpendicularly. For higher spin quantum numbers allowable directions increase one for each higher number.

Spin of quarks and hadrons

All quarks have spin $\frac{1}{2}$, which means that as they spin their spin can point only up or only down; i.e., their spin state can be $+\frac{1}{2}$ or $-\frac{1}{2}$. The spin number and direction of spin of a particle composed of quarks, i.e., a hadron, are determined by the total of the spin states of the component quarks after cancellation of quarks with plus spin (pointing up) by an equal number with minus spin. Thus, a nucleon, which has two quarks with spin pointing up and one with spin pointing down, has spin $\frac{1}{2}$ and one spin state; as it spins its spin can point only up or only down. A π meson (pion) has two quarks, one with spin up and one with spin down; the spin states of the quarks cancel each other, and so the pion has spin zero and no spin states; though it has angular momentum. A delta particle has three quarks all pointing up, so it has spin $\frac{3}{2}$ and four spin states (two times the spin number plus one); as it spins, its spin can point in one of four directions.

The foregoing analysis of the relationship between quark spin and hadron spin is somewhat detailed and complex, but it shows the significant impact of quark spin on nucleon and other hadron spin and structure.

Right and left-handedness

One is accustomed to regard spin as clockwise or counter-clockwise. It is more convenient in particle physics to view the spin of particles as right or left-handed. By convention, a particle whose spin points in the direction of its motion is right-handed, and one whose spin points in the opposite direction is left-handed.

In beta decay neutrinos emitted are right-handed, and that makes them antineutrinos since antineutrinos are right-handed. The electrons emitted in beta decay are left-handed.

Handedness, or "chirality", as it is called, plays a significant role in other instances of particle behavior and recognition. For example, in particle decay there is a seeming violation of chiral symmetry in that the emission of right-handed electrons and left-handed neutrinos has never been observed.

Decay and radioactivity

Reference to particle decay and radioactivity has been made on several occasions in the foregoing discussion of the subatomic and of particles. Radiation from radioactivity has impressed itself on the minds of all people as something that can, on the one hand, be useful and beneficial when properly used, and that is, on the other hand, dangerous and destructive, when not properly used or safeguarded against.

Our purpose is to complete our general picture of the interiority of matter by discussing briefly the duration of particles and their natural decay and also radioactivity.

Decay is a process in which an atom, nucleus or subatomic particle changes into two or more other like entities, emitting other particles or photons or both as it does so. Just what is meant by "decay" depends on the context, whether it is of an element, atom, nucleus or subatomic particle.

Most subatomic particles are unstable and decay into other particles. All hadrons, including the neutron and possibly the atom when outside the atom, do so. The electron, the massless photon and the massless graviton (if it exists) seemingly are stable, i.e., they do not decay. Neutrinos probably are stable in proportion to their lack of mass.

How long-lived are the proton and the electron? Much more so, we are told, then the present age of the universe.

The "ground states" of stable nuclei, atoms and molecules means that they continue as they are until they are excited into an excited state.

Radioactivity is the spontaneous and regular transformation over time of the unstable nuclei of certain species of atoms (elements), emitting radiation in the transformation. Radioactive radiation is both particulate and wavelike. That is, it consists of particles and is propagated in waves. Like electromagnetic radiation it can be beamed naturally or artificially. Also, it carries energy or, otherwise said, radioactivity radiates energy. The amount of energy varies with the kind of radiation and is inversely proportional to its wavelength.

Basically, there are five kinds, though many varieties of these, of radioactivity and its radiation. These five are alpha, beta, gamma, proton and spontaneous fission. In the first three, alpha, beta and gamma particles are respectively emitted in the decay process. In spontaneous fission a nucleus splits into two pieces of comparable masses and several neutrons. Nuclear fission can be triggered artificially in nuclear bombs and in energy production.

Alpha decay occurs through the strong force, beta decay through the weak, and gamma through the electromagnetic; and spontaneous fission also through the electromagnetic. What is important in our general depiction of radioactivity is that it is brought about by the fundamental forces; how need not be explained.

Radioactive decay occurs serially from one unstable nuclide (a species of nuclei with a certain number of protons and neutrons) in a chain of nuclear transformations until a stable nuclide is reached. The chain may lead, for example, from an unstable nuclide of uranium and thorium to a nuclide of lead in a ground state (the lowest energy state) or from an unstable nuclide of cobalt to a nuclide of iron in a ground state.

Only a few of the elements, mostly those of high atomic weight, are radioactive. However, many elements on earth not now having radioactive nuclides had them in the past, at least when atoms first formed. They decayed into stable nuclides too rapidly to exist naturally now. However, radioactive forms of most elements have been found through artificially induced transformations of them.

Radioactivity is absolutely regular and so is used in testing materials for their age. The time that it takes for different unstable nuclei to decay ranges from zero to infinity. For example, the half-lives of uranium radioactive isotopes range from an infinitesimal fraction of a second through seconds, minutes, hours, days, months and years to $4\frac{1}{2}$ billion years and stability. Likewise, the half-lives of radium radioactive isotopes range from almost nothing in time through minutes, hours, months and years to ten billion years and stability. Radioactive carbon 14 has a half-life of 5,568 years.

Half-life is the time required for half of the nuclei in an assemblage, large enough to be representative of the kind of nuclei involved, to decay. It is an accurate basis for predicting how many atoms of a material will decay in a year. It is impossible to determine how long a particular atom will endure.

Radioactivity plays a major role in the weaving of matter through the basic interactions of particles, and it also plays a major role in human understanding of that weaving.

God said

"Let there be particles interacting with one another energetically to burst into an expanding universe of spacetime throughout which the interacting particles will be woven into radiation and then into matter along with the radiation. The matter shall be made of leptons and quarks aggregated through the interactions of the particles into atoms, molecules, solids, gasses and fluids, cells and living beings, plant and animals. Let intelligence evolve in some species of animals, enough in some to contemplate the origin and nature of the universe and of themselves and to think of me with love and wonder. I shall love them in return and all my creatures and my works, but I shall leave them to the resources with which I have endowed them." Or did it all happen otherwise?

11

The Expanding Explosion

We look away from the earth in any direction and in doing so we look down in distancepast toward the Little Bomb that made the Big Bang. With telescopes we can see at least half-way there; and on our distance-past ladder we can intellectually climb down almost all the way there, though much is unclear to our minds as we descend, especially near the bottom of the ladder. Below 10^{-43} second after the Big Bang exploded, called Planck time, physicists tell us that they cannot now know what was happening in that explosion, that is, in the universe.

We realize, as we descend our ladder, that we pass through what we metaphorically have called the loom of spacetime upon which the fabric of matter and of radiation is being woven. We also realize that the loom is expanding and that, as it expands, the fabric expands with it in that the galactic patterns being woven upon the loom are continually being separated from one another by the expansion of the loom.

The expanding of spacetime, and so of the universe, is, metaphorically, the continuing Big Bang explosion. Thus, it is the power unleashed by the Little Bomb that keeps the explosion expanding; or, in other words, that keeps spacetime and the universe expanding. Gravity is a brake on the expansion, gradually slowing it down; and gravity is a glue holding together the expanding loom of spacetime and the fabric being woven upon it.

The expanding force apparently is consequential on the four fundamental interactions of matter, which may be less in number or only one, as previously discussed.

Science has no idea why the Little Bomb exploded, or why it did so with the force with which it did, to create our expanding universe. Or, if there was no Little Bomb, science has no idea why the Big Bang occurred, or why it did with the power that it had. We only know, which we do certainly, that the exploding power was sufficient to make the explosion, braked and held together by gravity, the universe in which we live. God may know why the cosmic event occurred, and he may have willed and caused it to occur, if there is a God. What does the event itself indicate? The answer depends perhaps on further knowledge of what transpired in the first 10^{-43} second of time (after the universe and time began).

The twin realizations of this century that the universe is exploding and that the expansion had a beginning in the Little Bomb, or without it if there was no Little Bomb, are among the most momentous events in the intellectual history of mankind. Previously, there had been no scientific evidence that the universe had a beginning, though that it had has been asserted often and long by religions and in mythology. That space itself is stretching three-dimensionally, that space and time, and thus spacetime, curve and are mutable everywhere, and that space and the universe are as immense as they are and are expanding steadily, but with gradual deceleration, are concepts of reality that the medieval Church fathers would have deemed cause for punishment and purification by torture and burning; and that people at most times and places would have derided, laughed or raged at and considered mad or even criminal. In 1930, however, intellectual society everywhere, though amazed at the report of the expansion of the universe and of its many concomitant cosmological facts and probabilities, and more or less aware of what its tremendous impact on mankind's outlook upon the universe and itself would be, accepted it as probably true if credible scientists so regarded it. To the public generally it was astonishing but not usually frontpage news. The reason why there was only a modicum of excitement, though very much interest, was that the public had become accustomed to the marvels of science and technology, and to the revolutionary theoretical discoveries of the great physicists of this century.

Edwin Hubble and his associate, Milton Humason, must be chiefly credited for the observational evidence that confirmed beyond a reasonable doubt that the universe is expanding as had been predicted theoretically by William de Sitter in 1917, Alexander Alexandrovich Friedmann in 1922 and Georges Lemaitre in 1927. The expanding universe as shown by observation corresponds most with the prediction of Friedmann.

Hubble was present at a meeting in 1914 of astronomers, at which Vesto Slipher reported his discovery that certain nebulae (now known to be galaxies) were receding from us at tremendous speeds. In 1931 Hubble and Humason in a joint publication reported the result of their many years of observation of the relationship between the recessional velocities and the distances of galaxies. The report established that, with the exceptions of some nearby galaxies and our own galaxy, the galaxies are receding from us at speeds proportionate to the increase in distance from us times a constant known as the Hubble constant. This relationship of galactic recessional velocity to distance is known as Hubble's law and is expressed by the equation $v = H_od$, v being velocity, d distance, and H_o the constant.

Extrapolating from the apparent recessional velocities and distances of galaxies from us, it becomes clear that all galaxies, excepting some relatively close to each other, are receding from each other according to Hubble's law, and the universe consequently must be expanding, beyond a reasonable doubt.

It should be mentioned here that Hubble in his investigation of nebulae concluded in 1917 that some nebulae were gas clouds in the Milky Way, though he believed that the spiral nebulae were beyond the Milky Way. By 1928 his observation showed conclusively that M31 in Andromeda is a galaxy similar to the Milky Way.

Hubble and Humason, observing with the 100–inch telescope at Mount Wilson, used the red shift to determine the recessional velocities of galaxies from us, and they used the intrinsic-apparent brightness, Cepheid-variable and other methods to determine their distance from us. It now has been concluded, with some dissent, that quasars are at a great distance from us and are receding from us at velocities proportional to their distance, in accordance with Hubble's law. They, too, like galaxies, are being carried apart by expanding spacetime. The dissent attributes the red shift of quasars possibly to gravity, rather than to cosmic expansion, resulting in their distances from us being far less than it would be in the latter instance.

Frequently it is said that the red shift of galaxies and quasars is due to a Doppler effect, but according to many astronomers, the red shift of greatly distant galaxies and quasars is due more to the expansion of space (concurrent with the expansion of the universe) than it is due to a Doppler effect. By this they mean that light or other electro-magnetic waves are flattened and lengthened by the expanding of space through which they travel, rather than by the relative velocities of the source of light or other radiation and the observer. The more distant from us the space through which the waves travel is, the faster the space is expanding, carrying the galaxies with it at its continuous accelerating expansion. The galaxies are being carried like passengers in an ever-accelerating car. The rule is that the more distant that a galaxy is from us, the more its red shift is due to cosmic expansion, and the less it is due to a Doppler effect, if any. Conversely, the closer a galaxy is to us, the more its red shift is due to a Doppler effect, though that effect is minimal except as to galaxies very close to us, like those in our Local Group.

Galaxies very close to us may actually be moving toward us with acceleration revealed by a blue shift. This is because their relative velocity in space toward us, caused by gravitation locally, suffices to overcome the overall rate of spatial expansion. They are like ships struggling to reach a harbor against a strong, outgoing tide.

An important consequence of the recessional red shift of galaxies being largely, indeed almost entirely, due to spatial and cosmic expansion, rather than to a Doppler effect, is that it explains how the recessional red shift of some galaxies and some quasars can show, as it does, that their recession from us is close to the speed of light. Indeed, one observed quasar has a recessional velocity of ninety two percent of the speed of light, which makes it the most pastdistant of any observed object. The rule that nothing can attain or pass the speed of light is inapplicable to the expansion of spacetime carrying galaxies and quasars with it.

The galaxies are nearly fixed in space, moving relatively little and slowly with respect to other galaxies in their local group, as in the case of the Milky Way and the Magellanic Clouds, or as to nearby local groups, as that containing the galaxy M31 in Andromeda. The blue shift of M31 evidences that it is approaching the Milky Way.

We can visualize the accelerating separation of galaxies from one another and the expansion of space and the universe by analogy with the accelerating separation from one another of raisins in a rising loaf of bread. The raisins are carried apart from each other by the expanding bread, which corresponds to expanding space carrying the galaxies apart from each other. As the bread uniformly expands, the raisins get farther and farther apart from each other, and as they do, their recession from each other accelerates even though the expansion of the bread is gradually slowing down. In the same manner, the galaxies are carried faster apart as their distance from each other increases, even though the expansion of space carrying them is gradually slowing down.

Hubble's law applies, not only to galaxies in expanding spacetime, but also to raisins in a rising loaf of bread, as well as to dots on the surface of an expanding balloon, and to any markers on any uniformly expanding two-dimensional surface or in any three-dimentional body.

It is spacetime rather than just space, as spacetime is a continuum, that is expanding and carrying the galaxies apart as it does so. Within the spacetime continuum, space continuously expands three-dimensionally and time continuously in the direction of the future, the temporal expansion being proportional to the spatial according to Hubble's law. That is, the rate of temporal expansion equals Hubble's constant (which depends on spatial distance from us, or from any observer in the universe) times that distance. The equation still is v = Hod, though it is spacetime rather than just space that is expanding.

The Hubble constant cannot precisely be determined, at least as of now, to give certainty to the Hubble law governing galaxies in space, because of the difficulty of precisely determining the distances involved, but it can be determined to give certainty to the Hubble law governing dots on an expanding balloon and raisins in a rising loaf of bread.

The age of the universe, the time that has elapsed since zero time when the Little Bomb exploded in the Big Bang, can be estimated from what has been observed and is known of the rates of expansion of the universe, and of deceleration of that expansion since that first event. But that age cannot be determined accurately because those rates are not accurately known. The expansion rate depends on the Hubble constant, which in turn depends on determinations of distances to the greatly distant galaxies. Revised distance measurements give a much smaller value now to the Hubble constant and, therefore, a much greater age of the universe than did distances as measured by Hubble. The value originally given the constant indicated that the universe was younger than the solar system and the earth, which discredited the Big Bang theory, but this difficulty has been eliminated by the revised estimated distances of the galaxies. It is known that there is a gradual deceleration of the expansion of the universe, but the rate of deceleration, or rates if there has not been a uniform rate, are unknown.

Allowing for the unknown and variable factors, the estimated age of the universe, calculated from its expansion, is now thought to be between ten and twenty billion years. Estimates of the age based on other methods are in accord with these figures. Some astronomers think that the latest observational data give an age of between eighteen and twenty billion years, which age we shall assume in this book to be correct.

What can be said as to the impact of the now known expansion of the universe and of its concomitant immensity, and of its long or ever-lasting destiny upon traditional concepts of the God-Creator and upon traditional proofs of his existence? Our previous discussion as to the impact of the Little Bomb and the Big Bang on these concepts and proofs is applicable here, also, since the expansion is the consequence of the magnitude of the mysterious and unknown explosive power of the Little Bomb when it was released, by what means we do now know, in the Big

Bang. It appears that God or nature (something natural that we do not understand) made the Little Bomb, jampacked it with protomatter-energy and set it off with the power to sustain and expand the explosion, perhaps forever. The expansion is restrained and kept in shape by gravity-glue, as discussed in the next chapter.

Neither the early and medieval Church Fathers nor anyone of their time had any inkling of the age, vastness and expansion of the universe, though they did have conceptions (mistaken) of absolute time and space, extending without limit, and of the eternity of God, often thought by them as by many until now, as independent of time and space. Nor did anyone until the twentieth century have any notion of the immensity and expansion of the cosmos; and concepts of the God-Creator and proofs and disproofs of his existence remained rooted in Christian, Jewish and Mohammedan theological and philosophical thinking of the past, without substantial modification since St. Thomas Aquinas, Luther and Calvin.

In the now-known expansion, greatness of age and unimaginable vastness of the universe, theologians and philosophers, disagreeing and disputing among themselves, will perceive evidence of God's existence or will perceive the lack of evidence. Some will see signs of divine design; others will not. Some, unaffected by modern cosmology, will regard our own existence—and indeed existence itself—as proof of God's existence. Others will accept his existence as explanation of the Little Bomb, the Big Bang, and its continuing expansion. We shall state our own view on these matters later.

12

Gravitation

The loom of spacetime and the fabric of matter and of radiation being woven upon it differ from an ordinary loom and the fabric that is being woven upon it in that it is continually expanding four-dimensionally. That expansion is kept in check by the gravitational force, just how much in check being most important though uncertain. That is to say, departing from our metaphor, the force that restrains the continuing explosion of the Big Bang—that is, the continuing expansion of the universe—is the gravitational force, which results, according to prevalent physical and astronomical theory, from the gravitational interchange of particles, one of the four basic interchanges of particles, as discussed in Chapter 8. According to the general theory of relativity, however, the gravitational force results from the overall, regional and local curvature of spacetime, caused by mass as noted in Chapter 6. There it also is noted that while spacetime curvature is caused by mass, spacetime curvature, in turn, causes mass to move and governs when, where to, and how fast it moves. Mass, in this context as always, includes energy, its equivalent under the special theory of relativity, and it also includes radiation, insofar as radiation is particulate, i.e., has mass.

Reconciliation of the gravitational force being a consequence of the interaction of gravitons and other particles with it and also being due to spacetime curvature will be discussed later.

The primary meaning of "gravity" is the attraction by the earth's mass toward its center, of particles and bodies on or above its surface and within it. More broadly, the word is used to mean "gravitation," the universal force of which "gravity" is the earthly manifestation. Generally, we shall use "gravity", "gravitational force", and "gravitation" synonymously to mean gravitational force, and we shall also use "gravitation" to mean the interaction of the force with spacetime and with matter. According to the general theory of relativity, there is some question, as we shall see, as to whether or not gravity actually is a force.

It is our intent in discussing the gravitational force, not to argue scientifically what it is or is not, but to note prevalent scientific views as to its origin, nature and effect, in our endeavor to look at the universe as it is, broadly and essentially, without unnecessary and confusing detail, in basic inquiry as to how it came to be, continues as it does and will be, whether through God, other cause, or no cause. No doubt, the gravitational force, whether obedient to non-divine natural law or to divine natural law, operates in opposition to the expansion of the universe, and together with that expansion creates the equilibrium in which the expanding universe exists and functions. In that equilibrium order is possible. There is a distancepast, spacetime and a distancefuture. All things instantaneously neither crash together nor infinitely disperse.

Strength and role of gravitational force

As discussed in Chapter 8, the characteristic strengths of the basic interactions of matter at a distance of 10^{-13} centimeter, equivalent to the diameter of a proton, are respectively: the strong interaction, 1; the electromagnetic, 10^{-2}; the weak, 10^{-13}; and the gravitational, 10^{-38}. Thus the role of gravity in the subatomic is negligible. On the other hand, the gravitational and the electromagnetic have major roles in the supra-atomic. Of course, since the supra-atomic is aggregated of the subatomic, all four basic interactions are involved in the supra-atomic. The role of the gravitational force as a check on the expansion of the universe has already been discussed.

Newtonian view

Between every particle, every physical body and every aggregation of particles or of physical bodies, there is an attraction, i.e. gravitation or the gravitational force, varying with the product of their masses and inversely with the square of the distance between them, expressed by the equation $F = Gm_1m_2$, where F is the attraction (force), G is a gravitational constant and m_1 and m_2 are the masses respectively of each of the two particles, bodies or assemblages of particles.

An obvious error in the Newtonian concept and equation, as Einstein discerned, is the assumption that there are absolute space, absolute time and an absolute present or "now," which is false according to the special theory of relativity. Also questionable and probably false is the assumption in the Newtonian concept and equation that the infinite effect of the gravitational force is instantaneous.

General relativity corrects the Newtonian equation by taking into account time as well as space, spacetime and spacetime curvature, and also the effect of constancy in the speed of light under special relativity.

The Newtonian concept and equation agree with general relativity in result, or nearly so agree, and can be and are used, where distances are not astronomically great. The Newtonian equation explains the orbiting of the solar planets precisely, or nearly precisely, except for the precession of Mercury's orbit, which general relativity explains much more precisely, indeed almost exactly. Accordingly, general relativity, embracing gravity as spacetime curvature (or as its effect), has replaced the Newtonian theory as basic in physical measurement and computation where masses and distances are vast. It has done so because determinations and predictions based on it have concurred, far more accurately than those based on Newtonian theory, with factual observation and investigation. This is true, for example, not only with respect to the precession of Mercury's orbit, but with respect to the bending of starlight toward the Sun during solar eclipse, to similar bending of radio waves from a quasar and to gravitational red shift, noted in Chapter 2 and also subsequently discussed.

Gravitational response of energy

Energy acts like other mass in response to spacetime curvature. The bending of starlight and radio radiation toward the sun confirms this fact as well as spacetime curvature. The same is true of increase of wavelength causing gravitational red shift, as subsequently discussed.

Gravitons as carriers of force

Theoretical physicists mostly agree that the gravitational interaction or force is effected through force-carrying particles called "gravitons", as noted in Chapter 8. No gravitons have been experimentally observed or detected sofar. Obviously, the gravitational force as a result of particles, bodies and assemblages of particles and bodies following the easiest curvature of spacetime to follow, just as water follows the easiest path downhill to follow, needs reconciliation, not yet understood, with the gravitational force as a consequence of the exchange of gravitons between particles. It could be, perhaps, that spacetime curvature by mass-energy and the following of it by mass-energy are effected through the intermediation of gravitons.

Spacetime curvature as cause

What causes and what is the nature of gravitational attraction? Newton's law of universal gravitation states the effect, but Newton gives no explanation of the phenomenon. Einstein's theory of general relativity gives a geometrical explanation of the phenomenon as being due to the curvature of spacetime caused by matter. How this can be, assuming spacetime does curve, is illustrated by the following analogy.

Two airplanes flying straight north (toward the North Pole) after taking off simultaneously from two cities, one due east of the other, naturally converge as they fly. Their convergence is due, of course, to the convergence of the meridians that they respectively are following, and is not due to any force other than the jet forces respectively propelling them straight north.

Similarly to this analogy, a bomb dropped from one of the airplanes and another dropped at the same moment from the other airplane converge as they plummet toward the center of the earth; and the convergence is due to the convergence of the curves they respectively follow toward the center of the earth. In plummeting straight down, the bombs follow the shortest curves possible to the center of the earth, which are their shortest possible routes there. These shortest possible curves are spacetime geodesics, fully analogous to the globular geodesics being followed by the airplanes in their straight north courses.

Escape, return and orbiting of bodies

Each airplane is steered on its course by its pilot, but why do the falling bombs take the courses that they do, as discussed above? The answer, according to the general theory of relativity, is that it is the nature of each bomb, as it is of everything on or near the surface of the earth, or in it, always to follow the shortest route to the center of the earth, unless it is prevented from doing so. It has been assumed that the bombs were simply dropped and not pushed before they fell. In fact, some force is essential to their release.

When a projectile is shot from a gun or a ball is thrown into space, a force has been applied to the projectile or ball, and Newton's three laws of motion are applicable. Under the first law, the projectile moves in a straight line with unvarying velocity until an external force acts upon it. Under the theory of general relativity, however, the projectile follows as closely as it can the shortest curvature of spacetime, which is the shortest route, toward the center of gravitation, which is the center of spacetime curvature caused by the earth and which is the center of the earth. If its initial velocity is sufficient, that is, if it has escape velocity, i.e., 11.2 kilometers per second, it will escape spacetime curvature caused by the earth (the earth's gravitational field), never completely, but enough to continue its course out into space.

Thus, man-made satellites and their debris orbit the earth for awhile and then usually fall back to it. If their velocity and acceleration, initially and augmented by employment (through scientific know-how) of gravitational fields of other planets, are sufficient, they continue in orbit (that is, continuing fall toward earth), like the two Voyager spacecraft, forever, unless captured by spacetime curvature (gravitational force) of some other body or assemblage of matter, in which event they fall into orbit about that body or assemblage or crash into it.

Cause of curvatures

What causes spacetime curvature and thus gravity? The answer, as often already said, is mass-energy. Mass-energy throughout the universe causes an overall curvature of spacetime, closed, flat or hyperbolic, depending on the amount of mass-energy in the universe.

The degree of curvature regionally or locally depends on the amount of distribution of matter in the particular region or place. Local is superimposed on regional curvature, and both on overall curvature.

All of the foregoing is repetitive of what previously has been said. It has also been observed above, that mass-energy may make spacetime curve through the interaction and gravitons and particles. It likewise may be the case that mass-energy follows spacetime curvature through the influence of that interaction. Our understanding is that physics does not have as yet an explanation of why mass-energy and spacetime thus interact. That explanation may only come with a comprehension of a basic single interaction, force and field, of which all other interactions, forces and fields are manifestations in the weaving of the fabric of matter and of radiation on the loom of spacetime.

Analogy illustrative of spacetime curvature

While it can't as of now be fully explained why mass-energy makes spacetime curve, the following analogy is illustrative of its doing so, and also of spacetime curvature making mass-energy move.

The analogy is the curvature of a stretched rubber sheet on which a metal ball or balls are placed. The balls depress the sheet, discernibly if the sheet is not too strong and tightly stretched. The most depression caused by each ball is directly underneath it and is a hole in but not through the sheet in which the ball rests. Each hole causes (is constituted by) curvature of the sheet into it. A heavier ball causes a deeper hole and more curvature than does a lighter ball of the same volume.

Each ball produces its own hole and curvature in the sheet, and all the balls produce an overall curvature that can be mathematically described. A marble placed on the sheet will roll, following the overall curvature until it encounters a distracting local curvature causing it to roll into the hole causing that local curvature. It is somewhat like this with assemblages of mass in spacetime. They cause and also follow spacetime curvatures.

The analogy is far from perfect. An important difference is that a rubber sheet has a two-dimensional top surface, a two-dimensional bottom surface, and four two-dimensional edges, whereas spacetime is four-dimensional and has no surface or edges. Nor do assemblages of matter come to rest in holes as balls do on a rubber sheet. We perceive the rubber sheet and can visualize it without perceiving it. We cannot perceive or visualize spacetime though we do conceive of it.

A ball or any object falls to the earth with the same acceleration irrespective of its mass, excluding the effect of air resistance, as Galileo reportedly demonstrated by dropping two objects of different mass from the Tower of Pisa. Scientists puzzled about this until Einstein explained that the phenomenon is due to gravitation being the natural tendency of an object to follow spacetime curvature where the object is, with acceleration according to the degree of curvature only, that is, irrespective of its mass. Curvature of spacetime due to the earth is more than that due to the moon, simply because the earth is more massive than the moon. Thus, gravitation is stronger on the surface of the earth than it is on the surface of the moon, although the moon's surface is much closer to its center than is the earth's surface to its center.

The illustrated principle is that all things respond to gravitation equally irrespective of their mass or, in Einstein's perceptions, they so respond to spacetime curvature.

The equivalence principle

Einstein realized that in an elevator moving in the direction of its top, that is up, somewhere in space remote from any mass so that gravitational attraction by any body or bodies or all bodies on it are negligible, acceleration of the elevator has an effect on its occupants undistinguishable from the effect of gravity on terrestrial occupants. They are pulled toward the floor just as occupants of the earth and things above on or in it are pulled toward its center. The elevator occupants feel "pulled" because the floor is accelerating toward them. Earthly occupants feel "pulled" by gravity, because their natural motion is along spacetime curvature toward the center of the earth.

The strength of the pulling of the elevator's occupants to its floor is proportional to the acceleration, just as the gravitational pulling by a body on an object is proportional to their masses and thus to the degree of spacetime curvature caused by their masses.

The principle of similarity of the effect of gravitation and of acceleration is the principle of their equivalence. It led Einstein to his conception of gravitation being due to spacetime curvature caused by mass-energy.

Einstein envisioned in effect spaceships in deep space, in which there would be felt neither gravitation nor anything like it in the absence of acceleration of the spaceship.

Proportionality to density of matter

The degree of spacetime curvature and thus of gravitation is proportional to the density of matter-energy causing the curvature. Thus, the degree of spacetime curvature and so of gravitation in the vicinity of a neutron star of the volume of the earth and of the mass of the sun is far greater than is the degree of spacetime curvature and thus of gravitation either in the vicinity of the sun or of the earth. In the vicinity of a black hole the degree of spacetime curvature and thus of gravitation is far greater than in the vicinity of the neutron star of the same mass as the black hole.

Gravitational force as real or apparent

Gravitational force is only an apparent force if it is only like two airplanes converging as they simultaneously fly north. It is a real force if it is due to gravitational interaction, that is, to the interaction of gravitons and other particles, or to the interaction of particles through the intermediation of force-carrying gravitons. There may be, as said before, a causal relationship between the interaction of gravitons and particles with mass-energy that explains why mass-energy makes spacetime curve and why mass-energy follows spacetime curvature.

It is possible that in time science will find that gravitation fundamentally is the same as the other fundamental forces of nature, and is only a different manifestation, as they may be, of a single underlying force.

This may be the result of a valid unified field theory, unsuccessfully sought so long by Einstein, accounting for gravitation, electromagnetic force and the strong and weak nuclear forces.

Gravitational fields

What we have been discussing is the nature of any particle or body to move, unless prevented, along the shortest possible curvature to the center of gravity of the gravitational field dominant where it is at the moment. By a dominant gravitational field we mean simply the one that governs a body or particle where it is in two or more gravitational fields. For instance, we are in the gravitational field of the earth and that of the sun, but we stay on the earth because its gravitational field here is dominant over the gravitational field of the sun. It is also dominant over the gravitational fields of the solar system, the universe, and every body or particle in the universe. Obviously, if Newton's law means anything, every body and particle in the universe, as well as the universe itself, has a gravitational field extending everywhere in the universe. This portrayal of a "dominant" gravitational field is our own interpretation of the situation.

A gravitational field is a region wherein there is spacetime curvature and thus gravitational force, real or apparent, due to mass-energy of a particle, object, assemblage of objects or the universe itself. In each instance the field is infinite. At each point in spacetime there is spacetime curvature, and thus gravitation, toward every other point, governed by mass-energy distribution, universally, regionally and locally, in accordance with Newtonian as modified by Einstein's theory.

Gravitational energy

Particles and bodies have potential gravitational energy, i.e., the potential to do work through gravitation, as by water falling or by driving piles with a falling weight. It usually is said that particles and physical bodies have gravitational energy by reason of being in a gravitational field. What usually is meant is a gravitational field that is not insignificant in effect on the particle or physical object.

Potential gravitational energy as other energy is equivalent to mass in accordance with the special relativity equation of $E = mc^2$.

An example of the conversion of potential gravitational energy into work is its conversion, through gravitational contraction of a star, into light and heat, or of a nebula into a star that radiates light, heat and other electromagnetic radiation.

It also is thought that energy is transmitted by gravitational waves, if they exist.

Gravitational waves

Since matter causes spacetime curvature and thus gravitation, it is to be expected that an extraordinarily sudden or violent and enormous behavior of much mass will be reflected in some manner in spacetime curvature, such as waves in that curvature and thus in gravitation, varying in length and frequency and following that curvature with the speed of light. To cause detectable gravitational waves the event would have to be something like a supernova, the swallowing of a galaxy by a black hole or the rapid spinning of a small object of enormous mass like a neutron star.

Einstein in 1915 predicted that gravitational waves might be caused in this manner, and for some time effort has been made to detect them. Now it seems that at least one rapidly spinning neutron star (a pulsar) in a binary system, which has been observed, is propagating gravitational waves, evidenced by its shrinkage due to loss of mass carried off as energy by the gravitational waves. The detection is made possible by closely monitoring the spin of the pulsar. Pulsars are discussed in Chapters 16 and 18.

Gravitational waves, if they exist, probably are weak in their interaction with matter, but they might cause slight motion in particles or slight stress in materials that possibly is detectable, but detecting them in this manner so far has not been successful.

Gravitational waves, if a reality, conceivably could affect the weaving of the fabric of matter and of radiation on the loom of spacetime in important ways. For instance, it may be that they disturb intergalactic clouds so that galaxy formation is started. It has been conjectured that our galaxy had its beginning in this manner. It could be that gravitational waves, penetrating or emanating from matter or radiation impenetrable to observation by light or to other electromagnetic observation, might further the investigation of black holes, the interior of supernova explosions and other phenomena, and even of the Little Bomb and the first moments of the Big Bang.

Gravitational red shift

This shift in the spectrum of light is not due to a Doppler effect, as noted in Chapter 2. Instead it is due to the effect of the gravitational force of the body on light as it leaves the body. The light loses energy just as a ball does when thrown upward. The ball returns to the earth because it does not have escape velocity. The light, of course, has escape velocity and escapes the earth. The light does not slow down under gravitational pull of the body. Instead, it loses energy by a lengthening of its wavelength, which causes the red shift.

The more massive the body from which the light comes, the greater is the lengthening of its wavelength and thus of its red shift as it leaves the body.

It has been asserted that the red shift of quasars is, or might be, gravitational rather than due to their great recessional velocity, as discussed in Chapter 13.

Gravitational lens

The bending of light from an astronomical object toward another astronomical object as it passes the latter can create double or multiple images of the light-emitting object as seen from earth. The gravitational field of the body causing the light deflection thus acts as a gravitational lens. Radio waves and other electromagnetic radiation than light likewise can be deflected to create double or multiple images of the object emitting them. The emitting and deflecting objects can be quasars, galaxies or possible other astronomical bodies or assemblages.

At least in one instance quasars seen close together have been deemed to be multiple images of a single quasar, caused in this manner.

Gravitation and God

Does gravity in its tremendous and many roles in the structuring and functioning of the loom of spacetime, and in the weaving of the fabric of matter upon it, give cause for re-thinking traditional concepts and proofs of God? It certainly makes one reflect upon the dexterity of the intellect, or of the non-intellect, or of whatever it was, perhaps only chance, that included gravity in creation (if it occurred) and in the composition of the universe. It would seem, if there were any intent involved, that it was that gravitation from the very first would restrain and shape the universe into the cosmos that it is.

We do not mean this book to be a portrayal of the wonders of the universe so that readers will be exulted, or be overcome by awe, whether or not they attribute the wonders to a God. Rather, we hope that it will contribute to their reexamination in the light of modern cosmology of thinking about God that largely has developed while knowledge of cosmology was scant and mostly erroneous, and that in large measure has been based on that inadequate and erroneous knowledge. Gravitation, nevertheless, cannot be thought about deeply without awe at its cosmic range and at its dexterious instrumentality, shared, of course, by the like range and instrumentality of the expansive power of the universe and of the interaction of all the fundamental forces of nature, in the evolution and shaping of the universe.

We shall have more to say in Part Two about the impact of modern theory and knowledge of the gravitational force, as well as of other aspects of modern cosmology, on our personal views as to God, his existence or nonexistence, and his nature, if he exists.

13

Quasars and Hyperactive Galaxies

The mental tour on the red-shift ladder to be taken in this chapter begins far down in the distancepast, deep in the loom of spacetime, when the fabric of matter and of radiation being woven upon the loom was wholly gas, enormously dense and hot, comprised of ionized hydrogen, deuterium and helium. Here and there, however, throughout the gas clumpy coagulations were forming, and these were to become the quasars and galaxies which constitute the pervasive and dominant macro pattern woven into the fabric of matter. This probably was over fourteen billion years ago.

On our ascent on the ladder from then to now we shall mentally observe the evolution and morphogenesis of the quasars and galaxies.

Protogalaxies

What caused the spotty and lumpy thickening of the gas to begin and to continue until the gas fragmented into protogalactic clouds is unknown. Nor is it understood what caused the protogalactic clouds to revolve on their axes, which property the galaxies have retained.

We mentally see that within the turning protogalactic clouds billions of gas assemblages are grouping and revolving on their own axes while orbiting about the protogalactic axes. These assemblages, we surmise, are the gathering stellar systems. They are sweeping up protogalactic gas as they move through it. Indeed, throughout these formative stellar systems we see stars already beginning to shine. Thus, across the dominant protogalactic pattern a secondary protostellar motif is being woven into the fabric of matter and of radiation on the loom of spacetime.

Primeval galaxies

Ascending the ladder toward "now," we mentally see the protogalactic clouds collapsing into primeval galaxies, in which the stellar systems are attaining more and more solidity and stability, with more and more stars starting to shine. These occurrences are too deep in the distancepast to be telescopically observed from the earth at the present time. We know that the collapsing of the protogalactic clouds into primeval galaxies is self-gravitationally caused.

Down from "now" on the ladder as we mentally gaze about us, we observe that gas and clumps are falling inward with great and increasing speed and crushing together toward the centers of the primeval galaxies, there causing immense density, heating, radiation and explosiveness. We understand that the cause is the continuing self-gravitational collapse that has reduced the protogalaxies into the primeval galaxies.

In the dense, hot centers of the primeval galaxies we mentally discern "powerhouses" or "energy engines" created, we believe, by the crushing together of gas and matter. These "powerhouses" or "energy engines" are prodigiously emitting radiation from relatively minute spots that they occupy, and that is why we have named them as we do. "Aha," we say, "these powerhouses or energy engines must be black holes, and are the quasars, or are within the quasars, those most distant of actually observed astronomical objects, first witnessed from the earth in the twentieth century." Why there should be prodigeous radiation from a black hole and its vicinity is explained in Chapter 18, which discusses black holes.

The primeval galaxies that we mentally are observing from the red-shift ladder over ten billion years ago will become the galaxies that populate the universe today. Furthermore, the overall distribution pattern of the primeval galaxies generally is the same as that of the galaxies now. There have been and still are collisions and commingling of galaxies, and probably cannibalism by galaxies of other galaxies in order to fuel their black hole engines. This colliding of galaxies and their occasional devouring of other galaxies occur notwithstanding the overall expansion of the universe. Apart from these happenings, however, primeval galaxies, once formed, have preserved their identities in the galaxies observed today, evolving and seldom dying; and the density of the galaxies they have become depends on whether the universe is open and infinite or closed and finite.

That is to say, it seems that the loom of spacetime has been arranged with galaxies only once, and that was when it was young and the fabric of matter and of radiation being woven on it was vastly denser than it is today. The intergalactic gas seemingly has become far too thin for further galaxy formation out of it to occur. It has been at least three billion years since the last galaxy formed, so far as is now definitely known, and we have been told that no more galaxies will ever be born, at least in this universe. The nearest quasar, which may be the heart of the last-formed galaxy, is about three billion lightyears away.

As recently as May of 1987, however, it has been suggested that an observed dark object, discovered in 1985, well may be a spiral galaxy in early formation that commenced only 715 million years ago. It has been named "Malin 1" and is in the direction of the constellation Virgo. It has a bright nucleus, a few faint stars and much of the gaseous material out of which stars form. It is by far the largest spiral galaxy now known, being 770,000 lightyears across and ten times larger than the average spiral galaxy. If it is true that it commenced to form recently in astronomical time, it could be that galaxies are still forming in dark seeming voids in the universe.

As we mentally look out upon the primeval galaxies from the red-shift ladder in the far distancepast, they appear to be globular like the protogalactic gas clouds out of which they condensed, but as to this we are uncertain because we cannot telescopically see the primeval galaxies today. We mentally see them, however, apparently evolving into their present configurations, with a variance that may depend on their mass, density, spin, rate of star birth, star sizes, proximity of other galaxies and other factors.

It has been suggested that the most critical factor in the shape assumed in galactic formation from primeval galaxies, and of primeval from protogalaxies, is the rate of star formation, that is, the rate with which gas is converted into stars. If most of the gas of a developing galaxy quickly is converted into stars before it has had time to settle into a disk, the galaxy will be elliptical without much galactic gas. Disk galaxies have more gas because less of their gas was quickly converted into stars and consequently there has continued to be more star formation in them than in ellipticals. Irregular galaxies result from extremely slow star formation, leaving them with much gas in various configurations; perhaps more than half their gas remains unconverted into stars.

Will the primeval galaxies, that is, galaxies in their embryonic stage, remote as they are in the distancepast, contemporaneous with or beyond quasars telescopically observed today, be telescopically observed in the future, possibly soon, with new and improved observational apparatus and techniques, perhaps with the space telescope when it is launched? Most likely, the answer is "Yes". However, to distinguish the primeval galaxies from quasars, when and if they are observed, may be very difficult. Nevertheless, it is anticipated that they will be distinguishable from quasars by their peripheral cloudiness and some detail in the cloudiness, by the peaking of their spectra and by not varying in brightness periodically as quasars do. Indeed, it has been predicted that the space telescope will clearly resolve the structure of a primeval galaxy at a distancepast as much as sixteen billion lightyears, distinguishing its bright nucleus, far brighter than the nuclei of closer galaxies; and that in time thousands of primeval galaxies will be observed in a square degree of the sky.

Techniques, including use of an objective prism, have been and are being developed for rapidly surveying the sky for indications of red shifts and spectra that might be those of quasars or of primeval galaxies amongst or beyond the quasars, so that observation can be focussed on the indicated points of origin of the red shifts and spectra. Orbiting apparatus for X-ray and far-infrared observation, now being used for quasar detection, may also be used for detection of primeval galaxies, especially for those having red shifts of more than 3.5, that is, beyond the realm of quasars, but not necessarily beyond where primeval galaxies are expected to be encountered.

No doubt, knowledge of the cosmos will be greatly increased when and if primeval galaxies are observed. There will be confirmation, qualification or repudiation of their anticipated features, such as an abundance of short-lived, massive and very bright stars, relatively frequent supernovae, interstellar gas being enriched with heavier elements by those explosions, and dense and active nucleii. The nuclei may be determined to be quasars, containing powerhouses or energy engines, ejecting plasma and emitting radiation prodigiously, which perhaps are constituted by black holes, or less likely, by something else.

Quasars

Further mentally ascending the red-shift ladder, we come next to the region of the quasars, by far the most distantpast objects observed. Many of them can be seen optically even with an amateur's roof top telescope, but radio, high-powered optical and X-ray observation have vastly increased our detection and knowledge of them. They optically appear only as points of light, even when viewed with the most powerful telescopes, and until 1963, though seen, they were not distinguished from stars.

The revelation of quasars began in 1960, when a radio source was identified with an object optically observed, that looked starlike but had a very unstarlike spectrum and radio emission far too strong to be that of a star. Nor did the object, 3C 48, have any fuzziness; it obviously was not nebulous like a galaxy. In 1962 another similar object, 3C 273, optically seen, was identified with a radio source; and soon more of these objects were optically identified with radio emanations. Astronomers were very curious, of course, as to what these most unusual things might be. They were truly amazed when in 1962 Maarten Schmidt of the Mount Wilson Observatory reported that 3C 273 had a strong red shift of .16, which meant, if the red shift was due to cosmological expansion, that 3C 273 was receding from us at a speed greater than that of any observed galaxy. Indeed, its recessional velocity was sixteen percent of the speed of light. The red shift also meant that the object was about three billion lightyears away. One reason that it and other like objects can be seen optically is that their red shift has moved from the ultraviolet to the visual range of the spectrum.

Numerous other quasistellar objects were quickly discovered, and the name "quasars," given them by Hong Yee Chu, an astronomer at the State University of New York at Stony Brook, seemed most appropriate at the time. It has developed, however, that many more quasars are radio quiet or silent than otherwise, though they are X-ray exuberant. Thus, the X-ray quasars sometimes are called "QSO's" (quasistellar objects) and the radio quasars sometimes are called "QSS's" (quasistellar sources). There has been some thought that the two classes of quasars may differ significantly in other respects, as well as in radio emission, but the consensus is that they are fundamentally the same. Generally, "quasar" is used with respect to both classes.

Quasars vary in red shift from .16 to 3.53, most having red shifts between 1.6 and 3.50, denoting that most are between ten and fifteen billion lightyears in the distancepast. Many have recessional velocities, if their red shift is mostly due to cosmological expansion, of over ninety percent of the speed of light. It is most surprising that a red-shift of 3.5, indicating fifteen billion years in the distancepast, is a limit, as it appears to be, beyond which there are no quasars. We now have or shall have observational apparatus and techniques to detect them beyond that limit, and it is anticipated that, after the space telescope is launched, primeval galaxies will be observed at this pastdistance.

Why should quasars suddenly have come into existence fifteen billion years ago? Is it because that then the primeval galaxies, or many of them, condensed from protogalactic gas clouds, with quasars as their nuclei or within their nuclei? Or is the 3.5 red-shift limit for quasars due to some obscuring condition of the universe that prevailed just beyond fifteen billion years ago, the universe suddenly becoming transparent on this side of the demarcation? An abrupt change like this in the composition of the universe seems most incredible. More likely, the quasars are the nuclei of primeval galaxies. As the primeval galaxies age, the quasars, which well may be their nuclei or within their nuclei, become dimmer; and, as the primeval galaxies become galaxies, the quasars become too dim to be telescopically observed, at least with the best telescopic equipment today. Most are too dim to be telescopically observed at less than ten billion years ago. As noted, the closest quasar (nucleus of an unobserved galaxy?) is about three billion lightyears away. Accordingly, the region of the quasars is mainly from ten to fifteen billion lightyears ago.

Are quasars actually as far away and are they receding from us with as much velocity and acceleration as their red shifts seemingly indicate? Or are their fantastic red shifts due, not to the expansion of the universe, but to their enormous mass and resulting tremendous gravity? Or are those huge red shifts due to great velocity acquired in the explosive expulsion of the quasars from the Milky Way and other galaxies? It has been urged or suggested that, indeed, their great red shifts are due to one of these causes, or to other not understood causes, and not to cosmic expansion, so that in fact they are much closer to us than usually is thought. The increasing consensus of scientific opinion, however, is that the huge quasar red shifts are caused by the expansion of the universe and cannot rightfully be attributed to any other cause, which means that their enormous distances and fantastic velocities and acceleration of recession are real. There remains, however, some respectable scientific scepticism.

How common and widespread are quasars, as we mentally see them from the red-shift ladder, in their region of the distancepast? Is their distribution random or patterned by some cause? Only a few quasars appear among thousands of stars and galaxies in any photograph of any small area of the sky. Nevertheless, radio, optical and X-ray probes of the sky, including one that covered one-fourth of the celestial sphere and including X-ray observation by the orbiting Einstein satellite, have disclosed that quasars are very common in their region of distancepast, perhaps as common as are galaxies in their later and nearer realm. The probes also show that quasar distribution resembles that of galaxies, but possibly could be random like that of grains of rice thrown on a table top. In fact, it is difficult to say whether or not quasar distribution is random or has been patterned by inter-gravitational attraction or other cause.

One of the most startling properties of quasars is their enormous output of energy, hundreds to thousands more than that of galaxies, from spots in space not much or no larger than that occupied by our solar system. The size of quasars is determinable from their variations in brightness, which, though not much in magnitude, are in time from a few days to ten years. Light or other electromagnetic radiation, the unobstructed speed of which is constant, emanating from a part of the quasar closest to us reaches us first; accordingly, the more rapid the variation, the smaller is the quasar. The rule is that light or radiation from the quasar cannot change in a time less than it takes light to traverse the quasar. Thus, if the variation is every two days, the quasar can be no more than two lightdays across.

Are the quasars galactic nuclei? If they are neither stars nor galactic nuclei, they must be a third category of concentration of matter on an astronomical scale. The evidence is uncertain, though a faint haziness has been detected about some of the closer quasars, very suggestive of a surrounding galaxy. These quasars resemble Seyfert galaxies, which have hazy and indistinct arms, but have nuclei that are bright, though not as bright as quasars. They have an even closer resemblance to BL Lac objects, the prototype of which, BL Lacertae, was thought to be a very odd variable star. BL Lacs have an unstarlike featureless spectra and are immersed in a glow disclosing a galaxy about them. Accordingly, it well may be that quasars and the nuclei of BL Lacs, Seyfert, radio and other galaxies are all fundamentally the same, diminishing in their activity and energy output with their age and with their proximity to us. All of them may centrally harbor black holes.

There is a universal X-ray background radiation, entirely different from the universal low-temperature microwave background radiation that constitutes well-neigh compelling proof of the Big Bang. The cause of the X-radiation background is not known with certainty, but an extended investigation has led to the conclusion that it may be due to "brehmstrahlung" ("braking" radiation) from an intergalactic medium consisting of hot plasma, in which free electrons passing close to free protons lose energy that is carried away in protons; or that the background X-radiation may wholly or in large measure come from the myriad of quasars in the far distancepast.

Next, we ascend the red-shift ladder to examine the array of observed galaxies on the loom of spacetime. While we mentally are still on the ladder and deeply down in the distancepast, we look about us and see that the regions of observed galaxies and of quasars, that are those that now can be observed from the earth, overlap each other to a considerable extent. This is not surprising since quasars very well may be the nuclei of otherwise unseen galaxies. The nearest quasar, 3C 273, as already noted, has a red shift of .158, and is about three billion lightyears away; and the most distantpast observed galaxy, 3C 184, has a red shift of 1 and is about $10\frac{2}{3}$ billion lightyears away.

Hyperactive galaxies

By "active galaxies," as they usually are called, is meant those that are extremely active and energetic compared to a galaxy like our own, which is far from being inactive. We shall call them "hyperactive galaxies." They have much of their enormous activity in dense, small places in their nuclei, which may be black holes or, less likely, some other kind of powerhouse or energy engine. Generally, hyperactive galaxies are very pastdistant, that is, very young, though the nearest, Centaurus A, is only about thirteen million lightyears away. Several kinds of hyperactive galaxies have been observed and classified, including BL Lacs, Seyferts, N-types and Markarians.

BL Lacs are extraordinarily optically bright star-like objects, varying rapidly and considerably in magnitude, often comparably to a change each day of twenty percent of the luminosity of the Milky Way, which is like turning ten billion suns on and off daily. The prototype, BL Lacertae, whose light variability was first noted in 1929, was at first thought to be a most unusual variable star. However, the spectra of BL Lacs are featureless and most unlike that of the star or of a galaxy. In time, detection of slight fuzziness about some BL Lacs and spectral analysis of the fuzziness definitely established that the BL Lacs are giant elliptical galaxies with little gas content. Light observed is from their centers, probably from sources no more than a lightday across, which also emit detectable compact radiation and possibly harbor black-hole or, less likely, some other kind of powerhouse or energy engine, putting out energy that is enormous though much less than that of quasars. The extraordinary brightness of their centers probably accounts for their featureless spectra.

It is difficult to establish the distancepast of the BL Lacs, over forty of which have been discovered, but the distancepast of one of them has been put at $1\frac{2}{5}$ billion light years.

Seyferts are mostly, if not all, hyperactive spiral galaxies. Short exposure photographs show them as starlike points of light, which actually are only their nuclei. Longer exposure reveals a haziness about them, evidencing that they are galaxies. Their nuclei vastly outshine the rest of them. Their variability of luminosity denotes minute central sources, at most only a few lightyears across, emitting light equivalent to that of a hundred million suns. Their spectra is not at all starlike. It is nonthermal and manifestive of a largely gaseous origin, indicating that star formation has not progressed nearly as far as in closer and older spiral galaxies. The Seyferts radiate strongly in radio, infrared and X-ray wavelengths. They are thought to have much gas and dust outside their nuclei, that swirls about randomly at immense velocities; and energetic photons heat dust particles, causing the infrared radiation. Starlight, synchroton radio emission and infrared radiation contribute to the continuous spectra of the Seyferts. About nineteen percent of all spiral galaxies are Seyferts. (Synchroton radio emission is explained subsequently.)

N-galaxies probably are Seyferts that are very distantpast with enormous energy output from their nuclei. They are tremendously optically bright, and they are starlike in appearance. The light from their nuclei varies considerably in its brightness over years and at time is so bright that the rest of them cannot be seen. They then look much like quasars, and, indeed, the first object classified as a quasar, 3C 48, has been reclassified as an N-galaxy.

Radio galaxies

We shall now ascend the red-shift ladder to the region of radio galaxies, which is a vast area of the distancepast extending from only 13 million lightyears ago to $10\frac{2}{3}$ billion lightyears ago. The BL Lac, Seyfert, N-types and Markarian galaxies are found at the lower depths of this vast region, and its greatest depths overlap the domain of the quasars.

"Radio galaxies" is another name for those "active galaxies" which manifest themselves and their hyperactivity by detectable radio emission, and most of the far distantpast galaxies so manifest themselves. Radio galaxies are distinguishable from nearer and older galaxies, which are called "normal," "typical," or "ordinary" galaxies. The nearby and older galaxies also have observable radio emission, but far less than that of radio galaxies, indeed millions of times less.

If radio galaxies are large enough, if their light is bright enough and if they are close enough to us, they are optically observable; then they are said to be optical counterparts. At least many, if not most, radio galaxies also emit X-ray, infrared, ultraviolet and gamma-ray radiation, disclosed in their spectra; and much of this radiation is observable by modern telescopic devices and techniques, including the use of satellites for observation.[1]

Radio galaxies were first observed by radio, beginning in 1950, and then some of their optical counterparts were found, beginning in 1954; and by now many have been identified optically, though they are of low optical luminosity.

Like quasars, radio galaxies have in their nuclei small regions, often less than a lightyear across, harboring a powerhouse or energy engine or the like, which perhaps is a black hole or, less likely, something else, producing energy prodigeously in radiation and frequently in tremendous ejection of gas in a jet out of the galactic nucleus, and often out of the galaxy and into spacetime for thousands or millions of lightyears. The smallness of the radiation sources, so enormously energetic, is determined, as said before, by variation in the brightness of observed light or of radio or other radiation.

Radio galaxies can be classified as (1) unlobed or core-halo, which are in the minority; (2) double-lobed; and (3) trailed or tailed, which are in the majority. The double-lobed sometimes are double double-lobed, meaning that they have two lobes on each of the opposite sides, the two lobes on each side being generally in alignment, one closer and one farther from the central galactic component.

Unlobed radio galaxies

The unlobed radio galaxies are elliptical with a strong but radio-emitting halo. An example is M87, a huge elliptical in the Virgo cluster, about 65 million lightyears in the distancepast. It is observable optically and by its powerful radio and X-ray emission. Its light emission is a billion solar luminosities, and its X-ray emission is fifty times more energetic than its light emission.

Probably, M87 harbors at its center a supermassive black hole. Its radio core is less than a half-lightyear across and contains a group of small radio-emitting sources, at least one of which is less that $1\frac{1}{2}$ lightmonths across. Its X-ray emission is from a more extended region.

A gas jet, observable optically and by radio and X-ray emission, emanates from its nucleus and extends six thousand lightyears into spacetime. The jet has been known since 1915 when it was observed by Heber D. Curtis. The jet is as optically luminous as a million suns. It contains six optically, radio and X-ray observable blobs, each less than ten lightyears in length, suggestive of explosive outbursts by its central powerhouse or energy engine. Another much fainter jet from the opposite side of the galaxy also has been observed.

The radio and X-ray emission and the entire spectrum of the jet look nonthermal, indicative that the jet is being ejected otherwise than by (1) nuclear fusion caused by concentration of mass or by (2) many supernova explosions in the small energy-producing region. Hence, the powerhouse or energy engine blasting out the jet probably is a black hole. The light, radio and X-ray emission may be by a synchrotron process, explained below, associated with the supermassive black hole. The light from the jet is twenty-five percent polarized, indicative of the synchrotron origin. The radio and X-ray cores are generally aligned with the jets, this also being indicative of their synchrotron origin and of the jets being ejected by the powerhouse or energy engine.

Though a minority of radio galaxies are nonlobular, there are many that are. Some of these may have lobes too faint to have been observed.

Lobed radio galaxies

Double-lobed radio galaxies typically have two gigantic lobes of gas, roughly symetrically on opposite sides of a central galactic component, usually elliptical, which may or may not be bright in optical and radio emission or in either. However, the lobes often, though not always, are exceedingly radio-bright. Indeed, some double-lobed radio galaxies are among the brightest radio objects in the sky. These galaxies sometimes are X-ray bright, and their radio and X-ray radiation may be more than a million times that of a normal galaxy.

The lobes invariably are far larger in spacetime occupancy than the parent component between them, called their "parent" because it has produced them. The lobes may extend for thousands or millions of lightyears beyond the parent galaxy and be separated from it by a distancepast of up to five times more than their extent in spacetime.

Apparently, the lobes are created and fed by jets of gas squirted as though from a nozzle by the powerhouses or energy engines or the like in their nuclei. The jets carry with them from the parent galaxy, and supply the lobes with, momentum, mass and energy, and they have magnetic flux. The corpus is gas, mostly hydrogen, constituted by agitated electrons and other particles, charged and uncharged.

Squirted out into spacetime, the jets have to push their way through it because they encounter hydrogen atoms distributed throughout it at densities ranging from one atom per cubic centimeter to one atom per million cubic centimeters. Sometimes the jets end in a hot spot, resulting from the heating of atoms being pushed through spacetime by the jet. The hot spots, found at the ends of the lobes away from the parent component, not only stop the jets, but cause the jet gas to flow back on itself toward the parent component and to spread out into the lobes. A shock wave results as the flow of the gas is suddenly reversed by the hot spot, and the wave agitates the electrons and other charged particles to swirl in the lobe's magnetic field with velocities approaching the speed of light. The rapid swirling in the magnetic flux causes the electrons and other charged particles to radiate, and this radiation is called "synchrotron" because it is the same kind of radiation as that produced by the Synchrotron. The synchrotron radiation is in radio, X-ray, light, infrared or other wavelength, depending on the velocity of the electrons or other charged particles in the magnetic flux.

Jets, blobs in jets, and inner lobes if any, that have been observed, evidenced or hinted at by radio, X-ray or visual observation of double-lobed or double double-lobed radio galaxies, invariably are aligned between their source and one of the large outermost lobes, though the jets sometimes have turns or bends. What produces the collimation of direction is not well understood, but it seems that the expulsion of gas from inside a galactic nucleus would follow the path of least resistance, which would be in both directions along the axis of the galaxy as it spins, so that the jets would emerge from the north and south poles of the galaxy. The same direction is always followed by the collimation, although expulsions tend to occur at great time intervals, signifying that the expulsion mechanism, whatever it is, has a built-in infallible memory for direction.

Cygnus A (or 3C 236), 450 million lightyears in the distancepast, one of the first-discovered double-lobed radio galaxies, the largest and one of the most radio-bright, has a giant elliptical central component. Each of its lobes is 55 thousand lightyears across, a distance approximately half that across our galaxy, and each is about 160 thousand lightyears from the central galaxy. The entire length of Cygnus A, including all its components, is about twenty million lightyears. Its radio luminosity is a million times more than that of a normal galaxy. Total energy in its lobes is at least that of two billion supernova explosions. No large-scale jets have yet been found associated with Cygnus A although there is observational evidence of collination indicative of such jets.

Centaurus A (NGC 5128), the nearest radio galaxy to us, only thirteen million lightyears in the distancepast, is a double double-lobed super-giant radio galaxy. Its outer lobes are respectively 650,000 and 1,350,000 lightyears in length, and each of its inner lobes is 33,000 lightyears in length and is aligned with the outer lobe on its side of the parent component.

The lobes of Centaurus A are radio faint, but the large lobes store enormous total energy in electrons and other charged particles in magnetic fields. When much younger, Centaurus A probably had far greater radio and light output; probably, its nucleus was a quasar. As observed now, that is, as it was thirteen million lightyears distantpast, it has a radio source only a lightday across and an X-ray source even smaller in area. It well may harbor a black hole that at one time was far more active than it is as we now observe the galaxy.

Does Centaurus A have a jet? Yes. There is observable radio and X-radio emission apparently from a jet, with a blob-like structure, to one of the inner lobes.

An exceptionally interesting double-lobed galaxy is an elliptical, NGC 6251, that is 300 million lightyears from our galaxy. It has a jet from its nucleus that is very straight, very narrow, and more than 400,000 lightyears long. The jet begins in a pointlike source, which itself is a narrow jet only three lightyears long, at the very center of the central component. It resembles a cosmic blowtorch. It points toward one of the lobes and most likely supplies it continuously with gas and energy. The lobes are very extensive. Their radio output is comparatively low, but they are packed with enormous total energy. It well may be that there is another jet, as yet unobserved and perhaps unobservable, from the opposite side of the nucleus, through the central component and out into spacetime.

Jets

Much has been said above about jets in galaxies, which are called "cosmic" jets. Over seventy large ones from double-lobed galaxies have been observed. At the cores of six of these, small jets aligned with larger ones beyond the cores of the galaxies have been observed, suggesting that they are emitted by something like a black-hole powerhouse at their centers.

Stellar jets also occur in the Milky Way, as will be discussed in Chapter 16.

Cosmic jets are not always straight; sometimes they have bends or turns and zigzag.

Cosmic jets vary considerably in length, as noted in the foregoing discussion of radio galaxies.

Tailed and corkscrew galaxies

The most common radio galaxies are those with a long tail or trail of gas curving away from the galaxy in direction opposite to that of the galaxy through space. Jets from opposite sides of the galaxy emerge, curve back around it and join in the tail, sometimes in a corkscrew manner. The tail probably is caused by the rush of space, not an absolute vacuum, past the speeding galaxy, much as a pocket of air trails a speeding truck.

How radio galaxies are fueled

How are radio galaxies fueled in their enormous energy production expended in radiation and gas ejection? An explanation could be the gravitational in-flow of gas and of torn-apart stars on and into a black hole, with resulting explosive outbursting or outpouring of gas that escapes ingestion by the black hole. Some of the energy could be provided by the black hole itself, as discussed in Chapter 18. Some of the fuel, perhaps much of it may be the dismembered remains of devoured smaller galaxies.

Summary: radio galaxies

In summary, radio galaxies are very common throughout a vast region of the distancepast. They are very diverse in configuration and behavior, but variations as well as similarities in their shapes and functioning are explainable, for the most part, by certain fundamental galactic properties and processes, including their galactic age; enormous but decreasing central activity; conversion of mass into energy by some kind of central powerhouse or engine, probably a black hole; and expenditure of that energy in the output of radiation and the ejection of gas in opposite directions along the galactic axes.

Note

[1] X-ray radiation, which is absorbed by the earth's atmosphere, is observable from satellite observatories. Infrared radiation is observable through the infrared telescopes on Mauna Kea in Hawaii, from a NASA airplane equipped for the purpose, by conventional telescopes and special techniques and by specialized telescopes. Ultraviolet radiation can be observed by the International Ultraviolet Explorer (IUE) launched in 1978 into a geosynchronous orbit so that it can be used for observation from both sides of the Atlantic. Gamma-ray telescopes must be above the earth's atmosphere, since gamma rays are absorbed by it. They have been little used for observation of galaxies other than our own.

14

Galaxies Generally

Normal galaxies

We mentally complete our climb up the red-shift ladder through the loom of spacetime, watching the galactic pattern emerge in the fabric of matter and of radiation being woven upon the loom. We reach the top of the ladder and step off onto the earth and into our present. Here we shall complete our galactic survey by perusal of the normal galaxies, meaning those that we can see optically and those that are like those that we can see optically. These sometimes are called "optical" galaxies, but the name is somewhat misleading because we can see some radio galaxies optically. We shall use "normal galaxies" rather than "optical galaxies."

We, and our readers, too, we trust, have kept in mind, as we figuratively have gone down and then climbed back up the red-shift ladder to now, observing during our ascent the formation of galaxies, the question whether or not that formation evidences the hand of God or something else basic to it.

The normal galaxies are comparatively close to us on the loom of spacetime; they are relatively inactive compared to hyperactive more distantpast galaxies; and they are "older" than those galaxies in the sense that we are seeing them at a later time in their lives.

The normal galaxies are so-called because they are those with which we first became familiar as we began to observe galaxies outside the Milky Way. Presumably, in their earlier and more distant lightyears they resembled very closely, if they were not the same, in hyperactivity and structure, as those more distant and more active galaxies that we have studied as we ascended the red-shift ladder from when the protogalaxies began to form until now.

These normal galaxies, even those closest to our galaxy, the Milky Way, are, of course, enormously distantpast from us, compared to earthly and solar-system distancepast, though they are very nearby on the cosmic scale. Also, with age they have become inactive on the cosmic scale, though they are enormously active compared to earthly and solar-system activity. Andromeda M31 and our Milky Way, for example, most likely have central activity and violence hardly imaginable by us, probably culminating in each in a central supermassive black hole, still hungrily sucking into its maw and devouring all gas and matter falling into its compelling gravitational grasp, though it has become tame with maturity compared to its voracity in its youth.

The normal galaxies are so far from us that we cannot see them with unaided eyes, except three, the great Andromeda galaxy, M31 (in our northern hemisphere's sky) and the two Magellenic clouds (in our southern hemisphere's sky). Galaxies farther away than these, though relatively nearby, can be observed and photographed, adequately for classification and study, only by optical, radio and other telescopy.

Classification of galaxies

Configurations of the Milky Way and nearby galaxies generally are the same as they have been since these galaxies coalesced some twelve to sixteen billion years ago out of the ionized hydrogen, deuterium and helium gas that then pervaded the universe. There are now, as there were then, elliptical, spiral and irregular galaxies, each class varying vastly in configuration and in size. Variations within these general classes have resulted from causes not well understood. Seemingly, however, as before noted, the chief factor has been the rapidity of star formation, causing the protogalactic gas and dust cloud to thin sufficiently and in time to overcome the tendency of the cloud to settle into a disk with arms spiralling about it.

Accordingly, ellipticals are galaxies in which star formation has been more rapid, and spirals are galaxies in which star formation has been slower. Thus, ellipticals generally have older stars and less left-over gas and dust, and spirals generally have younger stars and more stars being born out of their more abundant left-over gas and dust. Less than four percent of ellipticals and more than seven percent of spirals have gas and dust not embodied in stars and their attendant systems. Only about ten percent of ellipticals have discernible gas and dust.

Ellipticals have more older stars and are more orange and red than spirals, and their redness increases toward their centers where there are more red giant stars. Spirals, having more younger stars and stars being born, which are hotter than older stars, are more blue than ellipticals. Their newer and new-born stars are more populous in their arms, which have more gas and dust than their nuclei; more plentiful gas and dust favors star formation.

Irregular galaxies, which have some but little pattern permitting sub-classification, have even more left-over gas and dust after star formation than spirals; why they have not evolved into more regular shapes is unknown. They generally have more new stars and are bluer than spirals.

What portion of galaxies is in each general class, ellipticals, spirals and irregulars? The respective percentages are twenty, seventy seven and three, for all known galaxies, and thirteen, thirty four and fifty four for galaxies within thirty million lightyears of us. Small irregulars of low luminosity are more detectable when they are comparatively nearby.

The general classification should not mislead one into thinking that galaxies neatly fall into one or another of the three general classes. Many are most difficult to classify even generally. Some irregulars possibly can be viewed as ellipticals or as spirals. Spirals with bulging disks and scant arm formation can be considered ellipticals.

Ellipticals are classified according to their respective degrees of ellipticity as EO (globular) through E7 (very elliptic). Spirals sometimes have a prominent bar, thought to be dust-caused, through their nuclei, and are called "barred" spirals. It is possible that our galaxy is a barred spiral. Spirals and barred spirals are further classified according to the tightness (angle between arms) with which the arms spiral about the nucleus. Thus, they are classified as Sa, Sb and Sc, and SBa, SBb and SBc; "a" means most tight and "c" means least tight to the nucleus.

Spirals approach flatness, like a pinwheel; but their nuclei vary in thickness. Spirals also have a globular halo of gas and dust. The halo may contain far more matter and energy than the central component. The classification of galaxies is based on their apparent rather than their actual shape.

Size of galaxies

The size of a galaxy is determinable by taking into consideration its distancepast from us and its angular size as it is viewed; the angular size depends on its edge, which usually is hazy and uncertain. The largest galaxies are supergiant ellipticals, which may be as much as six million lightyears across, which is more than twice the distance from the Milky Way to Andromeda. Giant ellipticals range up to 200,000 lightyears, and average 130,000 lightyears across.

Large spiral galaxies, like our Milky Way, average 200,000 lightyears in diameter and 2,000 lightyears in thickness. More typical spirals have diameters of about sixty thousand lightyears. A recently discovered dark spiral named "Malin 1", is thought to be 770,000 lightyears across. Previously, the largest known spiral is 640,000 lightyears in diameter. Malin 1 also seems to be by far the youngest known galaxy, as noted in Chapter 13.

The smallest galaxies are small ellipticals and irregulars with diameters of ten thousand lightyears, more or less. Typical irregulars have diameters of about 23 thousand lightyears.

Mass and luminosities of galaxies correspond to their size. Typically, giant ellipticals have 10^{13} solar masses and 10^{11} solar luminosities; spirals have 10^{11} solar masses and 10^{16} solar luminosities; irregulars have 10^9 solar masses and 10^8 solar luminosities.

Colliding and merging

While generally galaxies have retained the configurations with which they developed from primeval galaxies and with which the primeval galaxies emerged from protogalactic clouds, there have been considerable colliding and merging of galaxies, and devouring of smaller by larger galaxies, notwithstanding the overall expanding of the universe. This colliding, merging and cannibalizing are observable in various places, especially in clusters with many galaxies, like the Como cluster. It has been speculated that the Milky Way and the Andromeda group, which gradually are approaching each other, may in the far distant-future merge and become a large elliptical. This suggestion, however, requires some reconciliation with the theory that spirals have been spirals, ellipticals ellipticals, and irregulars irregulars, since their formation.

Clustering

Under local and regional gravitational force, locally and regionally slowing the expansion of the universe, galaxies tend to cluster in groups and superclusters. That is, neighboring galaxies through their intergalactic gravitation *inter sese* tend to group themselves in clusters and supergalaxies. For example, the Milky Way and Andromeda M31 and their satellite galaxies together with a few other galaxies, about thirty galaxies in all, constitute our Local Group, which is on the outer fringe of the so-called "Virgo Supercluster." Many superclusters are enormous with vast voids among them.

Though galaxies tend to cluster and supercluster, the macrofabric of matter and of radiation over any large-enough area or as an entirety generally has a homogenous and isometric galactic pattern. From the earth or anywhere it looks much the same in all directions over large enough areas and distances. Photographs of millions of galaxies clearly display this homogeneity and this isotropism.

Internal dynamics

The internal dynamics of galaxies involve star formation from gas and dust and star disintegration into gas, dust and the heavier elements, from which new stars and planets, many mineral-rich, form. The dynamics further involve disintegration of some stars into neutron stars and black holes and of others into stellar slag; and also involve gradual entropy. These matters are discussed in subsequent chapters.

Number of galaxies

Probably, there are more than 200 billion galaxies in the universe. Some astronomers and physicists think that the number may be infinite, even though the universe began in a Big Bang from a Little Bomb. Their reasoning is that infinite matter and energy may have been compressed in an infinitely dense Little Bomb, dimensionless or nearly so. As time, space, matter, radiation and energy erupted and expanded, in an expanding and boundless universe, the early states of the universe, may each have been infinite; the early gas state may have been infinite; and the number of the galaxies that coagulated from the gas and the spreading spacetime among them may be infinite.

If there is insufficient matter and, thus, insufficient density in the universe, to cause enough gravitational force to reverse the expansion of the universe, it will expand forever. In that event, spacetime will expand forever, carrying with it the galaxies, which may be infinite in number, in their groupings, which will always recede from each other with increasing velocity. After that recessional velocity becomes greater than the speed of light, the groups of galaxies will lose sight of, that is, any communication with each other forever.

A difficulty with galaxies being infinite in number is that a finite number of galaxies is consistent with the universe expanding and groups of galaxies spreading apart with it, forever, if matter and density in the universe are insufficient to reverse its expansion. It is not requisite for this to happen that the number of galaxies be infinite, even though infinite matter in an infinite number of galaxies in a limitless universe would not necessarily entail infinite density, or enough density to reverse cosmic expansion, if the galaxies were spread out thinly enough in infinite spacetime.

On the other hand, an infinite number of galaxies emerging from an infinitely dense Little Bomb, dimensionless or almost so, could return to a similar compression in an oscillating universe if there is enough matter and density in this universe in which we live to reverse its expansion.

Observable galaxies

Whether the number of galaxies is finite or infinite, we can observe only those whose light is reaching us as we look out and so down into the distancepast toward the beginning of the Big Bang, from the earth or a spacecraft, or in the future from the moon, another planet or elsewhere that we might manage to be. What we see is the observable universe, observable to us at the time that we are looking. We see galaxies as they were when the light reaching us left them. We cannot see them as they were when light that has already passed us was leaving them nor do we see them as they have become after the light by which we see them left them. That is, our momentary view of the galaxies at any time is as they were at the moment that the light by which we perceive them left them. Each time that we look at them or at one of any of them, our doing so is like an instantaneous photograph of them.

How many of the galaxies can we see when we look at them by optical or other means: by radio, X-ray, infrared, ultraviolet or gamma-ray radiation, or (as may be possible in the future) by gravitational waves? Some theorists think that we cannot see or otherwise observe those whose light or radiation has not yet reached us. That is, if they are so far in spacetime from us that their light has not yet reached us, we cannot observe them. Under this theory, if we had looked out from the earth three billion years ago, we could not have seen as many galaxies as we can today, assuming that we then had equal means of observation. Likewise, if we should look out from the earth three billion years hereafter, with equal observational means, we would see more galaxies than we can now observe. Thus, the theory is that more and more galaxies become observable as time passes. The observable universe grows.

This view of the observable universe is difficult to reconcile with the fact that we now can "see" with optical, radio and other electromagnetic telescopy nearly back to before galaxy formation started, and may in time with improved telescopy and its use in spaceships see back to that time, when the universe was all gas or radiation.

Galaxies, God and life

The formation and continuance of galaxies, though not fully comprehended, has in this century become well enough understood, to support strongly the presumption that that formation is a natural, and probably inevitable, consequence of the particles and their interaction with which the Big Bang began and has continued. There seems to be no need of a God hypothesis to answer why galactic formation started and continues. Also, it seems unnecessary to invoke a God hypothesis in order to conjecture what ultimately will happen to all the galaxies in the universe. This is not to say that the God hypothesis is or is not reasonable as a basis for thinking, believing or betting that God caused the Little Bomb to be and to explode in the Big Bang, or that he in some other manner instituted the universe.

Why is there the vast multiplicity of galaxies? Again, it seems that it is the natural, if not inevitable, consequence of the endowment of the Big Bang as it began.

How about the repetition of the galactic pattern throughout the loom of spacetime? Again, it seems to occur naturally, if not inevitably, given the original ingredients and mechanics of the Big Bang.

However, are the multiplicity and universal repetition of the galactic patterns not evidence of divine design implanted in the Little Bomb or whatever it was with which the universe began? But for what purpose? Certainly not, a skeptic is compelled to say, for a divine purpose of creating human beings and like beings elsewhere in the universe, who, if they were good enough in their mortal life, would be rewarded with immortal angelic status.

Nevertheless, a reasonable sceptic must agree that not only human beings and other animal life in its own way, and plant life in its own way, are finding immense worthwhileness though also, of course, tremendous misfortune and suffering, in terrestrial abode. Like worthwhileness despite pain and suffering, at myriad other abodes in the billions of galaxies, seems to be most probable.

Nor would the reasonable skeptic deny that the worthwhileness of life, especially intelligent life, notwithstanding all harm encountered, recurrent throughout the galaxies as a consequence of galactic mechanics, could fit into divine galactic design if there is a God-Creator.

In any event most of us treasure our terrestrial life that has flowered out of galactic evolution.

15

The Milky Way and Andromeda

The Milky Way, our galaxy, often is called "our" or "the galaxy" because until this century it was thought to be the only galaxy; that is, "galaxy" was another word for the physical universe. Galaxies beyond it, though observed by telescopes, were thought to be nebulae, or clouds, of gas and matter within it. The realization that it is only one of two hundred billion, or more, galaxies in the universe dawned with ascertainment that many nebulae are vastly too far away to be part of it and that they are distributed everywhere in the distancepast for billions of lightyears away.

The suggestion that the Milky Way is only one of many or countless like systems in an immense or infinite universe, made first by Thomas Wright (1711–86), and echoed by Immanuel Kant (1724–1804) John Heinrich Lambert (1728–1777) and Pierre Simon de Laplace (1749–1827) has been largely substantiated by twentieth century astronomy. Wright suggested that the nebulae were other "abodes of the blessed" like the Milky Way in "an unlimited plenum of creations." Kant, who had read a review of Wright's book, suggested a hierarchy of systems of Milky Ways in infinite space. Lambert's suggestion was similar. Later Pierre de Laplace supposed the nebulae to be clouds of gas becoming solar systems.

A general portrayal of the Milky Way and of its travelling companion, Andromeda M31, most probably is a general picture of billions of other spiral galaxies. As Paul and Newton advised, we and our readers can look at this general picture, asking ourselves if indeed all that may be known of God lies plain within it, or, we add, to see if some reality or something else other than God lies plain within it. Or, we must further add, does God or some other explanation lie dimly or hidden within it?

As the solar system is immersed in the disk of the galaxy about one-third of the way (that is, about 28 thousand lightyears) from the center of the disk to its edge and as our view is obstructed by dust clouds within it, we can see into it with optical telescopes only a short distance and then often not clearly. In the last half century, however, radio telescopes, and in the last few decades new X-ray, gamma-ray, ultraviolet and infrared observational equipment and techniques, including the use of balloons, airplanes, rockets and satellites for observation posts, have enabled astronomers much better to observe the galaxy, both toward its center and in all directions. However, observation of the galaxy, even by these new equipment and techniques, still is beset with great difficulties, including that of determining the distance from us and from each other of observed objects and determining their velocities and directions of motion with respect to us and to each other. To some extent these difficulties are being overcome by the use of the Doppler effect of light and other methods for ascertaining the velocity and acceleration, direction of motion and distancepast of celestial objects.

No matter how much we improve our means of observing the galaxy, we cannot look down at it from above or up at it from below, as we can look down on the earth from a spacecraft. Perhaps in the future, although most unlikely, earthlings or their descendants will look at the galaxy from afar and from above or below the plane of its disk, seeing it as we can now view telescopically the great Andromeda galaxy, M31 (also catalogued as NGC 224) and many other spiral galaxies which we are reasonably certain resemble the Milky Way very much. Or perhaps earthlings will send an unmanned spacecraft with a camera far away to photograph the galaxy and transmit pictures of it back to the earth. It would take, however, over 2.2 million years for the spacecraft to reach Andromeda, going nearly as fast as light, and another 2.2 million years for the pictures to be transmitted from there to earth.

The Andromeda great galaxy is 2.2 million lightyears away from us, so we are seeing it as it was 2.2 million years in the past. Likewise, any beings in the galaxy "now" seeing the Milky Way are seeing it as it was 2.2 million years ago. But 2.2 million years are only a tiny fraction of galactic time, and a galaxy must look from afar much the same at one time as it will look from afar 2.2 million years later.

Excellent pictures of Andromeda M31 and of other galaxies that resemble the Milky Way abound and are widely available in books. Most are excellent authentic representations based on photography and on recording and electromagnetic radiation at all wave lengths. They are produced by scientific technology, including aerial and space flight observation and the use of computers. They exhibit artistic skill in composition and in coloring. The coloring sometimes is true, and sometimes it is false or enhanced in order to clarify or emphasize detail or relationship, to aid comprehension, to arouse and satisfy interest or to accomplish some other useful purpose. By these superb pictures anyone can easily see for himself how our galaxy probably would appear if it were observed from as far away as Andromeda M31.

M31 is the nearest large galaxy to our large Milky Way. The two are gradually approaching each other and may in the far distantfuture merge, perhaps to form a huge elliptical galaxy mostly depleted by star generation of the gas and dust now possessed by each. However, their approach to each other is so slow that their merger could not occur until after the expansion of the universe had reversed itself if the universe is finite or until the comparable passage of eons if the universe is infinite.

Observation of features of M31 and of processes and events in it often has preceded and facilitated knowledge of the occurrence and understanding of like features, processes and events, not observed easily or at all, though possibly anticipated, of or in the Milky Way. For example, observation and study of the characteristics and differences and of the distribution of Populations I (young) and II (old) stars in M31 initiated and aided the discovery and understanding of the distribution, evolution and nature of Populations I and II stars in the Milky Way. Also, observation and study of M31 has helped our understanding of the rotation and mass of our galaxy and our knowledge of the scale of the universe, as will be explained subsequently.

Travelling companions

M31 and the Milky Way are travelling companions as they have been since the protogalactic clouds from which they emerged coalesced out of the universal gas about fifteen billion years ago, and as they will be until they merge in either a collapsing or in an infinitely expanding universe. In their sojourn in spacetime they are accompanied by their smaller satellite galaxies and by all the few members of the Local Group of galaxies.

The Milky Way, Andromeda M31, their satellite galaxies and all the members of the Local Group are travelling together as passengers in expanding spacetime. They also apparently are travelling at more than a million miles an hour toward the center of the Virgo supercluster of galaxies, of which they are members. Their movement toward the heart of this supercluster is suggested by a slight asymmetry in the universal 2.7K background radiation that permeates the universe and is nearly conclusive proof of the Big Bang. The asymmetry has been detected by a sensitive radio antenna carried by an aircraft nearly to the top of the earth's atmosphere. This rush by the Milky Way and the Local Group of galaxies well may be a gravitational slide down the curve of spacetime to the gravitational center of the Virgo supercluster, caused by the immense mass of that supercluster.

Galactic rotation

The Milky Way and M31, like all galaxies, are rotating about their axes as they travel through spacetime. That is, their stars, planets and other stellar companions and their gas and dust orbit about the galactic axes, which in the case of disk and spiral galaxies are through their centers and perpendicular to the planes of their disks. The center of the Milky Way is in the constellation Sagittarius, where the galaxy is brightest.

The rotation is not like that of a solid wheel or like that of the partially solid earth. Stars and their companions, star clusters, gas and dust clouds and unincorporated gas and dust at different distances from the galactic axes theoretically may or may not orbit at the same speed, as the orbital speed depends both on the mass and nearness of the orbiting body and on the mass within the orbit. Surprisingly, the orbital speeds of stars, matter, gas and dust in our galaxy, in M31 and in other studied galaxies, do not in fact decline with their distance from the galactic centers, as the orbital speeds of planets do with distance from the sun. This fact has led to the conclusion that our galaxy and other studied galaxies have many times more mass then previously thought, as is more fully discussed subsequently.

In our galaxy, stars, other bodies, gas and dust as far from the galactic axis as the sun, i.e., about 28 thousand lightyears, orbit at a speed between 230 and 250 kilometers per second with respect to the distribution of globular clusters about the galactic center. (More will be said about these clusters.) The galactic rotation at this distance from the galactic axis would be twice as fast if a galaxy were a solid wheel.

At a rotational speed of 240 kilometers per second and at a distance of 28 thousand lightyears from the galactic center, the sun completes an orbit of the galaxy in 240 million years, which time aptly can be called a "cosmic" or a "galactic" year in the solar system and on earth. We shall call it a "cosmic year." In the sun's lifetime, i.e., approximately five billion years, it has completed about twenty one orbits of the galaxy, and, hence, there have been nineteen cosmic years on earth, which is about $4\frac{1}{2}$ billion years old.

There is random, as well as orbital, motion of stars and star clusters, other bodies, gas and dust in clouds and in rings and streams and unincorporated gas and dust in the Milky Way and in all spiral galaxies. The causes of this random motion include gravitational interaction and dominance, stellar explosions, electromagnetism and the nuclear strong and weak forces.

The nuclear forces are operative in microprocesses, which are basic to macroprocesses, such as star formation and activity in the weaving of matter on the loom of spacetime. Gravitational and electromagnetic fields when traversed by matter give rise to radiation and other particles.

At the center of the galaxy there seems to be an energy engine or powerhouse, perhaps a black hole.

The galaxy is a scene of tremendous activity, energy conversion and often violence; nevertheless, it is fundamentally cosmic, subject to natural explanation and law; and on the whole it is understandable and, when understood, predictable, though there remains much about it unfathomed and perhaps unfathomable.

Size and mass

The size and mass of our galaxy, of Andromeda M31 and of other spiral galaxies is unknown and may remain so, mainly because how much mass their coronae contain is not presently ascertainable. Furthermore, any demarcation of the outer boundary of our galaxy or of any spiral galaxy, that is, of the border between their coronae and interstellar space, necessarily is arbitrary.

Our galaxy, nevertheless, is among the larger spiral galaxies. Certainly, it is many times larger than it was thought to be in 1965, when it was thought to have a diameter of about 114 thousand lightyears, 300 billion solar masses and a hundred billion stars. It is now known that its diameter is at least three times, and its mass at least ten times, more than previously thought; and it is believed to have at least 200 billion stars. Indeed, it has much more extent and mass than it was thought to possess, even as late as 1975. Much more gas and dust have been detected than previously was thought to exist in it, and there is much hidden matter in it, especially in its corona. The hidden matter may be dark or barely luminous and may be slightly luminous stars or the dark embers of burnt-out stars, and may even lie in invisible black holes.

The orbital velocity of an object in a galaxy depends, as previously noted, on mass within its orbit as well as on mass in and about it. Because of this, many times more mass in the galaxy than previously it was thought to have necessarily is implied by discovery, chiefly by improved radio telescopy, that its rotational speed does not decline with increasing distance from its center as much as that decline would have to be if its mass were as little as previously thought. Indeed, it has been discovered that the rotational velocity, not only of the Milky Way, but of several other studied galaxies remains fairly constant with increasing distance from the galactic center. Rotational curves showing the relationship of orbital velocity to distance from the centers of the Milky Way and of these other galaxies approaches flatness, i.e., is a horizontal line, nearly straight, for a great distance out from the galactic centers.

There are enormous mass and luminosity in galactic centers, but in our galaxy and the other studied galaxies mass does not decline as does luminosity with increasing distance from the centers. Thus, there must be much dark and barely luminous mass in the outer stretches of the galaxies, essential to their stability.

The central bulge and disk of Andromeda M31 seemingly are at least twice as large as those of the Milky Way, and it has over 400 billion stars, perhaps twice as many as the Milky Way has. Orbital velocity of hydrogen in M31's outer reaches indicates that like the Milky Way it has a corona containing much dark and barely luminous matter.

Structural components

The Milky Way, M31 and other spiral galaxies are alike in that their main structural components are a disk, a central bulge in the disk, a halo about the disk and a corona enveloping the halo. The disk includes arms spiraling outwards from the central bulge.

The central bulge

The diameter of the central bulge, or nucleus, of our galaxy is about sixteen thousand lightyears, and the greatest thickness of the bulge is somewhat less than ten thousand lightyears. The bulge resembles a flattened but still inflated basketball spreading out circularly in spiraling arms about the galactic disk.

The bulge has gas and dust in layers, clouds and streams that greatly obscure our visual view through it. In the last fifteen years, however, the capability of optical observation of the bulge has greatly improved, and new and effective ways of looking at and through the bulge by electromagnetic wavelengths other than visual have been developed. There are excellent pictures based on radio, gamma-ray, ultraviolet, X-ray and infrared radiation reception, showing properties of the bulge indicative of its contents and how they would appear if we visually could see them. These pictures are enabling astronomers and others more and more to understand specifically what the bulge contains in stars, star clusters, gas and dust clouds, rings, streams and diffusion, and to understand the distribution and the orbital and random motion of these components. Likewise, the central bulges of M31 and of other nearby galaxies are being observed and studied by this improved optical telescopy and by new apparatus and techniques for observation by other than visual wavelengths.

In the Milky Way bulge old red stars cluster thickly everywhere, especially toward and at the galactic center, but there also are clusters of bright and blue new stars. Gas and dust are relatively thin in the bulge because so much gas and dust have been converted into stars. But there still are in the bulge gas and dust clouds, layers, rings and streams with random as well as galactic motions. At the galactic center in a small area the heavy concentration of stars, tremendous radiation emitted and some jetting and streaming of matter are very suggestive of the presence of an energy engine or powerhouse, perhaps a black hole, that may have been much more active in the past.

In M31 and the Milky Way, Population II (old) stars predominate in the central bulge. All of these are about twelve billion years old, which means that they formed as primeval galaxies were becoming galaxies.

The distribution of stars, gas and dust in the central bulge of M31 resembles that distribution in the Milky Way central bulge. It was noted previously that discovery of the distribution of Population I and II stars in Andromeda led to the discovery of a similar distribution in the Milky Way. It was Walter Baade's systematic observation of M31 with the 100-inch Mt. Wilson telescope, particularly during the Second World War when the sky above Mt. Wilson was brighter because Los Angeles' lights were dimmed, that resulted in his discovery of this stellar distribution. Later observation and study have confirmed that the components of the M31 central bulge and their dynamics are much like those in the central bulge of the Milky Way and that at the center of M31 there may be an energy engine or powerhouse, perhaps a black hole, considerably more energetic than that possibly at the center of the Milky Way.

Star clusters, groups and clouds

The stars of the Milky Way and of other spiral galaxies are in assemblages that bestow upon the macrofabric of matter a repetitive pattern with variability from galaxy to galaxy. The dynamics of the assemblages, insofar as discernible and understandable, enlighten us as to the weaving of matter within galactic regions on the loom of spacetime.

In both the Milky Way and in Andromeda M31 globular clusters of old red stars are distributed throughout the halo, disk and central bulge, congregating thickly toward and especially at the galactic centers. In the Milky Way the globulars number at least 131, and over half of these are concentrated about the galactic center in the direction of Sagittarius. The linear dimensions of the globulars range from ten to one hundred parsecs (a parsec is 3.26 lightyears). In the Northern Hemisphere of the earth, the Great Cluster of Hercules is a globular cluster barely seeable by the eye unaided, and in the Southern Hemisphere, Omega Centauri and 47 Tucanae are globular clusters easily seen by the naked eye.

The globular clusters generally are as old as the galaxy, perhaps originating in its primeval state, a few billion years after the universe began in the Big Bang. A few of these clusters, however, have enough metal content, though it is scarce, to indicate strongly that they are younger than most of the other globular clusters. Generally, the globular clusters have only traces of metal or none at all, the reason for this being their great age; metals in stars in sizeable amounts occur only in their formation from the debris of dead stars, and few stars have died in the globular clusters. The globular clusters far out in the galactic halo contain far less metal than do the globular clusters closer to the galactic center.

In M31 there are at least 355 globular clusters, nearly three times as many as in the Milky Way. Two striking differences between the Milky Way and M31 globular clusters are that the latter generally have much more metal than the former and that metal content is unrelated to their distribution in M31. This shows strongly that the evolution of M31 and that the Milky Way differ in respects related to their globular clusters.

Many Cepheid variables in globular clusters in M31 and in like clusters in the outer and inner regions of the Milky Way provided the means through the periodicity and the apparent and intrinsic luminosity of the Cepheids to establish distances among globular clusters in the Milky Way and between the Milky Way and M31. The distance to the Andromeda galaxy was thus found to be twice as much as had previously been thought; and the scale assigned the universe correspondingly was doubled.

The Milky Way has over one thousand open clusters of stars of varying age, as well as globular clusters of old stars. Generally these open clusters are asymmetrical and shapeless, and their stars are distributed loosely, making it difficult in determine the cluster termini.

A dozen open clusters are visible to the eye unaided, among these, the Hyades and The Pleiades.

The open clusters in the galaxy vary considerably in size and in from having a few to having several hundred stars, and they vary in distance from the earth. They congregate strongly in the galactic plane. Typically, an open cluster has a volume somewhat less than one hundred cubic parsecs and has several hundred stars; and stars in an open cluster range from bright blue young stars through old red giant stars to white dwarfs. Most of the stars are in the main spectrum-luminosity sequence, discussed in Chapter 16.

In Andromeda M31, 403 open clusters have been identified and studied. As in the Milky Way, the open clusters are concentrated in and along the galactic disk. In both galaxies these clusters are far younger than the globular clusters. In both galaxies most, if not all, stars in an open cluster probably formed about the same time. This fact has been helpful in determining the rate of star formation in both galaxies.

So-called "stellar associations" are aggregations of a few to a thousand stars, usually young and bright, originating in varied proximity to each other; but they are not strongly bound together gravitationally, so that they tend to disperse among the whole galactic star population.

"Star clouds" are large assemblages of stars numbering in the thousands or millions, which occupy vast regions of the galaxy. The largest star clouds are in the most heavily star-populated regions of the galaxy, e.g., Sagittarius, Cygnus and Carina.

In galaxies other than the Milky Way and Andromeda M31, even in greatly distant galaxies, thousands of globular clusters have been detected; and in nearby galaxies hundreds of open clusters have been identified. This discovery of clusters in other galaxies has occurred since 1970.

Spiral structure

Most probably, our galaxy has a spiral structure and is in an Sb, perhaps a barred Sb, galaxy. Andromeda M31 is classified as an Sb spiral galaxy. The spiral, elliptic and irregular galactic motifs, as previously noted, are universally woven into the macropattern of matter on the loom of spacetime.

The spiral arms of galaxies lie in their galactic plane about their disks, spiraling out from their central bulges or nuclei.

Andromeda M31 appears to be a two-arm spiral, but there is respectable contention that really it has only one arm. No other one-armed galaxy is known.

Our galaxy apparently has at least three arms or arm segments, and possibly it has a fourth arm segment. The sun is on the inner side of the Orion arm, one-third of the way out from the galactic center to the outer rim of the disk. That is, it is about 28 thousand lightyears from the galactic center.

The Orion sometimes is called the Cygnus arm. It is ill-defined and may be a spur from the inside of the Perseus arm, which lies farther out from the galactic center. The seeming joinder of the Orion spur with the Perseus arm is in the region of the Crab Nebula. Closer to the galactic center is the Sagittarius arm; and there possibly is an arm or arm segment even closer, the Carina arm, which possibly is only the end of the Sagittarius arm and properly should be called the "Sagittarius-Carina" segment.

The tracing of the arms in the galaxy has been optically possible by their blue-white supergiant stars and bright ionized hydrogen clouds about these stars, and by the dark nebulae between arms. Radio observation provides some corroboration of the existence of the arms. It discloses carbon monoxide, indicative of, because associated with, dust, between clouds of atomic hydrogen in a spiral pattern.

What has caused the arms to form and keep their shape? The most accepted theory is that the cause is density waves which exist in the plane of the galaxy. What causes the density waves is unknown. Gas, dust and stars move into, across and out of these waves very slowly. Stars form out of the gas and dust, relatively abundant in this region of the galaxy, as the gas and dust move across the waves. Accordingly, the arms are the scene of most recent and present star formation in the galaxy. The motion across the galaxy is so slow that the stars may be born and die in an arm before they cross it. The stars and observable clouds disappear from visual view as they move out of the arms into the dark clouds between them.

If the arms were only formations of gas, dust, and stars, streaming after the galaxy as it moved through space, they would wind into the nuclear disk and disappear in time, as the galaxy revolves.

Concluding remarks

The macropattern of matter in the Milky Way, Andromeda M31 and other spiral galaxies is intermediate between the larger-scale galactic and the smaller-scale stellar pattern in the weaving of the fabric of matter on the loom of spacetime. The same is true of the patterns woven into matter in the elliptical and irregular galaxies.

Proponents of arguments for the existence of God and his creation of the universe certainly will see in the structure and dynamics of the Milky Way, Andromeda M31 and other spiral galaxies divine design and divine direction in the evolution and functioning of these galaxies in accordance with that design. Opponents of this argument may see in the evolution, structure and functioning of our galaxy and of others only the weaving of matter on the loom of spacetime in accordance with natural law and natural explanation.

In regard to design and otherwise, whether God or something else, equally basic, is plain, dim or hidden, in the modern picture of spiral galaxies, typified by that of the Milky Way and Andromeda M31, is, in our view, a subjective matter and not objectively demonstrable.

16

Stars and Nebulae

Being woven throughout the fabric of matter and of radiation on the loom of spacetime are the hot and luminous stars and the intragalactic nebulae, many of them glowing with reflected starlight. The stars and nebulae emerge as two products of the weaving process of the four fundamental interactions of matter—electromagnetic, strong, weak and gravitational—continuing ceaselessly in their attachment of matter to the events of spacetime.

The weaving somehow, perhaps by gravitational instability or gravitational waves initially, thereafter by shock waves from supernovae after these stellar explosions began to occur from time to time in stellar evolution, concentrates the gas and dust of galaxies into billions of intragalactic nebulae; and then, mainly through self-gravitation, further contracts the intragalactic nebulae into denser protostars, and then the protostars into even denser stars, as the protogalaxies become galaxies. This weaving of nebulae and stars is continuing and will continue as long as gas and dust are available for it.

The weaving of the fabric of matter on the loom of spacetime has created, not only the stars and nebulae, but also humankind with eyes, ears, senses and brains by which they feel and know the radiant beauty of the star-and-nebula-studded universe. Are there other intelligent beings elsewhere than on earth, who see the star-lit fabric and know and feel it as we do? More and more it seems that intelligent life like ours must be rare in the universe, because requisite conditions for it appear to be a matter of slight chance or almost impossible occurrence. Many of us, nevertheless, have little doubt that we are not alone, inasmuch as there are 200 billion times 200 billion stars or more, millions of which, if not billions, should have planets on which life could emerge, at least by remote chance, and also become intelligent. In any case, we exist, and to us the burning and shining stars and the glowing nebulae are radiantly beautiful. Are we like gods or demigods in a Garden of Eden or on a Mount Olympus, who have come forth out of the earth and the cosmos and are alone therein? Our role and responsibility in the cosmos is further considered in Chapter 19.

If there were no humanity on earth or like intelligent life elsewhere, there still would be stars and nebulae, but they would be unappreciated except perhaps by God; and starlight, for want of a recipient, would communicate no information, though it still would warm, guide and comfort other life, like that of "our" animals and plants, if it existed in favorable range of a star.

To know God, if he exists, or to find a way to him, by knowing his universe, or to know the universe well if it exists somehow though there is no God, requires knowledge of the stars and of nebulae from which they have emerged and are emerging. Moreover, we must know something about how science has obtained knowledge of the stars if we are to share in that knowledge at all. So, in this chapter we shall discuss not only stars and nebulae, but also techniques by which that knowledge has been obtained.

Birth, evolution and death of stars

Stars are being woven into the fabric of matter from intragalactic nebulae of gas and dust, though the first stars were woven out of the protogalaxies, mostly hydrogen but containing some helium and deuterium, about twelve billion lightyears ago. Most of the first generations of stars have perished, being largely dispersed into the intragalactic gas from which they emerged, adding the heavier elements and dust to it, though leaving behind their dense remains as white dwarfs, neutron stars and, probably, black holes. Some of the earliest stars remain, however, as old red (Population II) stars, mostly in globular galaxies nearly free of gas and dust, or in globular clusters, also nearly gasless and dustless, on the outskirts of the spiral galaxies.

More recently formed stars (Population I), ranging from red dwarfs through yellow dwarfs to blue dwarfs and blue giants, stars on the Main Sequence (explained subsequently), mostly are found on the edges of the arms of spiral galaxies and in galactic central bulges and nuclei.

The weaving of new stars in the fabric of matter, insofar as observed, mostly is in and out of dark molecular clouds in bright nebulae like that of Orion. We cannot see these new stars until they begin to shine, as they are hidden in the darkness of their nebular womb.

The birth of stars begins with coagulations in the molecular gas and dust clouds, perhaps caused by density waves, shock waves from supernovae, gravitational instability or gravitational waves, the colliding of molecular clouds, or other cause, the exact causation not really being fully understood. The coagulating lumps gather increasing self-gravitational force as they sweep into themselves by their gravitational attraction all gas and dust within its compelling reach. The coagulation accelerates as the cloudy lumps become denser dark globs, which contract faster into protostars, and then into stars. These globs are observed throughout areas of star formation and are called "Bok globulars" after their discoverer, Bart Bok. The globs may, if their spin is too fast, become unstable so that they break up into two or more fragments that evolve into a binary or multiple-star system.

A protostar is deemed to become a star when in its self-gravitational compression it becomes dense enough and therefore hot enough to become self-luminous. If it is less than .01 solar mass, it ceases compression, and remains a red dwarf star, off the Main Sequence (explained subsequently), for billions of years until it finally becomes a black dwarf and ultimately a burnt out cinder. If, however, it is larger, its self-gravitational shrinking continues until after millions of years, thirty million if it is of one solar mass, its central temperature reaches fifteen million degrees Kelvin; and at this temperature nuclear fusion of hydrogen in its core commences. The nuclear burning is a continuing explosion, the pressure of which outward by light and other radiation and heat convection reaches an equilibrium with the inward crushing of gravity, and the star is then stable and will be stable for millions of years if it is a giant and for billions of years if it is a dwarf.

In a yellow dwarf star like the sun the nuclear reaction begins, as said, at fifteen million degrees Kelvin and is the so-called "proton-proton" chain in which hydrogen is converted into helium, the process releasing energy as photons, neutrinos and gamma rays. In more massive stars, when their central temperature reaches more than fifteen million degrees Kelvin, the reaction is the carbon-nitrogen-oxygen cycle, which is productive of the heavier elements, releasing energy in the process.

Smaller stars like the sun continue stable, on the Main Sequence, though in uneasy equilibrium between self-gravitation inward and nuclear explosive pressure outward, for billions of years. The uneasiness of the equilibrium is manifested in surface and atmospheric turbulence, discussed subsequently.

The sun's expected life on the Main Sequence is about ten billion years and is now half over. More gigantic stars live on the Main Sequence for only millions of years. A star ten times as massive as the sun is on the Main Sequence for only ten million years. After stars leave the Main Sequence, they degenerate into compact objects: white dwarfs, neutron stars and black holes. (These compact objects are discussed in Chapter 18.) Normally, however, a star like the sun will expand twice, the second time much more than the first, before it enters its final plunge into its ultimate compactness.

When the nuclear fire has consumed the hydrogen at a star's core, it burns hydrogen outward from the core, and this causes a star like the sun to expand a thousandfold into a red giant. Eventually most hydrogen in the interior of the star reachable by the nuclear fire is consumed (about fifteen percent of the star's total hydrogen), and the hydrogen fire begins to go out.

The process is complicated, but pressure, density and temperature at the core increase as the hydrogen burns outward away from the core. When the cores are hot enough, the helium ignites in a sudden flash into a new nuclear fire. In the helium flash the star in a matter of days drastically contracts. But as the helium continues to burn, the star again expands until it is far larger and brighter than it was in its first expansion. A star of solar mass becomes four hundred times larger, and a thousand times brighter, than the sun. It becomes larger than the orbit of Mars, though less than that of Jupiter. Eventually, its increase is so much that its self-gravity no longer can equalize its outward nuclear explosive pressure, and it explodes in a supernova. It blows off its outer layers in a planetary nebula into space; and its remainder self-gravitationally collapes into a white dwarf.

When giant stars have consumed their helium, converting it into carbon and oxygen, their cores contract until they are hot enough to ignite the carbon in them and convert it into magnesium. The nuclear burning and converting of elements into heavier elements continues until the core is iron, at which stage the chain process stops. As the iron cannot be converted by the self-gravitational force of the star into outward pressure, there is a sudden implosion of all the gas and matter outside the core into it, causing the gas and matter rushing together against the core to increase in density and temperature until it ignites in a nuclear supernova explosion. The size of the supernova is commensurate with the mass of the star. The star may be entirely destroyed, scattered into shells and fragments of gas and bits of matter spreading outward into intragalactic space for thousands of lightyears.

Starlight language

Starlight and other star radiation carry a huge amount of information, and scientists marvelously have learned to understand much, though far from all, that the light and radiation say as to the pastdistance, motions, birth, evolution, structure, dynamics, classes, volume, mass, color, temperature, constituents, ageing and death of the stars. Indeed, only through light and other radiation of the stars have we come to know them at all and as wonderfully well as we do, though much about them still is understood poorly or not at all. The remarkable aspect of all this is that astronomers, even with the most powerful telescopes, see the stars only as points of light (except for blurring by our atmosphere), and likewise observe them by other radiation only as points of origin of the radiation.

Light and radiation from or reflected by nebulae, gas and dust in our galaxy also have instructed scientists as to the existence, formations, motions, velocity and constituents of the nebulae, gas and dust, and have provided them with additional information about stars embedded and being born in the nebulae.

Starlight and other radiation from stars and from nebulae, gas and dust in other galaxies gives us information about them. Some individual stars in nearby galaxies, including M31 in Andromeda, can be visually discerned and otherwise observed, their light and radiation telling us much about them. The light and radiation of more distant galaxies inform us about their stellar and gaseous content, although their individual stars and nebulae cannot be observed, and they tell us much more about them, including their size, mass, temperature, motions and distancepast from us. It is by the red shift of starlight and other star radiation of distantpast galaxies that we know that they are receding from us, how fast they are receding, how much their recession is accelerating, and how distantpast from us they are; and that we know that the universe is expanding and know, with some uncertainty, the rate of its expansion and its age.

Some would say, though others would dispute, that scientific study of starlight and other radiation tells us much, not only about the universe, but about the possibility or probability of a God-Creator; and some might even say that astronomy and physics, edified by information conveyed by starlight and radiation and by observation of the microscopic world in the laboratory and by particle accelerators, constitute a far more illuminated and a far better way than any other to conceptualizations, proof and understanding of a God-Creator.

Distancepast of stars

The distancepast from us of stars and intragalactic nebulae is determined by distancepast markers discussed in Chapter 3.

The nearest stars to us are a group collectively known as "Alpha Centauri," about $4\frac{2}{3}$ lightyears away. Two of the stars are a binary system. The brightest, itself, also called "Alpha Centauri," is much like the sun. The component that comes closest to us is called "Proxima Centauri."

The next nearest star to us is Barnard's star, which is 1.84 parsecs away. Sirius, the brightest star, is 2.65 parsecs pastdistant. There are sixty one stars within five parsecs from us. A parsecs 3.2616 lightyears, which is equivalent to 19.2 trillion miles or 206,265 times the radius of the earth's orbit about the sun. Accordingly, these nearest stars are tremendously far from us by terrestrial standards.

The most pastdistant of the twenty most bright stars is Deneb, which is 450 parsecs away. Next most pastdistant of these brightest stars are Rigel, 250 parsecs from us, and Betelgeuse, 150 parsecs pastdistant.

How deeply into the distancepast can we optically view the stars? By parallax, using the diameter of the earth's orbit as a base, the greatest pastdistance of a star determinable is ninety parsecs; with the space telescope it will be 150 parsecs. By mean or statistical parallax the greatest pastdistance to groups of stars determinable is 480 parsecs.

The Hyades open cluster of stars is forty two parsecs pastdistant from us. As noted in Chapter 3, its distance is determinable by earth-orbit parallax and more accurately by the moving-cluster method; and by its known pastdistance the pastdistance of other open clusters is determinable.

Cepheid variable stars detectable because they are sufficiently large and luminous in fairly near galaxies are used for determining distance-pasts of galaxies not more than 3,904,000 parsecs away. The use of the angular size of hydrogen (H2) regions in galaxies as distancepast markers is limited to 24,925,000 parsecs. Beyond this distance individual objects in galaxies cannot be seen telescopically from the earth's surface, but the space telescope is expected to increase tenfold the pastdistance of optically seeable objects, including stars within distant galaxies.

Bodily properties

Stars vary in size, mass, composition, density, temperature, luminosity, color and other bodily properties. Our sun is an average star, a yellow dwarf, with a diameter of 865,000 miles. Red dwarf stars are about one-half its size. Compact stars, i.e., (1) white dwarf, (2) neutron stars and (3) black holes, which are the remains of stars after their final self-gravitational collapse, are respectively (1) earth-size, (2) as small as ten miles across, and (3) dimensionless or almost so. At the other extreme are the red supergiants, for example Anteres with a diameter about 285 times that of the sun and Betelgeuse, three hundred times more voluminous than the sun. Either of these is farther across than is the orbit of Mars.

Stars vary less in mass than in volume. The upper limit of stability for a star is about one hundred solar masses, and the minimum limit at which mass can self-gravitationally collapse and become luminous as a star is one percent solar mass. Within these limits, however, stars vary considerably in mass from star to star. Those on the Main Sequence vary from one-fourth to twenty solar masses.

The relationship of the massiveness to the luminosity of a star is discussed subsequently.

The more massive a star is, the shorter-lived it is, and the less time it spends on the Main Sequence. The more massive stars have much more hydrogen than less massive stars as they begin their lives, but they burn it much faster than the less massive stars burn theirs, in order to maintain outward pressure and stability against their much greater self-gravitational inward pressure. Hence, a star ten times more massive than the sun lives only ten million years before it leaves the Main Sequence on its way quickly to become a black hole, whereas the sun will live ten billion years before leaving the Main Sequence to become in millions of years a white dwarf.

The composition of stars is determinable from the spectra of their light. Stars are mostly hydrogen with some helium and very little of the other elements. The heavier elements are produced only in the nuclear furnaces of supergiant stars, as has frequently been said. Smaller stars like the sun terminate their nuclear burning on completion of conversion by their nuclear fire of helium, available in their cores as fuel, into carbon, the helium being there by conversión from hydrogen in the previous nuclear burning of hydrogen in and near their cores.

Since stars have stages of contraction and expansion they vary during their lives in density, pressure, surface area, temperature, luminosity and color. Those with the hottest surfaces are blue, blue-white or white, those with the coolest surfaces are red and those with surfaces intermediately hot range from blue through the yellow and orange hues to red.

On their surface, stars vary in temperature from two thousand degrees to 100,000 degrees Kelvin. The sun is a yellow dwarf with an average surface temperature of six thousand degrees Kelvin. Betelgeuse, the twelfth brightest star and a supergiant, is cool and red. Vega, the fifth brightest star, though with a diameter three times that of the sun, is a hot blue-white star. Capella, the seventh brightest star, is yellow.

Motions

Stars orbit about the galactic center, as discussed in Chapter 14. From our viewpoint, considering the sun as though at rest, stars have radial motions and velocities, that is, in the line of sight, and they also have proper motions, that is, across or at angles to the line of sight. They also rotate on their axes, those larger, and higher on the Main Sequence, spinning faster, and those smaller, and lower on the Main Sequence, spinning more slowly. The spin becomes too slow to be detectable in stars that are later in the spectral classification than GO. (This classification is discussed subsequently.) A protostar becomes unstable if it spins too fast and fragments into a binary or multiple-star system, thereby losing spin.

Luminosity

The brightest star in the sky is Sirius, whose apparent magnitude is −1.47. Its absolute magnitude is +1.4 and its visual luminosity is 23 (number of solar luminosities). The next brightest star is Canopus, whose apparent magnitude is −0.73. Its absolute magnitude is −3.0, and its visual luminosity is 130.

In measuring the magnitude of a star, lesser brightness is expressed in greater numerical magnitude. A first magnitude star is one hundred times brighter (that is, it gives one hundred times more light) than a sixth magnitude star, which is the faintest that a star can be and still be seeable by the unaided human eye. The first magnitude is an average of the magnitudes of the twenty brightest stars in the sky.

Since a difference of five magnitudes is a factor of one hundred, as above noted, a difference of one magnitude is the fifth root of one hundred or 2.512. Thus, a difference of two magnitudes is 6.31, the square of 2.512; a difference of four magnitudes is 39.82, the fourth power of 2.512 and a difference of five magnitudes, as said, is one hundred, or the fifth power of 2.512.

The use of "magnitude" by itself usually implies apparent magnitude. Absolute magnitude means the visual brightness of a star viewed from a pastdistance of ten parsecs.

"Luminosity" generally is used in astronomy to mean the total radiation from a star or nebulae, though sometimes it is used to mean visual radiation, i.e., that visually perceptive or light. The total luminosity depends on how much surface a star has and on how hot the surface is. The star may be a red giant with a cool surface but so much surface that its total radiation is immense. That is, the star is very bright. Or the star may be a white dwarf with little surface that is tremendously hot, but its total output of radiation is small so that it is dim even though any square mile of its surface is much hotter and brighter than any square mile of the surface of a red giant.

The mass and luminosity of a star also are related. If the star is stable (neither contracting nor expanding) because of equilibrium between self-gravity and outward expansive pressure, then its properties, including its luminosity, are determined by its mass and its chemical composition and distribution. This means that in a cluster or assemblage of stars with about the same chemical composition and distribution the mass of any particular star determines its luminosity. Under these circumstances its luminosity is approximately proportional to the cube of its mass. Thus, under these circumstances, a star ten times as massive as another is about a thousand times more luminous than the other. This mass-luminosity ratio determines the lifetime of a star on the Main Sequence, as discussed subsequently.

"Brightness," in referring to all radiation from a star, means the amount of that radiation in a given unit of time; that is, it depends on the "flux" of that radiation. "Brightness," in referring to light, means the flux of light; in referring to radio emission it means the flux of that emission; or, in referring to any other radiation, it means its flux.

"Apparent brightness," in referring to light from a star means the flux of that light upon the earth, or upon any area unit of the earth's surface, the lens of the telescope or the human eye, i.e., the total amount of light being received by it in a moment or other measure of time. Likewise, "apparent brightness" is used to refer to the flux of any other radiation or the total radiation from a star being received on earth or on a space vehicle in a particular unit of time.

Apparent brightness of a star in light or other radiation, or the apparent luminosity of all its radiation, depends, as one would expect, on its intrinsic brightness, i.e., the flux of light or other radiation, or the total radiation, from it, and on its pastdistance from us. Thus, two stars may have the same apparent brightness, though one is far more pastdistant and much brighter than the other.

The reason why the amount of light received from a star becomes less with increasing pastdistance is that light is dispersed in all directions from its source, and so the surface of an object receiving light from the star is less and less of the surface of the globular volume of light expanding about the star as the pastdistance of the star from the object increases.

Astronomy has classified stars according to their luminosity, as: Ia, brightest supergiants; Ib, less bright supergiants; II, bright giants; III, giants; IV, subgiants; V, dwarfs. The sun is a class V star. This luminosity classification does not include the compact body into which stars contract in their final self-gravitational collapse, i.e., white dwarfs, neutron stars and black holes.

The sun, an average dwarf and a Main Sequence star, has apparent magnitude of +4.8 and an absolute magnitude of −26.7. Stated previously were the apparent and absolute magnitudes of Sirius and Canopus, the two brightest stars. Alpha Centauri, the third brightest star, the nearest star to us and the most like the sun, has an apparent magnitude of −0.27 and an absolute magnitude of +4.7. It has a visual luminosity of 1.1, meaning that its output of light is one-tenth more than that of the sun. Arcturus, the fourth brightest star, has an apparent magnitude of −0.06, an absolute magnitude of −0.1 and a visual luminosity of 52,000. These figures mean that it is enormous and very far away; indeed, it is 250 parsecs in the distancepast. Its output of light is 52,000 times that of the sun. Vega, the next brightest star, is at the center of our supercluster of galaxies. Its apparent magnitude is +0.04, and its absolute magnitude is +0.5. It will become the polar star in twelve thousand years from now.

The above figures illustrate the wide range of the flux of light from stars and of its flux upon the earth.

Luminosity in connection with spectral class is, as we saw in Chapter 3, one of the distancepast markers in scaling the red-shift ladder and in scaling the universe.

Spectra

Starlight and radiation must be decoded in order to understand the information that they carry about the stars, the galaxies and the cosmos. Spectroscopy, H-R diagram interpretation and measurement of the flux upon the earth, that is, of apparent magnitude, of the light and radiation are modes of decoding them.

Spectroscopy is the study of the spectra of light and radiation from the stars, nebulae and other celestial bodies and from intergalactic and intragalactic gas and dust; and of the spectra of light and radiation from atoms and their constituents. Metaphorically, it is a mode of understanding both the macroscopic and the microscopic weaving of the fabric of matter through the four fundamental interactions of matter—electromagnetic, strong, weak and gravitational—upon the loom of spacetime. It is a most important means of comprehending how matter is woven into nebulae and stars and of knowing their form, composition, physical conditions, functioning, motions and velocities.

The spectrum of light is the hidden range of colors in it, individually unperceivable by the human eye until they are revealed by the passage of light through a prism or defraction grating and thereby dispersed into a rainbow-continuous band of colors. The light spectrum is the portion of the entire electromagnetic spectrum that is visible to the human eye, aided or unaided, that is, from infrared to the near-ultraviolet. The electromagnetic spectrum is the entire range of electromagnetic radiation from gamma rays to radio waves.

Astronomical optical spectroscopy utilizes a spectroscope or a spectrograph to record or photograph the spectrum of the light of the star or other celestial object. It is possible, in so doing from the surface of the earth, to record or to photograph the spectrum from infrared to near violet; and it is possible by other techniques to observe the spectrum to far infrared and radio waves at one end of the spectrum and to X-ray and gamma rays at the other end.

Usually in optical spectroscopy a reflector-type telescope is used, that gathers the light and focuses it on a slit of the spectroscope or spectrograph. The width of the slit determines the resolution of the star or object being observed. The light passing through the slit is directed through a glass or quartz prism or a defraction grating and by it dispersed into its spectrum, which is recorded or photographed. Electronic scanning devices and computers are employed in the recording.

Stellar and other spectra are classified as continuous, bright-line or dark-line. A continuous spectrum is a smooth continuity of colors with no color missing. In a bright-line spectrum, the bright lines of the individual colors appear across the continuity of colors, that is, not lengthwise with it. In a dark-line spectrum, dark lines appear across the continuity of the spectrum.

A continuum spectrum is emitted by any body, whether it is solid, liquid or gaseous, that is dense, opaque and incandescent with high heat. This is true of a light bulb's filament, a metal bar, a glob of dense gas in a laboratory or in space or a star. Atoms emit light in quanta (discrete amounts) at different wavelengths, determinative of discrete colors, which merge in white light when they are produced by tightly packed atoms. The white light, so produced, has a continuum spectrum.

A bright-line spectrum is produced by a body of gas thin enough to be transparent. When it is hot enough to be transparent, the atoms in it being widely dispersed emit their particular colors in separated bright lines, called "emission lines." This is true of a body of thin gas in space or in the laboratory.

A dark line spectrum results when light passes through a gas, including that in a solar, stellar or planetary atmosphere or that in intragalactic space, or in a controlled body in a laboratory, that is cooler than the solid, liquid or gaseous body from which the light emanated. The cooler gas absorbs some of the light passing through it, causing the color lines of its spectrum to dim, thereby making the lines appear dark. The lines appropriately are called absorption lines.

Bright lines across a continuum spectrum are also caused when light from a star or other incandescent body in space or in a laboratory passes through gas, as in the halo or the corona of the sun or a star, or in a laboratory, that is hotter than the body from which the light comes. These added bright lines across the continuity of the spectrum reveal the chemical composition of gas through which the light has passed.

The basic principles of astronomical and atomic spectroscopic theory were ascertained by Gustave Robert Kirchoff, in work done in collaboration with Robert Wilhelm Bunsen, and were enunciated by Kirchoff in 1859. They worked primarily with solar and with laboratory-produced light. Since that time the theory and technology to implement it have developed greatly, so that spectroscopy now is one of the most important means by which starlight and radiation are interpreted.

Because of the consistency of continuum spectra and of the number, nature and arrangement of emission and absorption lines across a spectrum, whether the spectra is of starlight, solar light or light produced in a laboratory, we know far more than we could otherwise about the distance, composition, physical properties, motions and velocities of stars. Moreover, this consistency in the spectra of starlight from stars anywhere in the distancepast, that is, in the universe, is strongly persuasive that the weaving of the fabric of matter on the loom of spacetime is fundamentally the same everywhere on the loom. In other words, the laws of physics are the same everywhere in the universe, though an exception may be in the singularity at the bottom of a black hole, including that into which the universe will descend if it is finite.

There are further specific observations that should be made about the reading of starlight language by spectroscopy. First, each kind of atom has, in effect, its own spectral fingerprint in that it has a unique set of spectral lines, which are in the same number and pattern though they are emission or absorption lines. Thus, emission lines reveal the composition of gas through which light passes, as above stated. The number of lines in these fingerprints of atoms vary from a few for hydrogen to thousands for a heavy atom like iron.

Secondly, a body that emits light at all wavelengths also absorbs light at all wavelengths, and a body that emits light only at certain wavelengths also absorbs light only at those wavelengths. Accordingly, emission and absorption lines in spectra are of the same number, strength and arrangement, if they are produced by the same chemical compositions, and they vary in the same way where the variance is due to the absence of the same chemicals. This correlation facilitates the interpretation of either emission or absorption lines.

Thirdly, the displacement of spectral lines denotes a red or blue shift, as the case may be, revealing the motion, velocity and acceleration of stars away or toward us, and revealing also the pastdistance of the stars, thereby providing us with a ladder by which we can mentally descend into the distancepast, to the galaxies, protogalaxies, quasars and the beginning of the Big Bang, observing the fabric of matter being woven upon the loom of history as we do so, which is what we have done in former chapters.

Spectral type

Since stars vary in the spectral lines of their spectra and that variation is informative as to their chemical composition, surface pressure and temperature and pastdistance and velocity from us, a classification of stars according to their spectral lines is helpful in discussing and understanding them collectively as distinguished from individually and in knowing how common or exceptional are their particular physical properties. The development of the standard spectral classification has developed from the pioneer observation and classification of thousands of stellar spectra, especially that done by Annie Jump Cannon of the Harvard College Observatory in a project instituted by its director, Edward C. Pickering, in 1886. The work culminated in a catalog classifying the spectra of 250,000 stars.

This original standard spectral classification of stars is OBAFGKM, in order of their temperature from hottest to coolest. Originally, the classification was meant to be alphabetical from hottest to coolest, but new knowledge about stellar spectra necessitated the reordering of the representation letters. Students memorizing the classification have for

generations used the mnemonic, "Oh Be A Fine Girl, Kiss Me." Added
to the classification are R, N and S, representative of stars with large
amounts of heavy elements, though having the same temperature as K
and M stars. R and N also are called carbon stars because of the
abundance of carbon in them, and S stars have much zirconium and
yttrium.

The classification is refined by the additions of subclasses 0 to 9
between the letters according to variation of spectral lines, as, for
example, the weakening of hydrogen and the strengthening of calcium
lines in the range of G. The sun is classified as G2. To the spectral
classification the luminosity classification I to V, discussed previously,
often is added. Thus, the sun is classified as G2V.

H-R diagrams and the Main Sequence

An H-R, or Hertzsprung-Russell, diagram or graph plots the brightness of stars on the vertical axis against their color or temperature on the
horizontal axis of the graph. These graphs are named after E. Hertzsprung of Denmark, and H. N. Russell, an American, who independently first constructed them, Hertsprung in 1911 plotting the apparent
magnitude of stars in each of the Hyades and Pleiades open clusters
against their color index, and Russell in 1913 plotting the absolute
magnitude against the spectral class (an effect of temperature) of nearby
stars.[1] The Hertzsprung and Russell diagrams have the same effect since
the stars in an open cluster are all about the same pastdistance from us,
so that their apparent magnitudes are directly proportional to their
absolute magnitudes.

H-R diagrams of a very large number of stars, of many of the brightest
stars or of many of the nearest stars always show a Main Sequence of the
stars running diagonally from lower right to upper left, that is, with
most of the stars more or less grouped in this arrangement with a few
stars out of the Main Sequence in the upper right region of the diagram
and a few stars out of the Main Sequence in the lower left region of the
diagram.

Stars in the Main Sequence are middle-weight stars ranging from
smaller and cooler red dwarfs in the lower right through larger and
warmer yellow to still larger and hotter blue dwarfs and blue giants in
the upper left of the sequence. As stars condense out of photostars,
most enter the Main Sequence at places according to their mass, size,
temperature and color. More massive, larger and hotter stars enter in
the blue dwarf and blue giant range; those less massive, large and hot,

like the sun, enter in the yellow dwarf range; or, if still less massive, large and warm, enter in the red dwarf range.

Stars in the lower left of the diagram, off the Main Sequence, are so-called "white dwarfs," which in fact may be any color as their surface temperatures vary widely. They are degenerate stars that have lived their lives as yellow dwarf stars, being no more than $1\frac{1}{2}$ solar masses, on the Main Sequence and have left it as white dwarfs, about the size of the earth but very dense, on their degenerative way to becoming black dwarfs or burnt out slag. Neutron stars and black holes into which still larger, hotter and bluer stars on the Main Sequence have condensed self-gravitationally after their departure from the Main Sequence do not appear in H-R diagrams. In the upper right hand region of the diagrams, out of the Main Sequence, the red giants and red supergiants appear, these being stars that have left the Main Sequence in their first or second expansions in their degenerate course toward final self-gravitational collapse into neutron stars or black holes; those more than three and one-half solar masses theoretically are destined to become black holes.

H-R diagrams since their origin have proved to be another invaluable tool in the interpretation of star language, and in thinking and talking, about the distance, velocity, mass, size, density, temperature, surface pressures and turbulance and other physical conditions of the star. An astronomer knowing one or more of these properties of a star and its place on an H-R diagram may read off or infer from the diagram most, if not all, of the others.

Variable stars

Stars periodic in intensity of their light are another important means of interpreting starlight language, not only about the variable stars, but about stars in general and about the galaxies and the universe. They tell astonomers much about themselves and other stars as to pastdistance from us, mass, radii, density, temperature, color, motion, velocity and other matters.

There are thousands, if not millions of variable stars, over 25 thousand of which have been cataloged, and they are being discovered, studied and cataloged in increasing numbers. The variability sometimes is due to pulsation of the star's surface; and sometimes it is caused by eclipsing in a binary system, as discussed below.

Pulsation of the surface of a star, causing variability in intensity of its light, is due, generally speaking, to the opposition of nuclear explosive expansion and self-gravitational contraction of the star, compression waves generated by that opposition and lag between the waves travel-ing outward in reaching the surface. The pulsation occurs on the surface only. The star because of the pulsation varies with time in size, temperature, color and brightness.

Cepheid variables, which are yellow supergiants, because of their luminosity-period relationships are pastdistance markers, as discussed in Chapter 3. There are additional correlations of their periods with their spectra, temperature, radial velocity and other properties, all helpful in understanding them and other stars, the galaxies and the universe. They expand and contract with the regularity of a normal heart beat, in periods between two and forty days and with brightness change of magnitude.

RR Lyrae variables are fainter pulsating stars with the shortest known periods, between three- and nine-tenths of a day. They are Population II (older red giants) and are found in globular clusters in the halo and nucleus of the Milky Way. They also are pastdistance markers as noted in Chapter 3.

There are other kinds of variable stars. Eruptive variables, flare stars, nova and supernovae are discussed subsequently. An opposite of flare stars are R Coronae Borealis stars, which suddenly, for unknown cause, decline in brightness for weeks or months before again reverting to their previous brightness.

Turbulence and explosiveness

The photosphere and surface of a star are violently turbulent because of hot gas, radiation and sound waves within it being pushed outward by nuclear explosive force against gravity in an uneasy equilibrium and through magnetic fields of varying intensity, which arise from the photosphere to the surface. There are shifting zones of varying activity and turbulance on stellar surfaces. (As to the photosphere and surface of a star, typified by those of the sun, and as to activity described above in regard to the sun, see Chapter 17.)

On other stars as on the sun, plages, prominences, flares and spots like sun spots are presumed, and in some measure observed or inferred, to occur. On flare stars, as many as five hundred being known, flares flash suddenly, making the star a hundred times brighter for a few minutes. These flares are thought to occur on young stars, and to become less frequent and less intense as the star ages until they are comparatively modest like flares on the sun.

What is said in Chapter 17 as to the surface and composition of the sun and activity on and in it is typical of other stars, at least of those like it in size and mass.

Turbulence is increased on stars in binary systems by inter-tidal pull of each star on the other and, also, if the stars are close together, by insufficient room for expansion as one of them expands in the normal course of aging, as more fully discussed later.

Explosiveness and implosiveness of stars result from phases of drastic disequilibrium or of total loss of equilibrium between nuclear explosive outward and self-gravitational inward pressure, and also from interaction of stars in a binary system.

Novae

Novae occur usually, if not always, in binary systems, and occur when gas from one star flows onto the surface of the other causing a nuclear explosion, small compared to a supernova, but still considerable enough to be observed, if unhidden and near enough, from the earth by the eye unaided. The brightness of the star increases in one or two days by a factor of a thousand or tens of thousands. Only a minute fraction of one percent of the star's mass is lost by the explosion, and some stars are observed to explode in novae repeatedly.

The flow of gas from one star onto the other, causing the explosion, occurs when one star is so close to the other that it deprives the other of room for expansion in its normal aging. The expanding gas, usually that of the larger component, is pulled by the gravity of the other component down into it.

Supernovae

These exceed novae in explosiveness millions of times, the brightness of the exploding star increasing by a factor of ten billion, often briefly surpassing the entire brightness of the galaxy in which the star is located. Their occurrence in our galaxy can be seen by the naked eye.

A supernovae seems to be a normal happening in the late evolution of a star having over four solar masses. Records indicate that they have been observed to occur in our galaxy in 185, 1006, 1054, 1181, 1572 and 1604, A.D., and they are thought to occur in it two or three times in a century.

The exploding star blows off all its mass except a core that quickly self-gravitationally collapses into a neutron star, perhaps one that is a pulsar, or into a black hole. Or the star may be completely destroyed, but this occurrence seems to be unlikely or infrequent. The remnant gas and dust blasted into intragalactic space in time becomes a nebula like the Crab Nebula, illuminated by light from the explosion and by the remnant neutron star.

Supernovae are essential, as we have observed frequently, to the formation of mineral-containing stars, planets and animal and plant life, as the minerals are manufactured only in the nuclear-fusion fire in and about the cores of the supergiant stars.

Jets

Many gas flows or jets in opposite directions, seemingly from protostars or young stars, have been detected in the last few years. The discovery has resulted from observation of radiation in the near and far infrared wavelengths and in the shortest wavelengths of the radio spectrum, the probe using particularly the 2.6 millimeter wavelength of carbon monoxide in search of that element as a tracer. The discovery resulted from observation of molecular clouds that are the sites of star formation. The flows or jets are based on observed spectral red and blue shifts. The observation has been aided by new observational apparatus placed on high places and also used in air and space vehicles.

The jets or outflows seemingly are emitted by stars in opposite directions along the axes of their spin, the least-resistant route. They are in many respects much like cosmic jets, i.e., those emitted by galaxies, discussed in Chapter 14. It has been suggested that stars of one or more solar masses emit jets in their early evolution.

Binary and multiple-star systems

Probably more than one-half of all stars are members of binary or multiple-star systems, in which two or more stars orbit about each other or, more precisely, orbit about a common center of gravitation. In a multiple-star system one component may actually be two stars orbiting about each other, so that there are three stars in the system. Or each of two components in a binary system may itself be two stars in orbit about each other, so that there are four stars in the system. Still other combinations of stars orbiting about one another occur.

Apparent closeness of two stars in the sky or their appearing to be one star may be due only to their closeness in our line of sight, though one is much farther from us than the other, and they may not be orbiting about each other. They appear to be traveling together if they have the same proper motion, and, if not, they appear to drift apart. The term "double star" is applicable to them as well as to a binary system in which the two stars appear close together or to be one star.

One must thank God or thank nature if it solely is responsible, for binary and multiple-star systems, as they are another valuable means of deciphering star language about the weaving of stars into the fabric of matter and of radiation, since often the information carried by their light pertains, not only to them, but to stars generally. Furthermore, observing stars in a binary or multiple-star system makes it possible to make determinations that are difficult or impossible to make by observing a single star not in such a system. These determinations may relate to mass, radii, temperature, color and other stellar properties, which can be compared to observational data relating directly to other stars, thereby refining and enlarging knowledge of the latter.

Binary and multiple-star systems, it has been theorized, may originate in more than one way. Binary systems may be due to the splitting of protostars into two stars as a result of spinning of the protostars so fast that they become unstable. Or their origin may be due to two stars being formed close to each other in an intragalactic nebula. It seems that binary stars with orbital periods of less than one hundred years originate in the former, and those with greater orbital periods, in the latter way. It may be that triple, quadruple or more numerous multiple systems result from successive fragmentation of protostars due to excessive spin or from their births close together in nebulae. It also has been suggested that capture of one star by another getting too close to it may explain some binary or multiple star systems.

The separation of stars in a binary or in a multiple-star system and the size and period of their orbits vary tremendously from system to system. The strength of the gravitational field of other stars about them, however, imposes an upper limit on the distance in which two particular stars can be apart and still in orbit about each other. The separation of stars in a binary system, nevertheless, may be so much that it takes hundreds, thousands or millions of years for them to orbit each other. Some may perish before completing a single orbit.

At the other extreme, two stars actually may touch each other and be in orbit about each other; and stars, usually a large and a small one or two small ones, may orbit each other in periods of days or even minutes. Discovery of extremely short orbits of degenerate dwarfs about each other has recently been made by X-ray observation from space vehicles.

If two stars are too close together or too dim or one of them is too dim, it is only by X-ray observation or by the spectra of their light that it can be determined that they are two stars rather than one and that they are orbiting each other, and it is only by their spectra that it can be determined what their orbits and many of their physical properties are. These binary systems are called "spectrographic binaries." They must be long watched, probably for years, to record and finally determine the orbital nature of their paths; at least ten percent of their orbits must be observed and recorded from time to time in order to make the determination. Binary systems so discovered are called visual binaries. About 75,000 have been cataloged, and of these orbits of seven hundred are known.

Binaries are called "eclipsing binaries" when they eclipse each other in our line of sight. Successive eclipses cause periodic changes in brightness, as the duller star passes in front of the brighter and then the brighter passes in front of the duller. These binaries usually are discovered easily, and as many as one thousand have been, though the orbits of only two hundred of these have been determined. Observation of eclipsing binaries is most fruitful in furnishing information about them, especially since their orbital periods often are only a few days, which facilitates the quick accumulation of observational data. The data permits determinations as to inclinations, mass, radii, density and other physical properties, helpful in understanding, not only the binaries, but also other stars, especially when or insofar as the evolution of one component of the system has not, as they are in the distancepast at which we view them, been affected by the other.

Binary systems substantially affect and modify the evolution of their components, causing it to deviate significantly from that of single stars. For one thing, a closeness of one component drastically restricts the normal expansion of the other in the latter's aging. This leads to gas flowing from the expanding star, usually the originally larger and brighter, to the smaller and dimmer until it becomes the larger and brighter. There is also much loss of mass from the system into space. Furthermore, the flow of gas onto the component causes it to flare up from time to time and to explode in a nova or successive novae. It is thought that most are so caused; supernovae are otherwise caused, as discussed previously. The loss of mass by the originally larger and brighter star to its companion and into space also makes it contract and more quickly become a white dwarf, neutron star or black hole.

More will be said about binary systems harboring white dwarf and neutron stars and possibly black holes, in Chapter 18.

Stars, starlight and God

Does starlight in what it tells us about stars, galaxies and the expanding universe communicate to us or evidence anything about God or an alternative to him as explanatory of the universe? Certainly, starlight and other electromagnetic radiation illuminate the universe for us so that we can look upon it, as Paul and Newton advised, in order to see God in his works; or, we add, to see if we do in fact see in it God in his works.

Proof by starlight and other radiation of the Big Bang from the Little Bomb strongly supports, for some, a cosmological argument that God created and governs the universe. The repetition of a like process in star formation and the repetition of stellar pattern with classifiable variations throughout the universe support, for some, the teleological argument that the God-Creator exists. Others find no reason thus to regard stars, starlight and other stellar radiation.

Notes

[1] The color index as defined about 1890 by W.H. Pickering is the difference between photographic (blue light) and photovisual (yellow light) magnitudes. The color index between any two wavelengths is now determined by the use of color filters, and seldom photographically.

17

The Solar System

The solar system is our neighborhood in the Milky Way, so tiny that it is virtually lost in the immensity of the galaxy, but so vast that compared to the earth, our abode, it is like the earth itself compared to a baseball. From the human perspective, however, the earth is the most beautiful and useful home in the solar neighborhood. Let us briefly survey this neighborhood, paying special attention to the sun, the gigantic heart of the system, whose lavish outpouring of energy is lifeblood to earthly inhabitants and seems to be otherwise wasted if life is all that counts, inasmuch as it is doubtful that life exists elsewhere in the solar system. Then we shall inquire and comment about the impact of modern knowledge of the solar system on religious thought and belief. The next chapter considers the earth as a Garden of Eden in the solar system, and as possibly a unique place in the universe.

Evolution of the solar system

About 4.6 billion years ago our sun probably began its birth in the center of a "cacoon nebula," sometimes also called a "placental nebula," an enormous dusty and dark globular gathering that somehow had formed in a vastly larger molecular gas cloud on the inner edge of the Orion arm of the Milky Way. The dusty gathering probably had dimensions many times those of the solar system, and had twice the mass of the present solar system.

When this birth process of the sun began, the Milky Way had been in existence for at least ten billion years; the galaxy was about two-thirds of its probably present age. The universe was about three-fourths of its present age of probably twenty billion years as a maximum. The earth and other planets of the solar system also were about 4.6 billion years old, being nearly as old as the sun.

What caused the dusty, dark placental globular cacoon to gather in a small locality of the galaxy? The cause is unknown, but one favored theory is that probably the cause was a shock wave from a nearby supernova that compressed neighboring molecular gas and dust into a placental globular gathering of sufficient density to initiate gravitational self-collapse.

The birth process of the sun is much the same as that of other stars. Stars continue to be born as they have been since galaxies condensed out of protogalaxies. In the Milky Way stars form in dark molecular clouds, especially along the edges of its spiral arms. They are hidden at first in their dark and thick cacoons or placenta, but as their luminosity becomes intense and as the placental gas thins, they become visible to us. Presumably, star births are similar in other galaxies; in the great Andromeda galaxy it can be seen that in fact they are.

The "nebular hypothesis" that the sun and solar system originated in a gaseous nebula, now generally accepted, was first suggested by Immanuel Kant in the middle of the eighteenth century and was more specifically developed by Pierre Simon de Laplace toward the end of that century.

As gravitational collapse of the solar cacoon or placenta continued, the gas ball contracted more and more, spinning faster and faster in order to conserve its angular momentum. The spin caused it to flatten into a disk, so that the sun, planets and other orbiting bodies are now substantially in the same plane.

Atoms falling inward toward the center moved faster and faster and collided with each other more and more frequently, causing increasing heat, especially toward the center of the solar disk. Much of the heat radiated away, blowing much gaseous material away with it. Much of the increasing heat in the center became trapped, however, by the increasing central density and opacity. Containing most of the mass of the cacoon or placenta, not left behind or blown away, indeed eventually 99.9 percent of it, the center evolved into the sun.

The tremendous luminosity of the young star evaporated most volatile matter (hydrogen, helium, water, carbon dioxide and methane ices) in relative proximity to it. The remaining rocky and metallic matter in this zone about the sun evolved into the terrestrial planets: Mercury, Venus, Earth and Mars. The planetary formation occurred through continuing gravitational attraction by larger and larger assemblages of smaller assemblages. To the eye, if it had been possible to witness the scene, it first would have appeared that a dark dust cloud was orbiting about a center hidden from view by the central thickness and opacity. Then it would have been seen that turning chunks began to form and to collide with each other in the orbiting dust, many sticking together in larger and larger chunks, the largest sweeping up other smaller chunks and unassembled dust. The dust becoming thin enough, the new-born shining sun at the center became visible from anywhere in the cacoon or placenta and from outside it for great distances. Eventually in this zone of relative nearness to the sun only the four terrestrial planets and their moons were in orbit about it.

As large masses formed into the terrestrial planets, they spun on their axes and became globular, but they were too solid and hard, and their spin was not great enough, for them to flatten into disks. The eye would have observed, if they were seen in their formation, the cratering of their surfaces by their constant bombardment by pieces of rocky and metallic matter, of varying size, attracted gravitationally to them. The cratering became less and less, but continues to occur as meteorites from the orbital zone between Mars and Jupiter wander into the orbital zone of the terrestrial planets. The eye then would have observed, if the watch had continued, wind, rain (on earth), volcanic flow or other eroding forces more or less obscure or completely obliterate the cratering features.

In the orbital zone between Mars and Jupiter chunks of rocky and metalic matter of varying size, for some reason, have not assembled into planets, although in this zone asteroids nearly planetary size have evolved.

Far away from the new sun, in the orbital area of the Jovian planets, the solar heat was insufficient to evaporate volatile matter, which remained essentially as it was originally in the cacoon or placenta, being mostly hydrogen and helium and ices of water, carbon dioxide and methane. Out of this matter large turning globular gas assemblages formed and through their gravitational force swept up and incorporated smaller assemblages and unassembled dust and gas until only the five Jovian planets, Jupiter, Saturn, Neptune, Uranus and Pluto, remained. Their substance is much like that of the sun, being mostly hydrogen and helium.

The satellites of the Jovian planets formed about them in a way somewhat resembling that in which the terrestrial planets formed about the sun. They evolved, containing much of the ices and a larger percentage of heavier elements than is present in the Jovian planets themselves.

Comets for the most part formed in the outer fringes of the solar system, and their composition is believed largely to be what it was originally, so that if they could be approached or visited, much could be learned of the composition of the original solar cacoon or placenta.

Halley's comet has now been closely approached, and observational data obtained on the visitation is being analysed and made known.

The sun

Ancient and noncivilized people have venerated and worshipped the sun or have endeavored by magic to affect its treatment of them and of their environment. Among civilized people, even today, there are many who in a secular way worship the sun and expend much time and money in order to bask in its radiation. Obviously, even to untutored primitives, the sun in many ways benefits or harms and governs people, animals and planets, and has many sanctions, either beneficient or punitive, to enforce its laws.

Today it is known that the sun is in effect a central energy and heating plant for the solar system, providing the earth with optimum energy and heat and bathing all the planets and their satellites, and all bodies in the solar system, with radiation and heat in a measure varying with their distance from the sun. The amount of solar radiation and heat transmitted to the earth is optimum from the human perspective simply because life and humanity evolved while accustomed to that amount.

The sun is a central energy and heating plant for the solar system because it is a star, and all stars, as previously discussed, emit radiation, light and heat as long as their central thermonuclear reaction continues.

The sun is a fairly typical, though rather small, star, a so-called "yellow dwarf," with a spectral classification of G2, as noted in Chapter 16. As noted above, it is located on the inner edge of the Orion arm of the Milky Way. It is about 28 thousand lightyears away from the center of the galaxy, that is, about one-sixth of the way out from the center of the edge of the galactic disk. Its average distance from the earth is 93 million miles, or eight and one-third lightminutes. The nearest star to us beyond the sun, as previously noted, is Proximi Centauri, which is $4\frac{2}{3}$ lightyears away.

The diameter of the sun is 865,000 miles. It contains 99.9 percent of all the mass of the solar system. It is 300,000 times more massive (heavier) than the earth, but because its average density is far less than that of the earth, it could contain the volume of a million earths.

Pressure and density increase tremendously toward the solar center and are greatest there, making the interior extremely hot gas and the central core a thermonuclear-fusion furnace. There is little nuclear fission because of the scarcity of heavy elements. Highly energetic radiation from the thermonculear furnace slowly makes its way to the surface, losing energy as it does, and emerges as the sunlight and other solar radiation that floods the solar system in every direction from the sun.

The photosphere

The surface of the sun, called the "photosphere," is a layer of dense gas, two or three miles thick. It pulsates and bubbles because of convective heat coming up through it from a lower zone in which convection occurs because its relative low temperature causes great opacity that blocks and traps rising radiation from the much hotter interior. The photosphere itself is relatively cool, averaging about six thousand degrees Kelvin.

The chromosphere and corona

Above the photosphere is the chromosphere, and above the latter is the corona. The chromosphere is ten thousand miles thick and is much more rarified than the photosphere. Surprisingly, it also is far hotter than the photosphere, and its temperature increases with height to reach one million degrees Kelvin. The corona is even more rarified and hot, in places being four million degrees Kelvin. Why the chromosphere and corona are so much hotter than the photosphere puzzled scientists for a long time, but they have decided that the cause is atmospheric waves, analogous to sound waves on earth. These waves are caused by magnetic and heat disturbances in the photosphere and in layers beneath it. In passing outward (upward) through the chromosphere and corona, they shock and excite the gas, causing the tremendous heat increase.

Solar wind

The corona streams away in a "solar wind" that "blows" out into the solar system one hundred astronomical units (an astronomical unit is the distance from the sun to the earth) at a speed varying between 220 and 500 miles per second. The solar wind has various effects on earth and in the solar system, including the "twinkling" and "fade out" of radio waves as they encounter irregularities in the wind; the pointing of comet tails away from the sun and knots in the tails; and polar aurorae.

Sunspots

These are caused by the behavior of the sun's magnetic fields. They are vast colder and darker regions on the photosphere, and they move over it in periodic patterns. Their occurrence is cyclical over an eleven-year period, and they are more than one hundred times as often at their highest than at their lowest frequency. There is, however, little, if any, evidence, that the present eleven-year cyclical periodicity is other than a relatively recent phenomenon. The frequency and cyclical behavior well may affect earthly weather; and long periods of little sunspot activity may be related to cold periods on earth, as between 1460 and 1540 and between 1645 and 1715, the latter being the so-called "Little Ice Age."

The solar constant

This is the total amount of solar energy received in a given unit of time by a given unit of area at or just beyond the earth's atmosphere. The accepted value of the constant is 1.36×10^6 ergs per second per square centimeter, which is nearly two calories per minute. From the solar constant the total energy emitted by the sun is calculated to be 3.8×10^{33} ergs per second. This value for the solar constant has been accepted for over seventy years.

Do the total energy output of the sun and accordingly the solar constant vary with time? Slight variations, e.g., one or two percent if for a prolonged time, e.g., ten years, could substantially affect earth's temperature. A long continuing decrease in the solar constant of five percent undoubtedly would cause another ice age. One of ten percent would be catastrophic; the earth would become ice-covered and probably beyond thawing by any likely increase in the solar energy output. In the past, adequate measurements for a sufficient length of time have not been possible to determine more than that probably there is some fluctuation of at least one or two percent for short periods. However, with continuing space-borne monitoring of the solar constant and with improved monitoring devices for the purpose, it is probable that soon more will be known than is now known in the matter. Undoubtedly, fluctuation in the solar constant is one of the most important things for humankind to know about the sun, the central power and heating plant of the solar system.

The sun's lifetime

How long will the sun endure much as it now is? In about five billion years, equal to the time that it now has existed, it will burn out the hydrogen at its core. It will then expand into a red giant perhaps extending beyond the earth's orbit. Then it will contract, expand again and contract again into a white dwarf. Then it will cool gradually until it is a dead black dwarf, a chunk of slag. Its fate is that of other yellow dwarf stars, discussed in Chapter 16.

Planets and other solar bodies

The .01 percent of mass of the solar system, not contained in the sun, is in bodies and particles that orbit the sun, including the nine planets and their satellites some of which are planet size; the asteroids the larger of which are in effect minor planets; comets; meteoroids; and dust particles. A meteoride is any small body in solar space, ranging in size from dust particles to asteroids. A meteor is a meteoride traversing the earth's or another body's atmosphere, candescent from the resulting friction. A meteorite is a meteoroid or a fragment of it or a fragment of a comet that reaches and strikes earth's ground without being consumed by friction-caused fire.

The "meteoritic complex" embraces dust particles, meteoroids, asteroids and comets. "Meteor" is derived from the Greek meteoron, meaning "in the sky" and meteoros, meaning "high in the air."

Many meteoroids, like most or all comets, have been in solar orbit since the formation of the solar system and consequently are specimens of that original matter out of which the planets formed, unaffected by geological processes that have transformed original matter.

Meteoritic bodies have been available for scientific study only through meteorites found on earth and more recently through meteoritic moon rocks. It is hoped that coming comet visitations will provide further opportunity for study of matter as it was when the planets formed. It may be that in the future meteoritic bodies may be utilized for space colonization, industry and mining.

The meteoritic complex, as above noted, has been the source of bombardment and cratering of those planets and satellites which have hardened surfaces, that has continued during the 4.6 billion years of their existence. The cratering and the peculiar geological, climatic and other formative processes of each of the planets and satellites and of the large asteroids have combined to give each its own peculiar surface.

On many bodies the cratering is very widespread and obvious. On others it has more or less been obscured by volcanic covering, wind or liquid erosion and other geological processes. On earth it is geologically detectable, but it is not easily discernible except in a few instances. It often is detectable from space despite obscuring, as its effect on the earth's surface is apparent or unmistakable.

Manned and unmanned space exploration and observation, utilizing photographic and electronic techniques, have enabled us to view most of the planets and their satellites and to know quite well how they would appear if we were close to, or on, them. Each is a vastly different world from the other. Life anything like life on earth on any of them other than the earth is most unlikely. Portrayal of these other worlds of the solar system has been considerable in books and on television, and further depiction of them here is unnecessary.

Impact on religious philosophy

A question that well may be asked in regard to the impact of modern solar and planetary knowledge on concepts and proof of God and on justification of belief in him and in his creation and sustenance of the universe is: Does the uniqueness in the solar system of earthly life and human intelligence and love have any probative or at least suggestive value in the matter? By "suggestive value" we mean the basis for a bet or a hunch in the absence of proof. This question will be kept constantly in mind in the ensuing chapter on the earth as a Garden of Eden.

Another observation that can be made is that the evolution and functioning of the solar system is very understandable physically, and seemingly are fully understandable physically if we knew enough physics, so that no hypothesis of God is necessary to explain them. If this be true, as apparently it is, the question of God must be related back to the Big Bang, the natural consequence of which is the solar system as it is.

A third observation to be made is that the orderliness of the solar system, and the repetition of planetary and other pattern in it indicate, at least to some, design or something much like that, suggestive of an intelligent intent and plan.

18

Black Holes and Compacted Stars

Black holes and compacted stars are the consequence of self-gravitational collapse of stars. Compacted stars are neutron stars, including pulsars, and white dwarf stars. They become compacted stars instead of black holes because they have too little mass for gravitation to compact them further.

Multiple stars, galactic gas and other matter may become so concentrated that it collapses self-gravitationally into a supermassive black hole. This may occur in quasars and in the cores of hyperactive galaxies.

Black holes are named as they are because at first it was thought that light and other radiation, as well as matter, drawn into them can never escape, and so they are black and invisible. Now it is theorized that in fact they subtly radiate a little slowly, and that they cause much radiation from their vicinity, as discussed later.

One can well ask why would God, if he made the universe, inflict on it anything as destructive as black holes are of his creation. Or why would he have his creation end in the collapse of all of it into an invisible black hole, the opposite of the "white hole" from which possibly it emerged in the Big Bang?

Self-gravitational collapse

The loom of spacetime and the fabric of matter and of radiation being woven upon it are afflicted with a disease, a malignancy; and that is self-gravitational collapse. The malignancy afflicts galaxies and stars but not lesser bodies. We call it as we do because it lies potential and dormant in galaxies and stars until conditions occur, as they inevitably do, that set it off in sudden compression of central matter within the galaxy or of all matter in the star. The compression may be into minuteness or even dimensionlessness. The star becomes a white dwarf about the size of the earth, a neutron star only a few miles in diameter or a black hole.

The dimensionlessness into which a star or into which matter and gas and gas in a galaxy is compressed by self-gravitation, if indeed it is so compressed, is a singularity, i.e., it is like nothing else. The singularity is at the very bottom of a black hole unless the singularity is "naked," i.e. unclothed by a black hole, which in all probability is never the case.

Once self-gravitational collapse has squeezed a star or matter in a galaxy into a black hole, the resulting gravitational force of the black hole attracts to it, and devours, all stars and matter within the compulsion of its gravitational reach. The consumed matter ends dimensionless in the singularity, according to the theory of general relativity. That is, a singularity has no volume but has infinite density, and all matter falling into a black hole must, according to general relativity, continue its fall into a singularity. But many physicists doubt that singularities actually exist in nature. What ultimately actually occurs in a black hole is unknown and may be governed by quantum mechanics instead of by classical mechanics and general relativity.

To call gravitational collapse a "disease," or "malignancy" is a human way of viewing this chronic affliction of matter and spacetime, but if the fabric of matter and the loom of spacetime could talk and laugh and noted our direful names for what we deem an affliction, they well might tell us laughingly that gravitational collapse is not in any way a disease or disorder, but, instead, is part of the orderly and healthy evolution of the cosmos. "We say 'healthy,' they would say, "because that is how you with your human sensibilities should regard it. The word does not really belong in our vocabulary."

The fabric and the loom might add, "After all, we and the cosmos exploded out of that singularity that in your book you call the 'Little Bomb.' And what do you imagine was the genesis of the Little Bomb? Do you not know that it was made by the gravitational collapse of another universe than the one in which you live? Do you not realize that we shall cease to be, as matter and spacetime, we and the cosmos, by self-gravitational collapse into another singularity, which will duly erupt into another universe? So it has been and will be endlessly."

"No, we do not know those things," we reply. "Because it is not possible for us to know what happened before the Planck time, 10^{-43} seconds after you began in the Big Bang. We do not even know that there actually was a Little Bomb, whether it was a singularity or an immensely dense thing with minute spatial and temporal dimensions."

We shall continue to regard, from our human perspective, self-gravitational collapse as a disease of matter and of spacetime notwithstanding any objection from them, and to consider its occurrence a catastrophe for them and for ourselves if it should occur in our sun or nearby in our galaxy. Nevertheless, we would not be writing or readers reading this, except for gravitational collapse, which has compressed supergiant stars until they exploded in supernovae, thereby endowing space, our stellar system, our earth, us and everything else containing the heavier elements with those elements, that indispensable enrichment, which is, indeed, most of what the inner planets and we are.

Insufficiency of nuclear fuel

There is another "disease" of matter that prepares the way for the ravage of self-gravitational collapse, and that disease is insufficiency of hydrogen and (when that becomes exhausted) of helium in stars to keep alive forever their steadily burning nuclear fire and thermal pressure outward to balance the squeeze of gravity and give them sustained stability. As their fuel becomes low, as their fire cools and as their internal pressure drops, drastic gravitational collapse suddenly befalls them. They become stricken with convulsions, contraction, expansion and again contraction, and then explosion; and their remainder, not blown off into space, collapses into a white dwarf or neutron star or possibly a black hole.

Are black holes factual or theoretical only?

What has been said so far and will be said and what is known about black holes is theoretical. Only their possible existence has been detected in some instances, discussed later.

In 1939 J. Robert Oppenheimer and Hartland Snyder were the first to theorize that black holes might exist, on the basis of Einstein's equations. On the basis of Newtonian mechanics, however, the possibility of density of bodies sufficient to prevent light escaping them was suggested by John Michell in 1784 and by Pierre-Simon Laplace in 1798. Laplace was in error because Newtonian mechanics do not support the non-escape of light from any body no matter how dense it may be, since speed attained by light in falling on any object should, according to the reversibility of Newton's laws, suffice to lift it off that object.

The consensus of theoretical opinion seems to be that black holes exist in fact. However, Robert Penrose, who has theorized how the spin of black holes could cause emission of energy, as subsequently discussed, considers it questionable that black holes are a consequence of Einstein's theory of general relativity and that they exist in fact.

In terms of spacetime curvature

Another name for self-gravitational collapse could be "spacetime-curvature collapse of mass self-caused by too much of it in too little spacetime." That certainly is an awkward name, but it expresses what in effect occurs in self-gravitational collapse. Too much mass in too little spacetime makes spacetime curve too sharply. The result is that the star or other mass follows highly convexed spacetime curvature back into itself. As all the mass easily falls down the steep curvature into itself, sudden enormous compression results. In effect, the mass is squeezing itself toward material and temporal extinction.

Why is it easy and compulsory for a star or other mass thus suddenly to reduce itself into a black hole? The theory of general relativity provides no full answer, but the ease and compulsion of its passage into the black hole through itself may result from the exchange among particles of force-carrying gravitons. These, as discussed in Chapters 8 and 12, have been theorized to exist, but they have never been observed or indirectly detected.

Fall of a star into its own black hole

This is to be distinguished from a star approaching a black hole and being drawn into and devoured by it.

A star of less than three solar masses on its final collapse becomes a neutron star or a white dwarf, as later discussed.

A star more than three solar masses, when it self-gravitationally collapses, quickly does so into a black hole. It is too massive to do less. It can't stop its self-squeeze and reduction at a white-dwarf or neutron-star size. Instead, it goes on self-squeezing until it disappears into the black hole that it has made for itself in spacetime, and it continues its self-compression until it becomes an irreducible minuteness or a dimensionless singularity. There is no reason under classical mechanics and the theory of general relativity to expect that it ever will stop squeezing and reducing itself after it has become minus-zero in size. However, as said before, the theory of general relativity may be no longer applicable after matter becomes, or is about to become, a singularity, and quantum mechanics may then govern its disposition.

Event horizon

Because the gravitational attraction of a black hole is so strong, light or anything pulled into it beyond a spherical surface limit, called its *event horizon*, cannot escape from it. The horizon is a spherical surface without an edge like that where the sky meets the earth. It is a one-way membrane through which matter and radiation can enter, but through which they can never emerge. Therefore, it is black and invisible. The event-horizon is so-called because no events within the hole can ever be observed from outside it; no information can ever emanate from it. Nevertheless, black holes radiate, as we shall see.

Growth of a black hole

A black hole once constituted pulls into itself all matter, light and radiation within the compulsion of its gravitational force. As it does so, it continues to grow, its mass and surface increasing even though matter and radiation that it ingests passes into its ultra-minuteness or its dimensionless singularity at its bottom. Its surface (event horizon) is proportional to the square of its mass. Its surface, like entropy, can never decrease; it can only increase or not change.

Properties of a black hole

A black hole has mass and spin (angular momentum); it has gravitational attraction (greatly convexed spacetime curvature into itself); and it has an electromagnetic field incident to any net charge that it has. It is escape-proof except by a subtle mode of radiation, later discussed.

Size of black holes

How large is a black hole? That depends on the quantity of matter and radiation that originally gravitationally collapsed into the black hole and thereafter gravitationally has been pulled into it. Black holes theoretically may range in size from that of an atomic nucleus to hundreds of millions of solar masses. As discussed below, the event horizon of a black hole may not diminish, though it may increase.

A black hole from collapse of a star of ten solar masses would be only thirty kilometers across. The sun and any star its size, if it could gravitationally collapse into a black hole, which it cannot, would be six kilometers across. The earth, if somehow reduced to a black hole, would be one centimeter across.

How numerous are black holes?

Scattered throughout the universe probably there are myriad black holes, ranging in size as said. Some possible black holes have been detected in the Milky Way, and they are as likely to occur in other normal galaxies. Supermassive blackholes that are far less active than they were once may exist at the centers of the Milky Way and other normal galaxies.

Supermassive black holes that are extremely active, prodigeously emitting energy in radiation, probably are quasars or are at the cores of hyperactive galaxies as they are now seen from earth.

It should be remembered that we see quasars and hyperactive galaxies in their youth and normal galaxies in an older age. It well may be that supermassive black holes at galactic centers decline in activity with age so that in normal galaxies they radiate less.

Radiation caused by black holes

Notwithstanding classical mechanics and general relativity theory that black holes allow no escape of anything once it is in their grasp, it seems that under quantum mechanics they do subtly radiate scantily and slowly. It also seems that they cause much radiation from about them, as will be explained.

Realization that, after all, black holes may both radiate and otherwise cause radiation is essential to our general portrayal of the universe, and some minimal explanation of how they may do so is helpful to that portrayal and will be undertaken.

The Penrose process

Surprisingly and contrary to what was at first thought, it has now theoretically been determined that a rotating black hole both can radiate and can lose mass. This is not true of a non-rotating black hole, but most black holes, like the stars or other matter from which they devolve, have spin.

Roger Penrose in 1969 proposed a process by which energy could be extracted from a spinning black hole and its ergosphere (ergon in Greek means work) assuming that we had the means to do it. The ergosphere spacetime outside the event horizon and within a so-called "static limit" is dragged along in the spin of the black hole. Outside the static limit it is possible, inside it impossible, for an observer to orient himself by distant stars, because inside the limit he is swept along in a swirl about the black hole.

Penrose has illustrated his process by the example of a spaceship carrying rubbish that enters the ergosphere and, after spinning with it for a time about the black hole, dumps the refuse into the hole in a direction that interferes with the hole's total angular momentum, and then leaves the ergosphere and the hole, taking with it an increase of kinetic energy greater than the total mass energy of the rubbish and taking with it also, some of the rotational energy of the black hole.

Repetition of the process in time would stop the spin of the black hole, after having extracted twenty nine percent of its mass-energy. By comparison less than seven-tenths of one percent of total energy is obtained by the hydrogen fusion process. Something like the Penrose process, if it exists in nature, could contribute to black holes being galactic powerhouses with enormous outpowering of energy.

The Penrose process, as Penrose himself notes, must conform with the second law of thermodynamics that entropy does not decrease, but the process satisfies that law when both the black hole and surrounding matter are taken into account. While the process demonstrates that a black hole can lose mass-energy, it is not clear that the process occurs frequently or at all in nature. The energy extracted by the Penrose process could be used for power, if all the financial and technical problems could be solved, perhaps at a space station for replenishment of the power supply of space ships.

Conversion of gravitational energy

It has been theorized that the potential gravitational energy of matter and gas caught by the gravitational pull of a black hole is converted into the energy of motion, heat and other radiation as the matter and gas fall faster and faster. By the time they enter the hole as much as ten percent of their mass thus will have been converted into radiation, which means that enormous energy has been produced according to $E = mc^2$. In the case of a supermassive black hole in the core of a galaxy, the conversion is of ten percent of millions or billions of stars and nebulae, which certainly should make the core intensely bright, as quasars and the cores of hyperactive galaxies actually are.

Radiation from accretion disk

It is theorized that as matter and gas approaches a spinning black hole, they whirl about it with, and in the direction of, the spin, in an accretion disk. The particles in them inevitably collide with each other, especially because inner and outer regions of the disk move with different velocities. The particle collisions produce radiation as they do when they occur elsewhere, as discussed in Chapter 10. In the case of supermassive black holes in quasars or hyperactive galactic centers, the production of radiation in this manner would, of course, be enormous.

Synchrotron radiation

This has been said to be the best explanation of those tremendous energy and radiation emissions by black holes, especially those presumably in quasars and at hyperactive galactic centers. It is theorized that the accretion disk has an electric field in the direction of the spin, which causes charged particles to move in opposite directions in the magnetic field, producing synchotron radiation of the same kind as that produced by the Synchrotron.

The Hawking discovery

Another way in which a black hole can radiate and lose mass-energy is as a black body, which, in fact, it may be. A "black body," as it long has been called, is one that absorbes all radiation falling on it and that in time emits the same amount of radiation as that absorbed. Its radiation covers the whole wavelength range, and for that reason it is also called a "full radiator."

S. W. Hawking discovered this nature of a black hole and reported it in 1974. He reasoned that a black hole was paradoxical if it absorbed all radiation reaching it and yet, unlike a black body, never emitted anything in return. His investigation of black body radiation led him to the inescapable conclusion that a black hole like a black body must similarly slowly radiate, losing energy and mass as it does so. His conclusion was consequent on quantum mechanics. Hawking was most surprised by his conclusion, as were other scientists when he reported it.

Basic to Hawking's discovery is the quantum-mechanics perception of any vacuum, empty according to classical mechanics, as in truth seething with virtual (almost) particles, a phenomenon noted in previous chapters.

These virtual particles are always coming into being, not only in a supposed vacuum, but also in supposedly otherwise unoccupied space, in particle-antiparticle pairs. The particle and antiparticle in each pair almost always instantly annihilate each other as they materialize, so that they hardly exist at all.

Their emergence and almost simultaneous cessation of existence is explained, we are told, by Einstein's equation, $E = mc^2$, and Heisenberg's uncertainty principle. In a bit of space there may or may not be energy; When there is, the amount is inversely-proportional to the bit of space. The energy when great enough becomes the virtual particle-antiparticle pair.

The mighty gravity of a black hole intensifies virtual pair creation and also tears some pairs apart before they inter-annihilate. Both separated particles or only one of them are swept into the hole. The escaping ones are the same as radiation from a black body.

Is this radiation from the black hole itself? Hawking proves that it is, he thinks, upon the basis of time reversal, as valid as time in quantum mechanics, and upon the basis of the Heisenberg uncertainty principle, which permits the "tunnelling" by particles of barriers otherwise impenetrable by them.

The separated particles going into the hole can be viewed in quantum mechanics as going backward in time through the event horizon to when it was torn apart from its twin particle; and, at this point it can be viewed as moving forward in time away from the black hole as radiation. Whether or not it is to be found on the exterior of the event horizon is uncertain, and accordingly, possible.

Radiation from a black hole, and resulting evaporation and shrinking of it, in this manner is extremely scant and slow. For a black hole of one solar mass thus to completely evaporate would take 10^{53} times longer than the universe has existed. The contribution of radiation and energy in this manner to the total radiation and energy caused by a black hole would seem to be inconsiderable.

Hawking's discovery certainly brings to mind the fact that God or nature works in mysterious ways, though accordingly to seemingly inflexible laws such as the conservation of energy, the equivalence of mass and energy, and the uncertainty principle.

Black holes in the Milky Way

There is an unusual compact radio source at the center of our galaxy, only a lightyear across, that could be a large black hole. However, it does not exceed five million solar masses and it could never have been particularly spectacular. Spiral galaxies like ours may be expected to have smaller central black holes than eliptical ones have, because their angular momentum is less than that of elipticals and so not as inhibiting of central aggregating of solid matter and gas.

In Milky Way binary systems

In our galaxy black holes have been sought and possibly found in binary systems, i.e., those in which two stars revolve about a common center of gravity. The components may be stars of almost any type, and one sometimes possibly may be a black hole. Often, one is a giant or supergiant star and the other is a compacted star, that is, a white dwarf or neutron star or possibly a black hole. Binaries are most common and many are visual; especially the larger companion may be. The binary or the compacted star often is first detected by its radio or X-ray emission. X-ray binary systems in which a neutron star or a black hole accretes gas from the atmosphere of its non-collapsed companion are often ten thousand times as luminous in X-rays alone as the entire radiation output of the sun, and they probably are involved with most, if not all, of the brightest X-ray sources.

The X-ray emission from a binary system, one component of which may be a black hole, is thought to be caused by an accretion disk about the black hole, constituted by material and gas drawn by the strong gravity of the black hole from the supergiant. The material swirls about the hole in the disk until it finally is sucked into the hole. The swirling heats the material enough to cause its emission of X-rays.

If the compact companion is more than three solar masses, the theoretical upper limit for a neutron star, it possibly is a black hole, as no other theoretical explanation for it is as good, at least at this time.

Cygnus X-1, eight thousand lightyears away, discovered in 1971, well may be a black hole in a binary system with a visible supergiant star. Evidence that it is a black hole, however, is not conclusive. Even less conclusive is evidence of black holes in other binaries in the galaxy. Remnants of supernovae sometimes include binaries, one component of which may be a black hole. Or the remnant binary may be a pulsar or other neutron star, as later discussed.

X-ray bursters

Are these the result of black holes? About thirty of them have been discovered in the galaxy, mostly near its center. Some have been discovered in the globular clusters about it. X-ray radiation in the bursters is in bursts, as would be expected from their name. One in a globular cluster is called the "Rapid Burster." Infrared as well as X-ray bursts from it have been observed. It is unknown what actually causes the bursts.

Black holes in normal galaxies

As before said in Chapter 14, beyond our galaxy upon the loom of spacetime galaxies for some distancepast include many like our own and others having different configurations and behavior, but their violence and energy productivity is far less than that of galaxies much farther down from us in distancepast toward the beginning of the Big Bang. Accordingly, in nearby normal galaxies it is to be expected that black holes are like those in the Milky Way. These galaxies like the Milky Way probably harbor massive but unspectacular black holes at their centers and solar black holes scattered in them. One would not expect them, however, to have at their centers black holes as supermassive as those seemingly existent in quasars and at the centers of hyperactive galaxies. Nevertheless, the galaxy, Centaurus A, only thirteen million lightyears away, and the galaxy, M87, 65 million lightyears away, in the Virgo cluster, may have supermassive black holes at their centers, as we shall see.

Spiral galaxies like the Milky Way well may not harbor as large black holes as eliptical ones do, because in the latter angular momentum may not be as inhibitive of centralization of gas and solid matter.

Supermassive black holes

The immense emission of energy by quasars and hyperactive galactic centers strongly suggest that supermassive black holes there exist. On the other hand, one would think that the tremendous gravitational attraction of supermassive black holes, equal to that of millions or billions of stars would have discernible tidal, distortional and chaotic effects upon galaxies and groups of galaxies, but this does not seem to be the case. Nevertheless, the consensus of scientific opinion appears to be that supermassive black holes very well may exist in quasars and in the cores of the distant hyperactive galaxies and also in the cores of some normal galaxies, at least those much like the Milky Way.

Some scientists call these supposed supermassive black holes "power-houses" or "energy machines." Whatever they are, they certainly are efficient in converting mass into energy. The black holes, if they are that, are of millions and even billions of solar masses, and their production of energy may be from one hundred to one thousand times that of a galaxy like our own, and from a region as small as our solar system or smaller.

How supermassive black holes formed

Alternative methods as to how this may have happened are (1) so much concentration of stars and gas in galactic centers that self-gravitational collapse occurred; (2) a black hole's growing supermassive by devouring stars and gas thickly concentrated about it at galactic centers; or (3) self-gravitational collapse at centers of protogalactic gas clouds as they were clumping and settling into galaxies.

Why supermassives radiate so much

How can the amazing amount of energy in radiation of quasars and hyperactive galactic centers be produced by something as small as two cubic lightyears? How can luminosity about a hundred times that of the Milky Way originate in such a comparitively tiny bit of spacetime? It seems that it can be only through the agency of supermassive black holes or at least of neutron stars, or other highly compacted matter.

An observational reason for deeming the powerhouses or energy engines in quasars or hyperactive galaxies to be black holes has been provided by study of the luminosity of M87, a gigantic and remarkable eliptical galaxy in the Virgo cluster, 65 million lightyears away. It was found, not only that the luminosity increased toward the center of the galaxy, but that at the center the increase was at a much faster rate than predicted on the basis of a model. Two independent investigations of the galaxy, one examining its inner brightness distribution and the other making a spectrographic study, agreed that the best hypothesis to explain their observations is that M87 has a supermassive black hole in its nucleus. It is not clear from these studies, however, that the high central luminosity is not due to a neutron star or other compacted object rather than a black hole.

Closer than M87, the galaxy, Centaurus A, about thirteen million lightyears away, may have the nearest supermassive black hole to us. It still shows the effects of accreting matter and gas. At its center a radio source only a lightday across and an X-ray source a few light hours across is indicative of a black hole of over ten million solar masses and is also indicative that the infall of matter and gas on the hole continues but has slowed down.

How supermassive black holes cause radiation has been discussed above.

How supermassive black holes are fueled

How are these black-hole powerhouses or energy engines fueled so that they continue for millions of years prodigeously to put out energy as they do? For their fuel they ingest all stars, gas and matter within the reach of their gravitational dominance, and they continue their output of energy until this fuel is exhausted. Actually, their fuel requirements are modest compared to their tremendous energy output. The digesting of a few solar masses per year keeps one of them most productive. However, in its lifetime conversion of mass into energy, one of them consumes matter of millions of solar masses.

How long superactivity continues

Eventually a supermassive black hole will consume most and then all matter and gas within its dominant gravitational reach, and it will then decrease and finally cease its huge energy productivity. Indeed, the lives of supermassive black holes as such are very short, ranging between ten and a few hundred million years. They are to be expected to be only in the very far distancepast when the universe and they were young. Seemingly, quasars are the youngest, most pastdistant and most powerful supermassive black hole powerhouses; those in the BL Lac and Seyfert galaxies are the next most powerful, younger and more pastdistant; and those in normal galaxies are oldest. As galaxies become older, they are closer to us in the distancepast.

In a black hole

We can only imagine what transpires in a black hole, and what it would be like to be within one. Though black holes can radiate and lose mass, it seems that the radiation they emit carries no information from within them. Theoretically, however, matter and spacetime continue to exist within a black hole until they fall into a singularity at its bottom, if they do that. The gravitational attraction within the hole toward ultimate minuteness or a singularity is enormous, though it decreases with the square of the distance from the minuteness or singularity. Any spaceship or spaceman caught in the gravitational suction of the minuteness or singularity, before ceasing to be matter, would be pulled into a long string because of the vast disparity in the gravitational pulls upon it or him, fore and aft.

In a large enough black hole, however, one, for instance, the size of the solar system, a spaceship could pass the event horizon without its crew knowing it or that escape had become impossible, and cruise about for awhile though pulled relentlessly toward the ultimate minuteness or singularity until its pull became an almost instantaneous intake into oblivion. Indeed, the density of matter in the outer regions of a solar-system-sized black hole would be no greater than in space between the earth and the moon.

Time would flow normally for the crew of a spaceship nearing or within a supermassive black hole, according to their watches made on earth. But their watches and all their bodily processes, including those within their bodily cells, would be running slow according to earth-time. The ship would enter the ergosphere of the black hole, swirl about the hole with the hole's spin and then pass beyond the event horizon, doing all this in minutes according to the crew and their watches. From the viewpoint of an observer on earth, however, the crew's time and watches would have slowed down so much that it would take eons for them and their spaceship to circle the hole and an eternity for them and the ship to enter the invisible hole.

Mini-black holes

At the other end of the astronomical scale, there may be mini-black holes, or there may have been in the past. Under present conditions in the universe, however, enough pressure to squeeze small quantities of matter into mini-black holes is not possible. But it is thought by some scientists, though doubted by others, that mini-black holes may have been created in the early moments of the Big Bang. If they were, they would be of the size of a proton with a mass of billions of tons and a density far greater than that of a neutron star. They could be detectable now through explosions caused by heat at the end of their decay, but so far they have not been discovered by radio and gamma-ray detection instruments or other means.

It has been conjectured that the Tonguste incident in Siberia in 1908 was the result of the impact of a mini-black hole on the earth. Trees were leveled throughout a vast area. It is most unlikely, though, that a mini-black hole was involved: the chance of an earthly encounter with a mini-black hole is infinitesimal, and a mini-black hole of small mass could pass through the earth undetected.

White holes

These are the reciprocals of black holes, though in some respects the reciprocity is unclear. Whereas black holes swallow matter-energy and quickly digest it into a minuteness or into a dimensionless singularity, white holes are singularities that explode mass-energy into spacetime. Black holes are created by self-gravitational collapse, triggered, in the case of stellar black holes, by hydrogen, and then helium, deficiency to maintain endlessly nuclear fire and thermal outward pressure. White holes eruptions, it must be surmised, are caused by some expansive force contained in the singularity out of which they come.

Black holes and white holes instance symmetry in the universe, which generally it prefers. They conform to the time symmetry of classical mechanics and of general relativity. They are symmetrical, one of them being white (visible) and the other of them being black (invisible). They are symmetrical in one being the entrance to, and the other the exit from, a minuteness or a singularity.

There is very good evidence of the probable existence of black holes, but there is no evidence whatsoever of the possible existence of white holes. However, if the Big Bang originated in a singularity, it did so in a white hole insofar as a white hole is deemed an exit of matter-energy from a singularity.

Wormholes

Black holes have been imagined to have passes or "wormholes" from this into another universe, or into another region of this universe, traverseable almost instantly; and white holes have been deemed exit doors from the same. The passages or wormholes, it is speculated, by-pass the singularity so that particles, bodies and radiation following them emerge through the white holes, more or less intact.

Compacted stars

Compacted stars are created by the same process that creates black holes, that is by self-gravitational collapse as an ultimate consequence of exhaustion of fuel to sustain central nuclear fusion, creative of outward pressure against gravitational pressure inward. Compacted stars are neutron or white dwarf stars.

It would seem that under similar circumstances solid matter and gas other than stars could be compacted into a small body rather than a black hole, but we have not encountered an explicit discussion of this.

Neutron stars

When a star one and one-half to three solar masses self-gravitationally last collapses, it becomes, after having blown off much of its mass, a neutron star, only about twenty kilometers across. It doesn't have enough mass to continue collapsing into a black hole.

Its density is greater than that of an atomic nucleus and 10^{14} to 10^{15} more than that of water. A speck of it weighs more than a million tons. Indeed, the density of neutron stars is the greatest known in the universe.

A neutron star has a solid crust, a kilometer thick, 10^{17} times stiffer than steel. Internally it consists of neutrons into which all electrons and protons have been compressed.

Neutron stars sometimes are components in binary systems. In this event matter and gas from the other component may flow onto the neutron star after swirling about it in much the same manner as incoming matter swirls about a black hole. Energy and radiation are produced prodigeously from the swirl in the same manner as they are produced in the swirling of matter about a spinning black hole. Indeed, neutron stars or like compacted matter, rather than black holes, may be the powerhouses in quasars and in hypergalactic centers, but it is more likely that black holes fill this role.

Cygnus X-1, discussed above, is in a binary system and may be a neutron star instead of a black hole. It is fairly certain that some neutron stars, or binary systems containing them, are supernova remnants.

Pulsars

These are neutron stars that emit short pulses of radiation. The radiation is in all wave lengths, but pulsars were discovered and they are mostly observed through their radio emission. In many instances pulsars or pulsar-like objects are observed by X-ray reception, particularly in binary systems. In a few instances pulsars have been observed optically, and in at least one instance by gamma-ray reception.

In 1967 Anthony Hewish accidentally discovered radio sources pulsing with seeming artificial regularity, which Thomas Gold theorized could naturally be caused by spinning neutron stars. Gold's theory was confirmed in 1968 by the discovery of a pulsar at the center of the Crab Nebula, which is the remains of a supernova observed in 1054 by Chinese and Arab astronomers.

The pulses of the Crab pulsar are observable by radio, light, X-ray and gamma-ray reception. The periodicity of the radio, optical and light pulses is the same.

By now over 330 pulsars have been discovered, and there must be hundreds of thousands of them in the Milky Way. Presumably, they must likewise abound in other galaxies, at least those much like the Milky Way.

Most pulsars are solo stars and not in any binary system. However, X-ray pulsars or X-ray pulsar-like objects mostly are in binary systems.

What causes the pulses? A newly formed neutron star must spin rapidly, as much as many times per second, because of tremendous reduction in size during its gravitational collapse, conservation of angular momentum and magnetic flux. Its magnetic field is extremely strong, a trillion times stronger than the earth's. The racing of electrons with the pulsar's spin in this magnetic field engenders synchrotron polarized radiation in a beam that sweeps spacetime as the pulsar spins. Receptions of the beam on earth or elsewhere is in pulses as the beam sweeps into and then out of view. The pulses are so regular that as a timekeeper a pulsar is surpassed only by an atomic clock.

The Crab pulsar is the most rapidly pulsing one known, with a periodicity of one-thirtieth of a second. Periodicity of pulsars ranges from that to 4.3 seconds.

The Crab nebulae is about 6,300 lightyears away, and the Crab pulsar as we see it then is about one thousand years old, which makes it the youngest pulsar known. These facts may explain why it is observable optically and by X-ray, as well as by radio reception.

The next youngest pulsar observed is in the constellation Vela and is about ten thousand years old as we now see it. It can be observed optically as well as by radio. The Sumerians six thousand years ago recorded what may have been the supernova giving birth to the Vela pulsar.

A pulsar's continuous radiation gradually reduces its mass, which in turn gradually slows down its spin and pulsation. After ten thousand years its radio pulses begin to fade. Consequently, older neutron stars become undetectable by radio, though they sometimes may be observable by X-ray emission, especially where they are binary components. In this instance, however, the pulses are not caused by synchrotron radiation. Instead, the X-ray pulses originated in the heating of gas falling on the neutron star from the other binary component.

Studying the pulses of pulsars gives atronomers not only much information about them, such as about their mass, density, crust, interior and distance from us, but also gives them like information as to neutron stars generally. It also increases their knowledge of the interstellar medium through which the pulses travel to reach the earth.

White dwarf stars

The sun or a star of about its mass, when it has its last collapse through self-gravitation, will be reduced to a white dwarf star, about the size of the earth, after having blown away much of its former mass. It lacks enough self-gravitation to be further reduced.

A white dwarf is far less dense than a neutron star but far more dense than the earth. A teaspoon of matter from a white dwarf would on earth weigh many tons, but a teaspoon of matter from a neutron star would on earth weigh billions of tons. The density of white dwarfs is a million times greater than that of water.

White dwarfs like black holes and neutron stars result from self-gravitational collapse as a consequence of their central nuclear fire burning out because of diminution at their cores of hydrogen and helium as nuclear fuel. They continue to shine because their thin atmosphere is illuminated by heat leaking from their interior. They are not necessarily white in color, and they vary in color according to their surface temperature. They lose luminosity as they become colder, and eventually they end as black dwarfs.

Internally, white dwarfs are degenerate in that the pressure of gravitational contraction separates electrons from atoms. As they cool their heavy atomic nuclei lose mobility and assume a lattice state.

About three percent of all stars are white dwarfs, but the number of them keeps increasing, and eventually all stars that are about the sun's size will become white and then ultimately black dwarfs.

Reflections on God and other ultimateness

What do self-gravitational collapse of stars and other matter and gas into black holes, neutron stars and pulsars and white dwarf stars evidence, if anything, as to God or other ultimate explanation of the universe? The process does emphasize the inevitability of the consequences of seemingly inflexible divine or natural laws governing the aftermath of the eruption of the Little Bomb and the Big Bang.

The gravitational force (or curvature of spacetime) is one of the essentials of the universe being at all and being as it is, but it also makes inevitable the occurrence of black holes theoretically and of neutron and white dwarf stars actually. God or nature, at least in this instance, is not capricious. The universe can exist only if gravitation is as it is, though that entails the ending of all stars in black holes or in neutron and white dwarf stars that eventually will become slag unless before they do the universe contracts and exits through a black hole.

Does not, then, this consistency of gravitation, evidenced by black holes and compacted stars, fit in well both with the design and the cosmological arguments for the existence of the God-Creator? Does not the clockwise preciseness of the pulsation of pulsars do likewise? The answer must be a subjective one or in the nature of guidance for a wager or for a determination of a jury verdict in a close case.

Of course, some might not regard the case as close. Some might think the black hole and compacted star evidence of no weight. On the other hand, many would say that it should be considered, at least in view of the lack of strong total evidence either way on the issue.

19

Earth, Humanity and the Cosmos

We now come to earth, terrestrial life and humanity in our general. portrayal of the cosmos. Accordingly, this chapter discusses earth and humanity in relation to each other and to the cosmos and God, if he exists. It questions whether humanity on earth is, as it were, in a Garden of Eden in the universe; or whether humanity, though mortal, otherwise is like the Olympic gods, who were thought to have emerged from a union of earth and the sky. It treats the Gaea hypothesis based on the seeming purpose of self-preservation of life on earth and in the universe; the role of humanity as observers and participants in the universe; and the anthropic principle that the emergence of life and humanity in the universe helps to explain it. The chapter also discusses the possibility of life elsewhere in the universe and the possible evolution of life in and from space as well as on earth. The chapter also includes commentary on a divine or other explanation of life and intelligence on earth and of their evolution on earth and possibly in and from space.

Earth as a Garden of Eden

Earth is a very special planet in that it has profuse life, human intelligence, a life-sustaining atmosphere and surface, and an interior contributing richly to the livability of its atmosphere, surface and water. Otherwise, it is much like Mercury, Venus, Mars and the Moon. Life of some kind on Mars has not yet positively been shown not to exist, and possibly may exist on satellites of the Jovian planets or in the Jovian planets' atmospheres. Its existence on Mercury, Venus and the Moon, in any way remotely resembling life on earth, is impossible.

Earth is a Garden of Eden in the solar system and perhaps in our galaxy and in the universe. That is, it is a garden abundant with plant and animal life and inhabited by intelligent beings who have awareness and much understanding of it and of the universe; and it certainly is the only garden like that in the solar system, perhaps in the galaxy and in the universe. God (if he exists) or nature (which can be defined as how the universe works) has placed in this Garden of Eden intelligent beings, humankind, to nurture it and live happily in it as theirs, at least for awhile, perhaps as long as it endures, which may be until the sun dies, five billion years from now.

Woman and man have eaten from the tree of knowledge in the garden, which it has been said God forbade them to do on penalty of expulsion from the garden. However, that God or nature would endow beings with compulsive intellectual curiosity and then prohibit or restrict their pursuit of knowledge on penalty of expulsion from their felicitous life-sustaining abode—that is, on penalty of their extinction—is unbelievable. Nevertheless, knowledge, when substantially attained, is patent with the warning that it must be used cooperatively and not antagonistically, on penalty of self-destruction of the human species, as by nuclear warfare. Knowledge, used cooperatively, as it should be used in United States and Soviet joint space exploration, would prolong the human species, say, in colonies in space, even beyond the death of earth when the time comes that the sun suddenly and enormously expands.

Earth as Mount Olympus

Earth, also, most aptly can be compared to the mythical Olympic home of the Greek gods who were the progeny of earth and the sky. Human beings, at least if in their intelligence they are alone in their galaxy or in the universe, can deem themselves, both with pride and with humility, to be gods, or vicars of God if he exists.

Human beings, like the Olympic gods, are the progeny of earth and the sky. Indeed, their ancestrage goes back through earthly matter to forging of the heavier elements in the interior nuclear furnaces of giant white stars, and beyond that to the primeval universal hydrogen of the Big Bang. We are earth dust and star dust forged from primeval hydrogen through hydrogen behavior under conditions arising from hydrogen behavior itself, consequent on we know not what.

Earth has become the human domain, notwithstanding human physical fraility, much human pomposity and arrogance, much cruelty of people to each other and to other life, animals and plants, and many other human faults. On the other hand, we, the people of earth, undeniably have many and great virtues and powers, too. Again like the Greek gods, we have both virtues and vices, strengths and weaknesses.

We are unique terrestrials and godlike in that we appraise ourselves and judge our virtues, vices and values, seek to control our emotions and thought and establish critiques as to the validity of our thought and knowledge. Thus, we appear to ourselves potentially to be gods of the earth and of the solar system, even of the galaxy, and even of the universe, if we are the only intelligent and contemplative life in the solar system, galaxy or universe.

Humanity, however, despite its realization of its mental power, must embrace its godlike role with humility and responsibility for the welfare not only of itself but of all terrestrial life and of all terrestrial physical matter; and, when and if the human domain extends beyond earth, humanity must, in order to be truly godlike, act similarly in its extended realm.

The Gaea hypothesis

This hypothesis is that the earth's atmosphere has a chemical circulatory system modified and regulated by the biosphere *in order* to keep the atmosphere in a state of disequilibrium and at a temperature that are optimum for life as it exists and evolves, whereas, in the absence of this influence by the biosphere, earth's atmosphere would closely resemble that of Mercury, Venus and Mars and be totally unavailable for an earthly kind of life. This hypothesis is named as it is because Gaea was the Greek goddess of earth and was the mother of the first generation of gods, the monstrous Cyclops and the giant Titans, one of the latter being Cronus, who sired Zeus.

Presumeably, Gaea would be zealous to preserve optimum living conditions for terrestrial living beings, and so the hypothesis has been named as it has.

This life-sustaining circulatory system of the atmosphere is comparable to the blood circulatory system of a mammal.

The Gaea hypothesis can be broadened to mean that the biosphere is an organization of all life forms that collectively function in order to foster optimum living conditions throughout the biosphere by regulating and modifying, not only the earth's atmosphere, but also its surface, hydrosphere (oceans and waters) and its lithosphere (soil).

To say that the biosphere functions *in order* to accomplish this result is to say that it acts according to purpose. Indeed, it appears to act in the same way that the cells of an animal or of a plant appear collectively to act in an endeavor to regulate and modify the organism's environment for the benefit of the organism. Likewise it appears to act as bees do collectively *as though* the collection were a living organism purposely or instinctively endeavoring to achieve optimum environmental conditions for the life of the collection.

Of course, not all life forms always act in consonance with the overall "purpose" and activity of the biosphere, just as not all cells in an animal or plant act in consonance with the overall "purpose" and activity of the assemblage of cells constituting the animal or plant. On the contrary, some life forms, including some cells in an animal or plant, sometimes act in opposition to the overall life-perpetuating *purpose* and activity of the biosphere, or of the animal or plant, in relation to environment. Sadly, humankind also all too often acts contrary to the overall seemingly purposeful activity of the biosphere to preserve a compatible environment.

It is the "lower" forms of life that more obviously participate collectively in the seemingly common effort of the biosphere to preserve an optimum chemical condition and temperature for the atmosphere, oceans and lands for the perpetuation and evolution of life forms. Indeed, it was photosynthesizing blue greens (cyanophytes) that, commencing 3.3 billion years ago, produced oxygen that over the millena accumulated in the atmosphere, making it possible for oxygen-using life forms to commence more than two billion years ago, and to evolve. Blue greens, somewhat more complex than bacteria, at first considered to be algae, still abound in moist environments, such as the bottoms of ponds and pools.

The atmosphere must contain the right amount of oxygen, neither too much nor too little, in order to be optimally suitable for the perpetuation and evolution of life. Too much would cause spontaneous combustion and sear off all plant life; too little would asphyxiate most animal life. This optimum amount of oxygen in the atmosphere and ocean primarily is maintained through (1) the production of vast amounts of oxygen by photosynthesizing algae in the ocean, (2) by consumption of much of that oxygen by zooplankton and (3) by marine bacteria's reduction of the zooplankton to a quantity favorable to non-consumption of that optimum amount of oxygen in the atmosphere and ocean.

How is it that the marine bacteria keep the zooplankton in the right amount? They do so because zooplankton need and consume nitrogen, and because the appetite of bacteria for nitrogen decreases as their supply of oxygen increases. Consequently, there is more nitrogen left for the zooplankton, who accordingly flourish and consume more oxygen, thereby diminishing it in the atmosphere and ocean. Thus, it is the effect of the supply of oxygen on the appetite of marine bacteria for nitrogen that is the key regulator of the amount of oxygen in the atmosphere and ocean.

The accumulation of oxygen in the atmosphere was followed and then accompanied by the formation of the ozone layer about thirty five miles above the surface of the earth. Ozone consists of molecules comprised by three atoms of oxygen and results from the interaction of high-frequency solar radiation with atmospheric oxygen. The ozone layer, as now widely known, is a shield protecting life below from deadly solar near-infrared radiation, thereby having made land as well as the ocean a region in which life emerged, evolved and spread.

Anaerobic bacteria (capable of living without oxygen), the first terrestrial organisms, came into being about $3\frac{1}{2}$ billion years ago and have continued to be, producing various gasses and supplying and removing them to and from the atmosphere, thereby contributing to its role in the biosphere. They and other bacteria and protozoans, algae and fungi contribute richly, by their interaction with one another and with organic and inorganic matter, to the complexity and fertility of soil and water, thereby making earth's atmosphere, hydrosphere and lithosphere unique in the solar system, as an abode teeming with life, or at least life as we recognize it. Among gasses released by microbial action in decomposition of once-living matter is ammonia, which neutralizes acidity, thereby contributing greatly to keeping the acidity of water, soil and air optimally favorable to life. Bacteria in the soil convert nitrogen to a form, such as nitrate, in which it can be absorbed and utilized by plants in growth.

Processes through which the biosphere, seemingly with purpose, controls its environment include symbiosis, ingestion, digestion, excretion, inhalation, respiration, fermentation, decay and decomposition.

Ecology as the totality of relationships among organisms and with their environment abounds with illustrations of the Gaea hypothesis; and some biologists and others think, or are strongly inclined to believe, that the biosphere is, in truth, a living organism that *intends*, and interacts in its parts and with the environment *in order*, to keep the environment optimally favorable for the perpetuation and evolution of life forms. Yet humans with their knowledge and power could misguidedly or evilly obstruct that purposeful biospherical activity, and despoil or destroy earth's habitableness.

How does the Gaea hypothesis bear on the conception of God, the creator, and on traditional proof of his existence? Obviously, it supports the teleological proof insofar as the apparent purpose of the biosphere to regulate and modify the environment for its own benefit is deemed to be ultimately extrinsic to it. However, that apparent purpose may be only apparent, something humans have subjectively read into the working of the biosphere, which in fact functions as it does solely as the result of evolutionary forces.

Observers and participants

People of earth observe, study and endeavor to understand earth, the universe and themselves; and they are, of course, part of earth and of the universe. Their activity is part of the total activity of earth and of the universe. They also act upon earth with greater impact than other forms of life other than insects and microorganisms. They cooperate and compete with other forms of life, not nearly as intelligently as they might, considering the intelligence that they have. In the end, they may destroy themselves and many forms of life in addition to those that they already have extinguished.

Their observation and interpretation of observed data are reaching far down into distancepast for billions of lightyears, about two-thirds of the way to the bursting of the Little Bomb in the Big Bang. They are now reaching out with manned and unmanned flights and probes beyond earth and even beyond the solar system into the galaxy.

What we have just said is nothing new to you, readers. Nor is the essence of what we said as to earth's biosphere unfamiliar to you. We could enlarge on how humanity is polluting and destroying earth's environment and ecology, and, on the other hand, we could say much about the effort of many people to stop the ravaging of this Garden of Paradise, our blue and green planet resplendent, also, with other colors of plants, rocks and soils. But you are familiar with it all. Why then do we dwell upon it? What has it to do with our quest for God, or for some natural ultimate explanation of all there is, if our scrutinizing of the cosmos should lead us to question or deny that there is a God who is immaterial, or spiritual as many would say?

You can answer, yourselves, readers, why we do so, we are sure, but we shall, nevertheless, state our reason. It is simply that we want to be certain, that you and we don't forget humanity itself as part of the cosmos in looking at it as the possible works of God or as something else.

In our quest we must reflect, not only upon life and intelligence, but also upon the heart, and not only upon the human heart. That is, what does feeling as well as thinking evidence as to their being God or a natural something of ultimate importance? It is religious and ethical reflection that we mention, and it is not for us to set forth our own reflection here except as to how thought and feeling in themselves evidence a Supreme Being or other ultimate explanation of the cosmos.

Many must see support for the teleological argument that God exists in earth's biosphere seemingly having intent to preserve itself. They must also see support for that argument in how the cosmos has produced the earth that is most suitable for human beings, and in how they adapt it for their purposes. There is no reason, however, to see divine purpose in spoliation of the biosphere. Kant saw evidence of God in the emergence of human ethics, as will be discussed in Chapter 25.

Others, including the authors, see no more reason that life and humanity evidence that God exists than that they evidence a natural origin of the universe. We so think because it seems to us that the occurrence of life and humanity is a natural outcome of the Big Bang.

The anthropic principle

In the last few decades some physicists, astronomers and cosmologists, many of them eminent, have been speculating upon the implications of human observation and participation in the universe as to its origin, some of the speculation relating to that origin through God. Their speculation has centered about the principle discussed in the prededing section of this chapter. That principle has been called by them the "anthropic principle" or the "anthropic cosmological principle." Largely, their speculation is a quest, the same as ours in this book, to find an explanation of the cosmos in its physics. However, their emphasis has been on the human role in the cosmos as explanatory of it, of its physics and of its origin, whether naturally or through a supernatural God.

More broadly stated, they have been looking for a biological explanation of physical phemonena, including the universe itself. They do not denigrate other explanations of physical phenomena. On the contrary, they are professionally occupied in pursuit of other explanations. They have become convinced, however, that biological explanations in cosmology should not be completely ignored, as for the most part they have been since Copernicus dethroned the earth as the center of the universe. On the whole, their speculation strongly supports the cosmic importance of man and woman and gives reason for their dignity. In effect, it views them as we have done in this chapter, either as in a veritable Garden of Eden through divine or natural favor, or as gods like those on Olympus, emergent from earth and sky.

These scientists have found biological explanation for physical phenomena, corroborating explanation through classical mechanics, relativity and quantum mechanics, as, for example, biological explanation of the expansion, age and size of the universe. The biological evidence refutes the steady-state theory and corroborates the Big Bang theory. Humanity could only occur in an expanding universe as old, vast and complex as ours is. The biological evidence corroborates physical evidence that giant stars exist for only millions of years, whereas stars of solar size exist for billions of years. Otherwise, we carbon-based writers would not be writing this. There is no end of biological evidence corroborating physical evidence as to physical happenings.

On the other hand, biological evidence, especially that of human intelligence, is thought by these scientists to explain some physical phenomena otherwise baffling or inexplicable to them, such as the strange occurrence of the same large dimensionless numbers in measuring values both in the subatomic and the supra-atomic. Life and humanity can occur only during the concurrence of these measures. Biology helps to explain the constants of nature, why they are precisely as they are. The strengths of the gravitational, electromagnetic and nuclear interactions must be close to what they actually are, or carbon and human beings would not have come about. Does this reveal physical phenomena as based on purpose of God or of nature to produce life and humans?

The biological evidence involves results as restrictions on causes, but the same is true of physical evidence explanatory of unobserved causes in distancepast. In both instances we have to reason back from observation in order to illuminate causation of what we observe.

We cannot too far pursue speculation centered about the anthropic principle. There are available books and articles dealing with it. We shall, however, take note of versions of the principle. It should be emphasized that the cosmologists, of whom we speak, regard their speculation centering on the anthropic principle as speculation only, and not as laws of physics.

The weak anthropic principle

Brandon Carter, who first took full notice of the anthropic principle, stated both a weak and a strong version of it.[1] The weak version, as he set it forth, is that what we can expect to observe in the universe can only be conditions necessary for our presence as observers. That is, a complete account of the universe must explain the fact that we live in it.

The weak principle, thus stated, is incontrovertible. Under it, the universe could have existed without producing us or any other observers.

Is the weak principle, so stated, trivial though true? Physicists think that it has far-reaching consequences for physics, which justifies stating it so that it will be kept in mind in investigation and interpreting physical phenomena. Keeping the principle in mind motivates us to search for error in cosmological views based on our selection of what we observe, where the selection is not of choice but because of physical limitations on us. Thus, before the telescope we could observe only through eyesight and other senses. It would be better perhaps to say that what we observe is restricted by our physical limitations than to say we select what we observe subject to constraints on our ability to observe.

Keeping the weak principle in mind also reminds us to look for means to escape restraints upon us as observers. In any event, many cosmologists find the weak principle of practical value in understanding the cosmos philosophically as well as physically. What does that mean? It means what it has always meant for philosophers, a search for truth beyond a mechanical understanding of how the universe and things work or for establishment of whether or not truth of that nature exists, in fact. It is an unending quest, because we will it to be so, but does that make it vain?

The strong anthropic principle

There are several varying versions of the strong principle. Brandon Carter's statement of it is that the universe must be such, or have such properties as to admit or allow life to occur in it at some stage in its development. It has been said by John Barrows and Frank J. Tippler that an implication of the strong principle, so stated, is that the constants and laws of nature must be such that life can exist.[2] This, they say, leads in effect to a teleological argument that the universe has a goal of producing observers.

J.A. Wheeler expresses the extreme view, a "participatory" version of the strong principle, to the effect that the production of observers at some stage in the universe or in any universe are essential to bringing it into being.[3] He reasons that through delayed choice the universe acquires reality, not only now but back to its beginning in the Big Bang, only when after eons it brings about observership. How this is true he illustrates by the well-known double-slit experiment in which an

experimenter decides, *after* a photon has passed through a screen with
two slits whether it *will* pass through both slits or only one. He makes
the decision by opening or closing a venetian blind beyond the screen,
after the photon has passed through the screen and before it reaches the
venetian blind. If he opens the blind, he records through which slit the
photon passes. If he closes it and uses it for a photographic plate, the
interference pattern shows that the photon went through both slits. In
the instance in which the photon passes through one slit, it's behavior
is particulate. In the instance in which it passes through both slits, its
behavior is wavelike.

Likewise, the occurrence of observers in the universe, determines
whether the universe was real when it began in the Big Bang, has been
real since and now is real.

The answer to the doubter is that his doubt is based on involuntary
selection by him of data on which he bases his doubt, i.e., decisions to
act precede the action. He resists avoidance of this constraint on his
decision as to the reality of the universe.

What do we think of the strong principle? Obviously, observers are
necessary to an observed universe. We cannot accept, however, that the
emergence of an observer is necessary for there to have been a universe.
While it is necessary for an explanation of an observer-containing
universe to account for the fact that the universe has observers (the
weak principle), it may not be necessary for the universe to have had
observers. The necessity that attaches to the explanation does not
automatically attach as well to the universe.

On the other hand, if the strong anthropic principle holds true, if (that
is) the universe must have produced us as observers,then the question
arises for the theist, does not this necessity apply to God? That is, if the
universe must have produced us as observers, then could God, who,
according to the theist, created the universe, have created the universe
without us? For it would seem that he too would be bound by the
necessity of the strong anthropic principle, if the principle holds.
Likewise, to maintain that he was not bound, is to say that the principle
does not hold as to the universe.

Life elsewhere in the universe

Mathematically, since there are hundreds of billions of galaxies with
hundreds of billions of stars, it would seem that planets like earth with
life and intelligence like ours must abound beyond counting. Mathematically, also, since life and intelligence, or something resembling

them, could possibly be based on elements other than carbon, the probability of life and intelligence or their like elsewhere in the universe is even more enormously increased. However, careful analysis of apparent requisites and conditions for life and intelligence or something like them reduces drastically the number of places in the universe in which life and intelligence or their like could occur. Nevertheless, even if only one or a few planets or places in a galaxy or in a supercluster of galaxies could possibly produce life or intelligence, the number of such planets or places in the universe could still be in the millions if not billions.

For decades we have been listening for artificial radio transmission from elsewhere than earth, and have not found it, but that failure may not be significant in view of the immensity of the galaxy and of the number of stars in it, to say nothing of the immensity of the universe and of the number of galaxies in it.

If life and intelligence exist in millions or billions of places elsewhere than on earth, what does that mean as to a God-Creator? Certainly it means, if he is a reality and if he is something like human intelligence and feeling, that he is not content with being God only of the people of Abraham or of the earth or that they are his favored people. It also may mean that living and intelligent beings are to him no more than mortal flowers are to us.

On the other hand, the religionist may reply, his ways and purposes are inscrutable, and what is ridiculous to the self-adjudged critical mind is no disproof of divine wisdom in creating a vast multiplicity of habitations of life and intelligence in the universe and in endowing billions time billions of mortal beings with souls having angel potentiality. Also, the religionist may add, there is of now no concrete evidence that life and intelligence exist elsewhere than on earth.

If life and intelligence exist only on earth, the religionist may ask, is that not strong evidence that God has, on earth, this speck in the cosmos, brought about for his purpose the emergence of human beings? Is not the earth obviously a Garden of Eden created by God in which he has placed man and woman?

A cosmic biosphere

Is the Gaea hypothesis applicable to the entire universe and not only to earth's biosphere, but to myriad other biospheres in the universe? Sir Fred Hoyle and N.C. Wickramasinghe, in *Evolution from Space: A Theory of Cosmic Creationism*, argue that the entire universe well may have within it what we, the authors, call a "biosphere" of biotic material diffused and moving throughout extragalactic and intergalactic gas and often locked within bodies and clumps of solid matter.

According to their speculation, this biotic material is swept into interstellar gas clouds, wherein it circulates in a life system from interstellar gas to protostars, stars, planets and comets, and then as amplified biotic material back from planets and other habitations into interstellar gas. In bits minute enough to ride stellar winds and other radiation, it rains upon planets and other bodies, the rainfall never ceasing for long, but varying in intensity. Whenever it encounters favorable conditions, as on earth, it reacts with inorganic matter, and with organic matter if that already is present, so as to institute, modify and redirect the evolution of life. At times, through various occurrences such as the passage of a comet through planetary atmosphere or the collision of great masses of matter in space, biotic material amplified by evolution already instituted and developed, is returned to interstellar and intragalactic gas and in this amplified form again rains upon planets and other bodies.

The original biotic material, they theorize, is constituted of biomolecules containing genetic information. Amplified by mutations, it returns from planets or other habitations to interstellar and intergalactic gas and again rains down on planets and other places as genetic fragments, viruses and even protozoa and bacteria. In favorable places upon which it falls, it thrives and evolves into new and various life forms.

Since there are over a hundred billion stars in our galaxy and a hundred billion times that in the universe, the number of places suitable for life upon which the cosmic biotic material continually descends is correspondingly enormous, making it most probable that the universe is rife with life and intelligence—that is, if this theory of life in and from space is sound.

Hoyle and Wickramasinghe think that their theory of "evolution from space" is a far more satisfactory explanation of life on earth than is the Darwinian theory of evolution of life on earth from the original chemical constituents of earth in reaction to earth's environment. It explains gaps in evolution of earth's life forms, they think, that are completely unexplained by the Darwinian theory such as, for example, the sudden emergence of humans on earth with a brain development nearly or actually as great as their brain development is today. Many biologists question this gap, in the light of recent anthropological discoveries. However, there still are great gaps in the fossil and physical record as to the evolutionary emergence of humans, apart from any gap in the record as to the development of their brains.

Hoyle and Wickramasinghe theorize that genetic material arrived on earth from space, coded with information to produce us much as we now are, only a few billion years ago and billions of years after life forms had first occurred on earth. They also theorize that the rain of genetic material on earth from space resulted in the occurrence of life on earth very soon, i.e., within millions of years, after the earth formed; and they think that this early occurrence of life on earth is absolutely unexplainable by the accepted theory that life began on earth.

Hoyle and Wickramasinghe recognize that their theory of evolution from space requires an answer to how biotic and genetic material first came to be in the universe. The chance of its origin and codification with information in random physical and chemical activity, they think, is less than one in $10^{40,000}$. Conversely, they say, the probability of the origin and codification of biotic out of nonbiotic material of the universe through intelligent or divine guidance is greater than $10^{40,000}$ to one. These odds, of course, should please believers in the God-Creator.

What is the nature of a God who supposedly somehow is responsible for the origin of biotic out of the nonbiotic material of the universe and who supposedly coded the biotic material with information for the beginning and evolution of life, so that biotic material should rain on planets or other places suitable for that evolution to begin and flourish? Is God's purpose implicit in the purpose of the biosphere of biotic material of the universe, to foster evolution of life whenever possible? Are the myriad stellar circulatory systems of biotic material from gas to stars, planets and comets and back to gas imbued with, or controlled by, this divine purpose?

Hoyle and Wickramasinghe's answer as to the nature of this God is much like Paul Tillich's conception of God as being itself, beyond any symbolism of him; yet it also reflects the pantheism of Baruch Spinoza; and also it embraces Miguel de Unamuno's belief that God is the consciousness of the universe. Hoyle and Wickramasinghe think that the long sequence of one why and how to another goes back ultimately to an idealized "limit that is God" and that "God is the universe." The questions nevertheless remain: Why is there anything at all? Why is there God?

God and evolution of life on earth

Is God manifested in any degree by evolution of life on earth, as evolution was perceived by Darwin and is now viewed by science? It seems clear enough, despite gaps in the fossil and other physical records, that life has evolved naturally in accordance with a straightforward process of natural selection, so that it is unnecessary to postulate intervention by God to account for the proliferation of earth's life forms. It is another question, however, whether the evolutionary process discloses a divine design culminating in the emergence of intelligence. We'll discuss the design argument that God exists in Chapter 23.

Notes

[1] See M.S. Longais, Ed.: *Confrontation of Cosmological Theories with Observations*. Dordrecht, Reidel, 1974.

[2] See *The Anthropic Cosmological Principle*. Oxford, Clarendon Press; New York, Oxford University Press, 1986, p. 21.

[3] See "Beyond the Black Hole," in H. Woolf, Ed.: *Some Strangeness of the Proportion: A Centennial Symposium to Celebrate the Achievements of Albert Einstein*. Reading, Mass., 1980, pp. 356–363.

PART TWO
GOD AND PHILOSOPHY

20

Concepts and Realities

Throughout this book the discussion has assumed the reality of the cosmos. Is there another reality, perhaps on a higher level, represented by God or gods and souls or spirits, and that is sometimes called "the beyond," "heaven," "another dimension," or the like?

The reality of the material world

The evidence of the existence of the material or physical universe is our sensory perception and mental cognition of it. Whether or not physical objects can be known really to exist outside us is a difficult issue, of course. Descartes, the first modern philosopher to consider the issue in a systematic way, did not think his perception of the apparent physical world established its existence beyond all doubt. Sensory evidence proves the existence of objects outside the mind, he said, only if one assumes that God exists and does not permit us to be deceived in the matter. British empiricists, to whom the question has been of paramount importance from Hume onward, have been unwilling to grant Descartes's assumptions, and have held until only recently either that the existence of physical objects is not really knowable or that, if it is, it is only because these objects in fact "reduce" to sense-data.

The view of many current philosophers is that physical objects must simply be assumed to exist if we are to make an adequate account of the coherency and predictability of our perceptual experiences, and it is for the same reason that we, the authors, affirm the existence of physical objects on the basis of our sensory perception. It is conceivable (if only barely so) that physical objects do not exist; but the explanation of perception as due to sensory stimulation from external physical objects is inherently credible and is far better than any alternative explanation of perceptual experience. It is the best explanation because it involves the fewest unnecessary metaphysical assumptions, and has the greatest predictive power and reliability. The complex explanations that idealist and phenomenalist theories must incorporate, in order to account for the orderliness and coherency of our sense-data during stretches of perception that are interrupted and noncontinuous, as well as to avoid solipsism, are notorious.

While we believe in the reality of the cosmos, of physical objects outside the mind, we would not say that there is a mirror correspondence between it and phenomena (perceptual experience). How the external world is represented within the human brain is an issue of great current controversy and discussion among cognitive psychologists, linguists, computer scientists, artificial intelligence researchers, brain scientists and philosophers. How the world is "in itself," apart from all representation, is, we maintain with Kant, an idle speculation. But the cognizable cosmos, as we may refer to the universe as it is represented within the human mind, is, we say and assume, as a mature physics would describe it as being. It is a part of that description, of course, that if we could perceive the objects of physics with far keener senses than we in fact have, they would seem to us very different from the way they do.

Thus, while we do not know that the cosmos is real, we presume that it is and that our mental image of it through optical, radio and other observation, subject to interpretation by our knowledge of physics, is a "true" image (though it may not be a mirror image of things as they are in themselves).

There are those, however, who consider the physical realm to be illusory. For example, outside the Western philosophical tradition, Shankara, Hindu spiritual leader and philosopher of the ninth century, A.D., taught that, not only the world including our physical selves, but also the Gods, including Vishnu and Shiva and their various manifestations, are all an illusion (maya). Brahman is the true reality that permeates the illusory reality, which is, like a mirage, seen as a true reality. We ourselves are divine, being essentially Brahman. What we see in the cosmos and in our physical selves is thought by us, in our ignorance, to be real, though what we see in truth is Brahman, or God, just as what we see in truth in a desert mirage is desert atmosphere.

An opposing Hindu viewpoint is rooted in the thinking of Ramanuja (twelfth century, A.D.) that there is a real world and beyond it a real God.

In the West, Berkeley maintained that nothing exists except ideas in the minds of percipients, and that nothing can be known to exist except by conscious apprehension of these ideas by percipients. Thus, the Berkeleyian idealist maintains in effect that the external world (the cosmos including our physical selves), when interpreted as something that exists outside the mind, is nonexistent. But Berkeley would have no quarrel with the findings of scientists; he would maintain merely that their theories in fact apply only to "ideas." However it is inappropriate and unnecessary in this book further to discuss philosophical realism and idealism. We presume the reality of a non-illusory and non-ideal world and assume that the general portrayal of the cosmos by astronomy and physics is a true one. As to the possible existence of God as an immaterial, non-physical or transcendent entity, which is an issue distinct from the question of whether the universe we perceive is material or ideal, we shall inquire in this part of the book.

First-hand encounters with God and other spirits

Many persons have reported or believed themselves to have had personal encounters with God or with beings from a spirit or immaterial order, by means of miraculous or paranormal perception or supernatural communication. But such reports are sometimes incoherent and almost always lack credibility, leastwise to others, since they are unverifiable memory reports usually made by single individuals, whose observations frequently were made under less than optimum conditions, and whose perceptions may have been impaired by emotional distress, fatigue or drugs, if not outright mental imbalance.

Therefore, one is well advised to follow Paul's and Newton's advice, as we do, especially in this part of the book, and look for evidence of God in his works, i.e., in nature, though we also shall discuss the *a priori* ontological proof of God.

As for proofs of the existence of other supposedly nonphysical entities—deceased spirits and the like—one of us has examined them elsewhere and found them lacking.[1]

Concepts of God

Concepts of God (as well as concepts of souls and spirits) as developed by religions or held by individuals differ considerably, and some religions lack objects or concerns that easily fit Western notions of what "God," "souls," and "spirits" mean. For example, Confucius was concerned primarily with social relationship and conduct, especially of gentlemen, in which relations with heaven and ancestors were central; and the only God Confucianism recognizes is heaven. Taoism involves an eternal and unchanging way which exists both within and beyond the changeable material world.

In Buddhism, for a further example, Guatema, the Buddha, and other Buddhas are beyond the Gods and yet are not Gods. A human person or other living creature, even a worm, can through recognizing the Four Noble Truths and following the Eightfold Path, the last element of which is concentration and meditation, achieve higher and higher forms of life and ultimately enlightenment and Buddhahood with entry into nirvana and therewith oblivion to the material world and release from the round of rebirth (samsara) and from suffering (karma).

Rebirth in modern Hinduism is not viewed as reincarnation of one's soul in, or as its migration to, another living body, as it, roughly speaking, was viewed at the time of Guatema. Rather, rebirth, as Ninian Smart has said in *The Long Search*, involves "just a swirl of events conventionally referred to by my name."[2]

In Western thinking God has been thought of variously as personal or living and as having personal attributes resembling or transcending human attributes, such as intelligence, consciousness, power, emotion, love, hate, presence and omnipresence; as impersonal, pantheistic or deistic, i.e., creative but not supportive of the cosmos; or as an ultimate immaterial reality conditioning and making truly real material reality (the cosmos).

Discussion in the following chapters is addressed mainly to persons thinking of God and souls in the Western mode, whether they are theists believing in a personal or living God, who is creative and supportive of the universe and communicative from or with people; theists or deists believing in an impersonal God, a pantheistic God, or a God creative but not supportive of the universe and noncommunicative with people; or agnostics and atheists.

Organization of Part Two

In this part of the book each of the important traditional Western philosophical arguments for God are examined, in connection with our discussion in Part One of the origin, evolution and structure of the universe. In particular, we consider the ontological argument, the teleological argument, and the cosmological argument. In addition, we consider the will to believe in God independently of, or despite any failure in, the traditional proofs. The will to believe, as we discuss at that point in the book, is predicated variously on the necessity of emotionally exercising a "live" option to believe or disbelieve; on the prudence of wagering; on the postulation of God and immortality as necessary to explain and justify ethical conduct; or on the weight of the evidence.

Throughout these chapters there are three major foci. The first is on the true reality of the supposed immateriality represented by God. Those who accept the existence of this immateriality generally deem it to condition material reality. The second focus, in keeping with the main purpose of this book, is on the philosophical consequences of acceptance of recent cosmological findings on traditional proofs of God. The third focus is on the cause or explanation of the physical universe and its continuance.

In the closing chapters of this book, the authors set forth their own considered opinions relative to the question of God's existence. As noted in the preface, one of us is a lawyer and the other a professional philosopher, which may have some bearing on our respective opinions in the matter.

Notes

[1] See Brooke Noel Moore: *The Philosophical Possibilities Beyond Death*. Springfield, Charles C. Thomas, 1981.

[2] Boston, Toronto, Little, Brown and Company, 1977, p. 73.

21

Religious Language

By "religious language" we mean both the language in which religion talks about God, the soul and its other concerns and the language in which these are discussed by philosophy and otherwise. Religious language, thus defined, is imbued with human idealism inasmuch as it has largely developed to express human aspiration for the highest good. Consequently, it tends strongly to influence people to live and act ethically, although religion itself sometimes does not have this benevolent effect, and sometimes it degenerates into bigotry and becomes pernicious.

On the other hand, religious language has great difficulty, as we shall see, in talking about an immaterial God and immaterial souls in a language based on experience with the material world.

Loss for words

When religious language seeks to discuss a living or personal God who is immaterial, it is beset with the difficulty that while all language relates to what has been experienced, people have not experienced sensorially a deity of this nature. The same is true of language that seeks to depict God otherwise than as clearly immaterial, as by depicting him as the object of ultimate concern, as intelligence or conscience of the universe, as the substance of infinite attributes or as something else having reality different from, or on a higher level than, the reality of the material world as commonly experienced. Consequently, religious language is at a loss for words.

Some will contend that they have had experience of a living or personal God, who, though immaterial, appeared as material; or that in some way they have experienced him sensorially without his having been even apparently material. However, any claim of this nature lacks credibility, as we explained in the last chapter.

It may be urged that the reality of the physical cosmos and of its physical content is also uncertain and could be illusory, but this ground for questioning religious disbelief was discounted in the preceding chapter because the reality of the material cosmos establishes itself as the best explanation of perceptions. Our perceptual experience does not require postulation of any supposed immateriality or of any reality or level of reality different from that of the physical cosmos.

Even though testimony of personal encounters or communications with an immaterial God is regarded as credible by some, religious language remains at a loss for words to describe the experience or the immaterial object of the encounter. The reason is that words have evolved in, and relate meaningfully only to, normal experience of the material cosmos. True, thoughts and other mental phenomena are deemed by some to be nonmaterial, but there seems to be no convincing reason to regard them in this way, though the issue is difficult and subject to some current controversy.

Self-contradiction and vacuity

Religious language, if taken literally, often seems self-contradictory, ambiguous and vacuous. The reason for this is that it tries, in one direction, to dehumanize God while at the same time it tries, in the opposite direction, to humanize him. That is, it tries both to make him like and to make him unlike a human person. Further, religious language tries, in one direction, to describe a supposed immateriality or another reality in terms wholly relational to our sensory perception of the physical world. At the same time it tries, in the opposite direction, to depict the immateriality or the different reality as unknown or as completely different from the reality of the physical cosmos.

Certainly, the appearance of self-contradiction, ambiguity and vacuity inevitably characterize discussion of a personal God who is immaterial. The same is true of discussion of an impersonal deity that is immaterial. Likewise, it is true of discussion of an ultimate concern with what is beyond our experience of the material cosmos, as the perspective of religion; and it is true of an ultimate concern without specification of the object of the concern, as that perspective. No person credibly has experienced an impersonal God or an ultimate concern with something known by him to be beyond or other than normally real, though some people do ultimately concern themselves with nonsense or imagined things. Nor is ultimate concern in itself, relating to nothing, a normal or meaningful experience.

Accordingly, any discussion of an impersonal deity that is immaterial inevitably tends to contradict its impersonality and immateriality since to say anything it must use words that garb it in personality and materiality. Likewise, any discussion of ultimate concern tends to make the object of the concern personal or material. Paul Tillich admits this fact, but views the personalizing and materializing of the concern as ritual and symbolism of the ultimate concern, which is always beyond what is being said. In other words, the object of ultimate concern is nothing sensible and knowable. This, we think, makes it difficult to distinguish from nothing or nonsense.

The word "God" and the terms "personal God" or "living God" have for most people, though they may not admit it, meanings of something that is both humanlike and unhumanlike or, in other words, that is both personal and impersonal. That is, God, or a personal or living God, is held to differ from people, from matter and from ordinary reality, and to be immaterial, or to be an extraordinary or a different reality from that we know, and at the same time to have attributes like those of people, matter and ordinary reality. He is deemed to originate and sustain causation, to exist and have essence, or to have location by transcendence or diffusion. He is deemed in many respects to act like human beings and to have properties resembling theirs, e.g., to act in creating the cosmos as they act in making buildings or machines. He is said to have intelligence and emotions, to think, to love and to hate.

God's acts and properties are believed to differ, however, from those of people in that they are "perfect" in goodness and in being unobservable except perhaps by their effects. The "perfect goodness" of God is assumed to be that which people, when they think rightly, consider perfect goodness.

God's acts and properties are thought to differ from human acts and properties in that they are unobservable except by their effects. But all his supposed effects arguably are wholly or potentially scientifically explainable. It is, moreover, unverifiable to relate material effects to immaterial causation. Nevertheless, in Chapter 27, one of us wagers that there is a God.

"Soul" like "God" is a word seemingly loaded with self-contradiction, ambiguity and vacuity because the word means for most people something both personal and impersonal and both material and immaterial. A "soul" devoid of personality or of anything like the attributes of matter is characterless, invisible. Thus, believers in the immaterial soul must describe it in the garb of personality and matter, or they cannot describe it at all.

Consider also "supreme" and "being." It would seem that these words have meaning for us with respect only to tangible things and with

respect to human and animal feeling and thought. We have no difficulty, of course, in applying "being" to material things. "Supreme" we
apply mostly to persons or abstractions such as "quality" or "sacrifice."
When we apply these terms to God, we necessarily impute to him what
they mean with reference to our experience. Thus, when we call him the
"Supreme Being", we garb him with personality, materiality and normal
reality, though our purpose may be otherwise.

Even "exists," when it is applied to God, necessarily retains those
physicalistic connotations that it acquired for us as we have come to
learn the meaning of the word in application to empirically observable
entities. When it is said that God exists, "but not in time," it is most
difficult to attach literal significance to what is said. The same is true
when it is said that God is atemporal, although some saying this
distinguish "is" from "exists" and "atemporal" from "not in time."
"Is," when used in the noncopulative sense, is the same as "exists" in
our experience. "Atemporal," like "immaterial," is not within our
experience. Other well-known perplexities attend "God as atemporal."
One of these is causation of a material effect by an atemporal being. If
atemporal, how does he cause what is temporal? How can God's love,
if he is atemporal, be indicated temporally? Some religionists well may
contend that these questions beg the question, which is whether or not
the material world is contingent on an atemporal and immaterial God.
However, "atemporal" and "immaterial" have no meaning for us in our
temporal and material experience. That is, they have meaning, but only
that an atemporal God is not within our experience of anything, and is,
as he is beyond our experience, indistinguishable from nothing. All of
what we have said as to "atemporal" is demonstrative of our contention
that religious language has difficulty for want of words and in being
meaningful.

In fact, there is perhaps no word in religious language, where the
ultimate religious concern is with an immaterial deity, that is not subject
to the strain of contradictory purposes of depiction and of inherent lack
of clarity. Also, discussion of the impact of modern cosmology on
concepts and proofs of God, or on religion generally, unavoidably
encounters loss of words, difficulty not to be self-contradictory and
unattainable clarity.

Ritual, symbolism, analogy

Religion and religious language endeavor by ritual, symbolism and
analogy to justify and encourage religious belief and comprehension

and worship of a personal God who is immaterial or of a nonpersonal deity that has a reality different from that of the material cosmos and things in it.

Religious ritual is manifestation by repeated words or acts, or by use of physical objects, of affirmation or reaffirmation of religious conviction and belief without any, or further, intellectual inquiry, investigation or discussion.

Religious symbolism is the use of objects, acts or words to represent or point to a deity, an immateriality or a reality or level of reality different from normal reality, or to an ultimate concern beyond normal experience, that is conceived to be worthy of veneration as the creator of the cosmos, the supreme being, the sustainer or ultimate explanation of everything or the ultimate goal of human beings. It assumes that the reality of that it represents or to which it points has been demonstrated or is manifest without demonstration.

Attempted analogy is employed in religious and philosophical language to demonstrate and to explain the reality and nature of a personal or nonpersonal immaterial God. It helps to understand something unknown or unfamiliar to have it compared analogically to something that is known or familiar. But whether or not an analogy is accurate, whether or not it truly represents the unknown term, can be determined only by someone who is familiar with both terms of the comparison. Unless some people already possess knowledge of God independently of that supposedly gained through analogy, it must remain forever unknown to all whether or not any comparisons made between God and things within the natural order are correct or enlightening. The history of theology contains ingenious attempts to circumvent this problem, but the fact remains that analogy is of dubious value in clarifying or explaining the nature of God.

Thus, ritual, symbolism and analogy, for various reasons, are essentially vain as efforts to clothe in meaningfulness an immaterial deity, whether personal or nonpersonal. They may indeed fuel the imagination with respect to the nature of the supposed deity; and undoubtedly they inspire emotion and conduct deemed good. They also may serve an important expressive purpose for believers and may have other functions besides.

None of this is to say that modern cosmology has no impact on concepts and proof of God and of his creation of the cosmos or on religious belief. Nor is it to say that religious language is without meaning. To say that there is a cause or explanation of the universe is not to say nothing. To say that the cause lacks characteristics of materiality is not to say nothing. To say that it is conscious or intelligent is not to say nothing, though here the speaker encounters the difficulties of loss of words, attainment of clarity and avoidance of self-contradiction. To say that God is conscious or intelligent entails assertion that he is human-yet-not-human, and physical-but-not-physical, overtones that characterize much religious discourse about the deity.

When, therefore, people talk about God, though what they say must be viewed in part as ritualistic, inspirational and expressive of moral insight, it cannot be regarded as wholly nonassertive or as assertive but vacuous. However, what is being said about God, when people speak of God, is mostly unclear, and any discussion of the philosophical consequences of cosmology on religious thought necessarily faces this obstacle.

Accordingly, you, readers, and we shall encounter these difficulties pertaining to religious language in the ensuing discussion of the traditional proofs of God and of refutation of those proofs, and of the impart of modern cosmology on those proofs. They are well to be kept in mind, though further specific reference to them will be seldom.

22

Ontological Argument

"Ontological" means related to or based on being, and an ontological argument that God exists is one based on a particular conception of his being.

Anselm

An ontological argument was first systematically propounded by St. Anselm (1033–1109) Abbot of Bec, later Archbishop of Canterbury, though antecedents of his argument are found in Plato, Aristotle, Augustine and others. Anselm stressed the conception of a Supreme Being rather than being itself in his argument.

Most people, when they first encounter Anselm's argument or other argument modeled on it, regard it as little more than a clever play on words, a philosopher's curiosity, not to be taken seriously. Indeed, the argument does have the effect of a magical trick: the conclusion of the argument—that God exists—seems to materialize almost out of thin air. Yet, the argument has been accepted as sound by some of the most brilliant minds in history, including Anselm, Descartes, Spinoza and Leibniz; and versions of the argument have been staunchly espoused by some eminent modern philosophers, notably Charles Hartshorne and Norman Malcolm.

Think of God as a being than which no greater being is conceivable. Then realize that he must be incapable of not existing if he is that than which no greater being is conceivable, for, if he is capable of not existing, he is not as great as he is if he is incapable of not existing. Therefore, he exists and is supreme and eternal, without beginning, end or interlude in his existence. Moreover, to be unsurpassable and supreme, he must possess omnipotence (except for the power not to exist), omniscience and all the virtues ordinarily attributed to the God of the Jews, Christians and Mohammedans.

Anselm made it clear, and it was obvious even if he had not, that in his proof of God's existence, he was (in the Augustinian tradition) thinking philosophically in order to prove that which as a believing Christian he already believed, i.e., that God exists. He stated one version of his argument in Chapter II of his *Proslogion* and another version of it in Chapter III, and he recapitulated the argument still again in Chapter IV, of that work. All of *Proslogion* Chapters II, III and IV require for publication only about three pages or a little more than a hundred lines of print.

Anselm's argument is concise, comprehensive, clear and cogent, but not convincing to nonbelievers or to many believers, including St. Thomas Aquinas (1227–1274). Nor was his argument convincing to Gaunilo (dates unknown) a monk of Marmoutier and a contemporary of Anselm, and like Anselm a believer in the Christian God. Gaunilo's famous reply to Anselm's argument and Anselm's response to the reply were by direction of Anselm made appendices to his *Proslogion* and usually are published with it. Both Gaunilo's reply and Anselm's response and the *Proslogion* must all be read together, in order fully to appreciate Anselm's argument and proof. The *Proslogion*, reply and response require only about twenty five pages of print. The writing about them in books and articles over the centuries, including many published in recent decades, certainly would fill a large library. While Anselm stated his argument succinctly and clearly, writers interpreting what he said, conjecturing what he meant to say or making inferences from what he said, often have needed lengthy articles and chapters and entire books in their discourse about what he said so tersely.

The argument set forth in the *Proslogion* in Chapter II and that stated in Chapter III often are regarded as separate arguments, but they are intrinsically related, the argument becoming decisive and culminating in Chapter III, though it is again stated in Chapter IV.

The argument in Chapter II begins with the definition of God as a "being than which nothing greater can be conceived." The argument continues in the following vein. Even the fool who in his heart has said that there is no God (Psalm XIV) understands this statement although he does not understand that a being so defined exists in fact. However, a being so defined that exists only in the understanding and not in fact is not that than which nothing greater can be conceived, because a being so defined that exists in fact can be conceived and is greater than a being so defined that exists in the understanding only. Accordingly, only a being so defined that exists in fact and is so conceived conforms to the definition of that than which nothing greater can be conceived. So, God necessarily exists in fact.

No doubt, a being than which nothing greater can be conceived must, as Anselm clearly demonstrates, exist in fact as well as in the understanding in *order to conform to the definition* of God as that than which nothing greater can be conceived; but that such a being exists in fact is an obvious nonsequitur, which clearly has been seen by most philosophers and theologians. To exist in fact in order to satisfy a definition is one thing. To exist in fact is another that does not follow from the former.

Anselm continues his argument in Chapter III of the *Proslogion* with the contention that God, in order to be a being than which nothing greater can be conceived, cannot be conceived not to exist, because, if he were able not to exist as well as being able to exist, he would not be as great as he is if he cannot exist. Ergo, God necessarily exists. By this conclusion of his argument Anselm more precisely than in Chapter II denotes what God must be in order to conform to the definition of him as that than which nothing greater can be conceived. Again, however, that God exists in fact is a nonsequitur.

Gaunilo's reply

Gaunilo saw the obvious nonsequitur that God exists in Anselm's argument. In his reply Gaunilo distinguished between understanding what is meant by what is said about God or about anything and believing or knowing that God or the thing exists in fact. He argued in effect that one can understand the words "a being than which nothing greater can be conceived" or "a lost island more excellent than any other country," but that his understanding the words is not tantamount to conceiving the being or the island as one conceives that which he knows from experience, i.e., of his own knowledge as lawyers say.

Gaunilo denied that because he understood the words of Anselm's argument, he had to accept it. It might be better, Gaunilo said, rather than to say that the nonexistence of this being is inconceivable, to say that its nonexistence is unintelligible, for unreal objects are unintelligible, though their existence is conceivable.

Anselm's response

If anyone claims he conceives a being greater than which nothing is conceivable not to exist, he either conceives of a being than which a greater is inconceivable or he does not conceive at all. If he does conceive of such a being, he cannot conceive of it not to exist as he claims. This was the heart of Anselm's response to Gaunilo. It seems to mean that one contradicts himself when he says that he both conceives of such a being and also conceives of its not existing.

In regard to Gaunilo's lost island, Anselm promised to give it to him if he could show how Anselm's reasoning applied in anyway to anything other than that than which nothing greater can be conceived. Of course, Anselm admitted, nothing other than God, i.e., that than which nothing greater can be conceived, can be proved to exist by defining it or conceiving it to exist; but God, i.e., that than which nothing greater can be conceived, can be proved to exist by conceiving it to exist, which necessarily entails conceiving its existence in fact and its impotency not to exist in fact. Later defenders of Anselm's argument have accepted his disclaimer of the applicability of the argument to all contingent and passable things.

St. Thomas Aquinas

Aquinas accepted that God is that than which nothing greater can be conceived but not that this concept of God in itself proves his reality. He said, stating more precisely that which Gaunilo had said, that one cannot argue that what is meant by the word "God" actually exists unless it is first admitted that there actually exists a being than which no greater can be conceived, which is not admitted by those who contend that God does not exist.[1]

This rejection of Anselm's ontological argument is applicable in principle to any ontological argument for God's existence based on any possible concept of his being or existence. No matter how logical a deduction of God's reality from any conception of his being or existence may be, it has no probative force for a nonbeliever, or for many believers, unless it first is established that a being exists in fact, to which the particular concept applies.

Aquinas further distinguished between the intrinsic self-evidence of the proposition, "God exists," which one must affirm, and the extrinsic self-evidence of the proposition, which one must deny. The proposition, "God exists," is intrinsically self-evident, because the predicate is included in the subject. Therefore, it is self-evident to all who know, but not to those who do not know the essence of the subject and the predicate. Because we do not know the essence of God, that he exists must be demonstrated to us by his effects that we know. Aquinas thus agrees with Paul and Newton. As we have reiterated, this book is a quest for God, or alternatively for nature without God, through the effects of the acts of God or of nature without God.

Aquinas' statement that the predicate is included in the subject anticipates one basis of Kant's deprecation of the ontological argument, as is subsequently discussed.

Descartes

Rene Descartes (1596–1650) in his ontological argument stresses the conception of God. His use of the argument to prove that God exists, that he created Descartes and that he created the world is subtle and complex, though Descartes' conclusion, simple enough, is that God's existence and his creation of the heaven and world and of all things therein necessarily follow from our certain knowledge of him as a perfect being. True, we often enough think that we know the truth when in fact we are in error, but in these instances we do not truly know the truth. Nevertheless, the ultimate test of truth for anyone is not what he is told by others, or tells himself, but what he clearly perceives and knows for himself.

Descartes' method was to reject everything as false unless he could not deny it in his own mind, such as: "I think, therefore, I am" (the *cogito*). The existence of God is a fact because it is clearly perceived that it is in the idea that a thinking person necessarily has of a perfect being. That is, to the thinking mind God, the existing perfect being, is like the *cogito*, and he is like the sum of the angles of a triangle equalling two right angles, though he is not like a triangle itself, which may or may not exist.

Why this truth as to the existence of God is not clearly perceived and known by some, Descartes says in his *Discourse on Method*, is because they are so accustomed to thinking about material objects that they cannot imagine that an immaterial thing can be intelligible and real.

Since Descartes could not conceive God without existence, inasmuch as he must think of a perfect being as having existence, he intellectually could do no other than to conclude that God exists in fact. Anyone who thinks soundly about God on a purely intellectual level must arrive at the same conclusion, Descartes was sure. Certainly, it was not within Descartes' power, he affirmed, to conceive of a God without existence, that is, of a supreme being without perfection, any more than he could conceive of a horse with wings.

In an appendix to Descartes' *Reply to Second Objection*, he summarizes his proof of God's existence. (1) It derives from the mere consideration of God's nature. (2) It derives from the mere fact that the idea of God exists in us. (3) It is proved because we, who possess that idea, exist. A corollary of (3) is that God has created the heaven and earth and all that are in them. Another corollary of (3) is that God can bring to pass whatever we clearly conceive, exactly as we conceive it.

It is proposition 2 that distinguishes Descartes' ontological argument from that of Anselm. The ultimate basis of the ontological argument to Descartes is the fact that the idea of God exists in us, whereas to Anselm it is the formulation of the idea as a being greater than which nothing can be conceived.

One fundamental objection to Descartes' ontological proof is that not all of us think that the idea of God is innate in us. Another is that not all of us clearly perceive that the "concept of God as a perfect being," though we understand the words as well as he or Gaunilo could have, proves God's existence in the same way that one clearly perceives that the sum of the angles of a triangle equal two right angles. What Aquinas aptly said of Anselm's argument can be said of Descartes': nonbelievers will require that it first be proved that a perfect being exists, even though existence is necessary to his perfection.

Spinoza

Baruch Spinoza (1632–1677) stresses being in his ontological argument to prove the existence of God. He describes God as an absolute infinite being or substance that consists of infinite attributes. Each attribute expresses eternal and infinite essence. For Spinoza, God is the one substance; there is no other substance and no duality of substance. God as infinite substance is uncaused.

Individual and finite things, which are caused by other finite things, *ad infinitum*, come into, and continue in, existence only through God or substance. They are "modes," that is "affections," of God or substance, through whom they are conceived. It pertains to the nature of substance to exist. Thus, God exists, and the existence of God and his essence are one and the same thing. If it be denied that God or substance exists, it would follow that God's essence does not involve existence, but that is absurd.

Spinoza also sought to prove God's existence by what he called an *a priori* argument that because we ourselves exist, either in ourselves or in something else which necessarily exists, being absolutely infinite, that is to say God, necessarily exists. If there is nothing which necessarily exists except finite things, then they are more powerful than the absolutely infinite being, but self-evidently that is absurd.

Leibniz

Gottfried Wilhelm Leibniz (1646–1716) accepted the ontological argument of Anselm and Descartes as an incomplete demonstration, denying that it is a paralogism as it had, he thought, been consistently misunderstood. That is Leibniz did not regard its conclusion that God exists as a nonsequitur. Instead, he asserted that the argument demonstrates that according to the present state of our knowledge God exists, save only that the proof is that, presuming that God is possible, he exists. One is entitled, Leibniz thought, to presume that God possibly exists until the contrary is proved, but, he added, it is desirable, nevertheless, that it be proved that it is possible that God exists, thereby making the ontological argument complete and irrefutable.

By "that God possibly exists" Leibniz means that the concept of him as a supreme or perfect being is not self-contradictory. The concept embraces the conception of two perfections: (1) a supreme or perfect being and (2) existence. Leibniz regarded a perfection as a simple quality that is positive and absolute or that expresses whatever it expresses without any limits. Two or more perfections, he contended, cannot be demonstrated to be incompatible without resolving them, which by his hypothesis as to their nature cannot be done. Therefore, perfections are compatible, and so the concept of God is not self-contradictory. By this argument Leibniz thought that he demonstrated the possibility of God's existence, thereby making the ontological argument complete and irrefutable.[2]

Hume

David Hume (1711–1776) and Immanuel Kant (1724–1804) demolished the ontological argument. "Demolished" is not too strong a word.

It is absurd, Hume wrote, to pretend to demonstrate or prove a fact by any argument *a priori*. Nothing can be shown to be true unless the opposite implies a contradiction. Anything that can be conceived to exist can also be conceived not to exist, and this is true of God. While it is pretended that God necessarily exists if only we knew his essence or nature, obviously we can't know that through our faculties, Hume observes; and, he adds, that although we conceive God to exist, we can thereafter at any time conceive him not to exist, and it follows that his "necessary existence" has no meaning or, which is the same, that the term has no consistent meaning. Moreover, Hume asks, may not the material universe be the necessarily existent Being, according to this pretended explanation of necessity?

Kant

Kant, who acknowledged Hume's influence on his own critical thinking, found the ontological argument to be meaningless because the concept of existence adds nothing to the concept of God or of anything. To say that "God exists" is like saying "God is God." "Exists" like "is" is a mere copula, not a predicate that adds anything to the concept implicit in the word "God." No matter whatever else is said about God, that he is a being greater than which nothing greater can be conceived, that he is the supreme or perfect being, that his nonexistence is inconceivable because if it were he would be less than a supreme or perfect being or less than that which nothing greater can be conceived— saying that he exists adds nothing to the concept of God, and certainly does not prove that the concept has a counterpart in reality. What is said is only word play with the copulative, "God is God," in order to prove that he exists in fact as he is described by the word "God" to Christians, Jews and Mohammedans. As Kant himself succinctly says:

> By whatever and by whatever number of predicates—even to the complete determination of it—I may cogitate a thing I do not in the least augment the object of my conception by the addition of the statement, this thing exists. Otherwise, not exactly the same, but something more than was cogitated in my conception, would exist, and I could not affirm that the exact object of my conception had real existence. . . . Now if I cogitate a being as the highest reality, without defect or imperfection, the question still remains—whether this being exists or not.[3]

Kant illustrates that "exists" adds nothing to God in "God exists" or to a thing in "the thing exists" by the example of one hundred thalers which are the same concept whether or not they exist in fact. That is, to say that "one hundred thalers exist" or that "one hundred thalers do not exist" adds nothing to the concept of one hundred thalers. Neither statement makes the number of thalers more or less; nor does either statement in itself make one hundred thalers exist or not exist.

Whether or not existential statements are indistinguishable from predicative statements in that they add nothing to the concept of the subject of the statement has been debated by logicians and need not be pursued here.

Even though existence be regarded as a predicate that adds something to the concept of God, if that predicate and the subject (God) of the concept are both annihilated in thought, no internal contradiction can arise, Kant argues. Therefore, the concept that God exists or that he is that than which nothing greater can be conceived to exist or that his nonexistence is inconceivable does not in itself prove the existence of God. Kant wrote:

> But when you say, *God does not exist*, neither onmipotence nor any other predicate is affirmed; they must all disappear with the subject, and in this judgment there cannot exist the least self-contradiction.
>
> . . . you [advocates of the ontological argument] find yourselves compelled to declare: There are certain subjects which cannot be annihilated in thought. But this is nothing more than saying: There exists subjects which are absolutely necessary— the very hypothesis you are called upon to establish. For I find myself unable to form the slightest conception of a thing which, when annihilated in thought with all its predicates, leaves behind a contradiction; and contradiction is the only criterion of impossibility, in the sphere of pure *a priori* conceptions.[4]

Hartshorne

Charles Hartshorne agrees with Anselm's argument in chapter III of the *Proslogion* that God, in order to be a being than which nothing greater can be conceived, cannot be conceived not to exist, and accordingly must exist, although Hartshorne disagrees with Anselm's conclusion in Chapter I of the *Proslogion* that the existence of God in fact follows from the conception of him as that greater than which nothing else can be conceived.[5]

The necessary existence of God, according to Hartshorne, means that he is somehow actualized in a suitable contingent concrete reality and is more than a mere abstraction, which is nothing. The actualization need not be in a particular way or in a particular contingent and concrete form. In cases other than divine existence, the contingency of actualization relates both to the particular concreteness in which the actualization occurs and to whether or not it occurs at all. In regard to divine existence, the contingency of actualization relates only to how it occurs and to the particular concreteness in which it occurs, but that it occurs in some way and in some concreteness is necessary.

The quality that makes God necessarily existent Hartshorne calls "greatness" rather than Anselm's "being than which nothing greater can be conceived." Hartshorne also refers to this greatness as "Mind as Great." "Matter" and "forms" are only words in the absence of "Mind as Great." If the universe itself is conceived of as this "Mind as Great," it is conceived of as God. Hartshorne, however, seems to think of the universe as actualized by God, although apart from this actualization "God" is a mere abstraction and nothing. This conception of God as Goodness and Mind actualized in concrete things, (the physical universe?) brings to mind Unamuno's similar view of God, discussed in Chapter 25.

That Hartshorne's God exists in reality is plainly required by his conception of him, but that God exists by necessity to satisfy Hartshorne's conception of him and that he exists in fact are two different things, the latter not following from the former.

Malcolm

Norman Malcolm, like Hartshorne, accepts Anselm's argument in Chapter III of the *Proslogion*. Malcolm asserts that the only way to disprove the necessity of God's existence is to show that Anselm's concept of God as a being greater than which cannot be conceived is either self-contradictory or nonsensical.[6] This cannot be done, as Malcolm says, but Malcolm, like others who accept Anselm's argument, fails to see that God's necessary existence to satisfy a definition of him is one thing and his existence in fact, extrinsically to the definition, is another, which does not follow from the former.

One who understands Anselm's conception of God may be an agnostic or atheist and still recognize that logic requires that Anselm's conception of God, which generally is held in the Judeo-Christian-Mohammedan religion, entails that God exists in fact. He can honestly understand the concept and not know whether in fact there is a being described in it though the concept logically requires that there is the being in fact. That logic requires that a proposition entails a consequence that is true in fact makes neither the proposition nor the consequence true in fact if the proposition, in the first place, is either false or unproved. The same is true of any concept and its effects. If the guilt of a defendant could be proved by a concept of him as the one who committed the crime, from which concept that he was guilty would be a necessary deduction, or rather a bare tautology, that would prove neither that the concept nor its consequence was true. This analogy seems completely applicable to Anselm's proof and Malcolm's use of it.

Malcolm, assuming that Anselm's concept of God is not self-contradictory or in some way logically absurd, thought correctly that it follows that God necessarily exists. No doubt he necessarily exists within the logical necessity of the formulated concept, but that he, as conceived, exists in fact and apart from the formulation seems a nonsequitur.

Malcolm says that he knows no way, or is any easily perceived, to demonstrate that the concept of God is self-contradictory. He correctly thinks, however, that the demonstration is unneeded. As above said, however, that does not prove that God exists in fact.

One still wants to know, as Malcolm says, why human beings have come to have conceived of God in this way. Malcolm suggests strongly that the concept has arisen from a feeling of guilt for great wrong-doing and intense desire for removal of the guilt by forgiveness by a God conceived as Anselm and Christian theists conceive him. At a deep level, Malcolm thinks, the ontological argument is fully understandable only by those who have a view of life that gives rise to the traditional Judeo-Christian-Mohammedan concept of God and who have some inclination to participate in religion centered on that concept. "The inclination," in Kierkegaard's words, is "from the emotions." Malcolm and Kierkegaard in this view are in effect basing God's existence on their will to believe in him irrespective of proof or disproof of his existence. Justification of such will to believe is discussed in Chapter 25.

Ontological proof and the cosmos

The ontological argument stands or falls on its own merits, regardless of the way the universe is and regardless of the way it is conceived to be. Even if the universe were radically different from the way we depicted it in Part One, even if it were much smaller, or closed and finite, or steady-state, that would not bear on the validity of the argument. The argument is immune to physical matters, to the change in understanding of the universe wrought by recent cosmology, to current views as to the size of the universe and its expansion, its evolution and dynamics, the Big Bang, the fundamental interactions of nature and the microworld of the atom. Having disclosed our own exceptions to the validity of the argument, we turn to one or two tangential matters.

First, it would be amazing that on this earth, this one small speck of matter in this vast universe of billions time billions and more of stars and other pieces and bits of matter, the human mind should have found God in Anselm's discovery, i.e., a few words or ideas in a certain arrangement. That the human mind has found that God exists simply by examining itself and its concepts would, perhaps, be almost as amazing as the existence of the universe itself. This reflection does not bear on the validity of the argument, of course, though it may add to the suspicions of those who already are disposed to reject the argument.

Second, the ontological argument exists in splendid isolation from human attempts to understand the world. It assumes that it is possible to find proof of God's existence while disregarding his great creative handiwork, and thus, in this sense at least, it treats God's work with disdain.

It is also vain, for it assumes that human thought can find that God exists simply by examining itself and its conception of God. Of course, even before Anselm's time, and indeed until this century, there was forceful, if not necessarily good, cause to regard the mind and its thought as far more important than the human body and the physical universe. It was obvious that it was by the mind that humankind has achieved dominion over the earth and its other creatures and has constructed civilization. So it was natural that humans should seek God by introspection. But today most people find it surprising that a few eminent theologians and philosophers still should pursue this way to God. Again, these thoughts do not bear on the validity of the argument.

Finally, it must be remembered, in looking for God in words or concepts only, that the words and concepts have originated and developed in relation to the world of experience. As we have noted, for this reason religion is at a loss for words. The main importance of recent cosmology to the ontological argument therefore seems to us to lie in this, that now, more than ever, the most overwhelming and awe-inspiring entity, i.e., the greatest entity, of which we have experience, as well as conception, is the physical universe itself. Suppose we define God as that than which no greater can be conceived. That in effect would be describing the universe as God, though greatness for Anselm meant something other than it means when we speak of the universe as great. That definition does not, however, make the universe exist in fact.

Notes

[1] *Summa Theologica*, Part I, Question 2, Article 1.

[2] See *New Essays Concerning Human Understanding*.

[3] *Critique of Pure Reason*, Part II, 2nd Division, Book II, Ch. III, Section V.

[4] *Ibid*.

[5] See Charles Hartshorne: *Anselm's Discovery*. La Salle, Illinois, Open Court Publishing Company, 1955.

[6] Malcolm's Statement of Anselm's Ontological Argument, in Alvin Plantinga, Ed.: *Ontological Argument*. Garden City, New York, Anchor Books, 1965.

23

Teleological Argument

Manifest design throughout the universe evidences that there is a divine Designer. This is the teleological argument or proof that a God-Creator exists.

> Look round the world . . . The curious adapting of means to ends, throughout all nature, resembles exactly, though it much exceeds, the productions of human contrivance; of human design, thought, wisdom, and intelligence. Since therefore the effects resemble one another, we are led to infer, by all the rules of analogy, that the causes also resemble; and that the Author of Nature is somewhat similar to the mind of man, though possessed of much larger faculties, proportioned to the grandeur of the work, which he has executed.[1]

Many people think that the phenomena of nature are so well suited to an obvious purpose that they must surely have been intended to serve that purpose by the Designer. Could natural causes by themselves possibly account ultimately for the remarkable suitability of an animal's digestive system for converting organic matter into physical energy? For the eye to see? For the unique appropriateness of the human brain to think, to relate thoughts as well as things, to seek and discern truth and to censor and regulate emotional drives in the development of morality? For the amazing fitness of the earth to sustain life? Many people think not. This amazing "adapting of means to ends throughout all nature," they believe, could only be the handiwork of a divine intelligence. Divine design, it is contended, is obvious both in the universe as a whole and in all its parts.

This argument was espoused by many noteworthy thinkers in the seventeenth and early eighteenth century, including John Locke, Robert Boyle, Robert Hooke, John Ray, Joseph Butler and Sir Isaac Newton. However, supporters of the design argument met a formidable opponent in the latter half of the eighteenth century in David Hume, who, in his *Dialogues Concerning Natural Religion*, impugned the analogy of design in the physical universe with that of human artifacts, arguing that there is no basis for concluding that world-orderliness is design, viz., an intellectual plan with a goal, rather than a natural outgrowth of matter itself. "The whole presents nothing," Hume wrote, "but the idea of a blind nature, impregnated by a great vivifying principle, and pouring forth from her lap, without discernment or parental care, her maimed and abortive children."

Notwithstanding Hume's criticisms of the design argument, and further criticisms raised a little later by Kant, the argument had many adherents in the early nineteenth century. William Paley (1743–1805) called attention to many instances in which a bodily organ possesses a structure remarkably appropriate to its particular function, and others emphasized the striking suitability of nature for life as further clear indication that the world was the result of intelligent planning by a divine mind.

Nevertheless, Charles Darwin, (1809–1882) made it clear that biological adaptation was fully explainable as a natural evolutionary process not involving or requiring the agency of God, at least after the beginning of that process in an early epoch of the earth (or, we should add in view of what we know now, after the beginning of that process in the spewing by supernovae of metals into interstellar space). Why are bodily organs suited to their function? Natural selection, not God, is the answer, at least the answer since the universe began in the Big Bang. There are several versions as to how natural selection works, but most involve genetic mutations resulting in organic changes that are inherited and become prevalent in a species because they are advantageous to its survival or that become prevalent in a species for some other physical reason or by physical chance bearing no indication of divine intervention.

Why is the earth so acutely fit for the sustenance of the life upon it? The answer again is natural selection. The forms of life, no matter how natural selection works, developed under earthly environment and conditions; obviously, failure of a form of life to accommodate to earthly environment, conditions or happenings (such as the ice ages) results in its extinction.

Going back, however, to the beginning of the evolutionary process of earthly life in the pre-oxygen epoch of the earth and beyond that to life's roots in the forging of metals in the nuclear furnaces of supergiant stars before they exploded in supernovae, the design-argument adherent well might comment: "It is here that divine design manifests itself." Darwin himself, in the last chapter of *Origin of Species*, expressed the view that the best argument for God's existence was the improbability of the great and wonderous world rising from chance, but his agnosticism in the end is apparent in the unexpurgated edition of his *Autobiography*.

Frederick Robert Tennant (1866–1957) has presented a systematic presentation of the teleological argument, in Volume II of his *Philosophical Theology*. He regarded theology as an extension of scientific knowledge, and he predicated belief in God on cosmic theology. Also, he was concerned with probability in the ordinary and not in any mathematical or technical sense, rather than with conclusive demonstration of God's existence and role as the Designer of the universe. The probability is that justifiable by reason.

Examining the universe for such a reason, he found it, not in a single category, but in several interwoven categories, of design or adaption for purpose, as follows:

(1) The cosmic rather than chaotic nature of the universe.
(2) Adaptation of animal organisms through evolution in respect to their design and directivity in the process.
(3) Emergence of life and intelligence out of inorganic matter and conduciveness of the inorganic world to the development of life and intelligence.
(4) Production of beauty in abundance for human appreciation, providing also with intelligence a theater for moral and religious life.
(5) The whole process of nature being viewable as instrumental to the development of intelligent and moral creatures.
(6) Suggestion by the foregoing categories of a cosmic purpose to use nature for the production of humanity. The more that is learned about the complexities involved before humanity was produced, the less credible becomes an alternative theory of cumulative groundless coincidence.

Tennant's first point, that the cosmic, nonchaotic nature of the universe is evidence of design, deserves extended consideration, and we return to it below. His second and third points, as they relate to the emergence of life and the adaption of organisms to their environment, involve matters discussed in Chapter 19.

Tennant's third and fourth points, as they pertain to the idea that design is evidenced by the aesthetic value of nature, and also by the suitability of nature for the development of intelligence and morality, are interrelated and call for a brief comment. The seat of human intelligence is the brain. That the natural order is well suited for the emergence and development of the human brain is no more surprising than that the oceans are well suited for the development of creatures with fins and mechanisms for extracting oxygen from water. Fins, mechanisms for extracting oxygen from water and brain components are all in their own ways advantageous, within a particular environment, to the creatures within those environments that have them. They, and other organs, emerge and develop in response to the extant conditions: therefore those conditions seem well-suited to them. Would it be reasonable to say that there are oceans in order that fish can have fins, i.e., to believe that the aptness of oceans for creatures with fins is evidence of design? It seems no more reasonable to find evidence of design in the suitability of the environment in which humans find themselves for the organs they have.

"The moral law within" is sometimes referred to as evidence for the existence of God, but the argument under Tennant's fourth point is that the suitability of the earthly environment for development of that law evidences design. Here again, however, what this suitability evidences is that human morality, i.e., the propensity of humans generally to seek norms and standards, and to govern their behavior in accordance with them, is advantageous to the survival of the species within its environment.

As for the aesthetic value of nature as evidence of design, as mentioned by Tennant, true, humans do derive pleasure from interacting with their environment. Much of this pleasure, of course, is not aesthetic, as when nature brings pleasure by satisfying biological needs. Often the pleasure derived from satisfaction of biological need goes beyond the mere removal of that need and is something positive, as when water not merely removes thirst but provides positive enjoyment, but these surplus pleasures, again, are not aesthetic. Aesthetic pleasures result principally when the mind beholds the world without and perceives in it proportion, harmony, order and the like. Thus, whether or not the beauty of the world gives evidence of design rests largely on whether and to what extent the universe is cosmic, and not chaotic. This question is discussed subsequently.

Tennant's sixth category brings to mind the anthropic principle discussed in Chapter 19. There it was noted that, since the universe contains us within it, necessarily any explanation of the universe must account for that fact. This is the weak anthropic principle. It also is certainly true that, since the universe contains us, necessarily it must have originated and evolved so as to give birth to us. But it doesn't follow from this that the universe necessarily must have originated and evolved so as to give birth to us (one version of the strong anthropic principle).

Let us now consider directly the question whether or not the universe as a whole or in its parts give evidence of intelligent planning toward some goal.

Undoubtedly, there are many people, but perhaps only few other than those who accept God on faith alone, who would attempt to specify the goal toward which the universe trends or state its purpose. But then it isn't necessary to specify the goal toward which something is aimed in order to know that it is directed to some goal or serves some purpose. If the first humans to visit Titan (a satellite of Saturn) should discover the remains of a complex technology, they would assume that some unknown intelligent being had used the artifacts for some purpose, even if they could not fathom what that purpose might be. That the artifacts had been used to some end probably would be clear from their nonchaotic structure.

The physical universe as a whole appears to the human mind to be cosmic rather than chaotic. The universe is the Big Bang still going on, and the Big Bang has within it both expansive and restraining forces. The expansive force is not well understood, but it is real, witness the expansion of the universe. But the restrained expansion is cosmic in character, not chaotic.

The cosmic restraining force chiefly is gravity, though the other forces of nature have cosmic effect within the weaving of the fabric of matter on the loom of spacetime. Except for gravity, the Big Bang would have reached infinity instantly and would never have been. The restraint on expansion gives birth to spacetime, which we perceive as three-dimensional space and the one-way flow of time. Spacetime expansion and its gravitational restraint also generate the moving present, that will-o'-the-wisp, gone as it arrives, that dimensionless division between distance-past and distancefuture.

The electromagnetic and the strong and the weak nuclear forces (the so-called "forces of nature" other than gravity) function, on the one hand, to keep atoms together and, on the other hand, to cause them to emit particles and waves and to decay. These forces also affect particles and radiation behavior; they contribute with gravity to galaxy, star, planet and other formations and to star explosion and grey-dwarf death of stars; and they operate in many other ways in the weaving of matter on the loom of spacetime. The interaction of these forces with matter and radiation in accordance with discoverable laws contributes to the cosmic character of the universe as a whole, though that interaction involves to some extent uncertainty, randomness and violence. The uncertainty and randomness do not preclude overall predictable patterns of behavior, e.g., determinable half-life, which is the time in which half of the nuclei of a radioactive substance will decay. Violence, too, has cosmic consequences in some, if not all, instances, as is discussed below.

The physical universe appears to be isotropic (the same in all directions) as a whole. However, as we have seen in Chapter 13 and 14, galaxies and groups of them vary much in configuration, although they lend themselves to general classification in this respect. Voids among groups and supergroups also vary much, both in extent and in shape.

Everywhere the universe seemingly is homogenous (the same in structure and substance). Matter, radiation and the laws of physics apparently are the same everywhere, though perhaps they were different within 10^{-43} seconds after the Big Bang began and are different at or near the singularity or compact minuteness at the very "bottom" of a black hole.

For over two hundred years Newtonian mechanics were deemed correct in their application. Einstein's theories of special and general relativity have proved to be more accurate in application, especially where great distances and masses are involved. Quantum mechanics likewise has replaced classical mechanics as to the interiority of the fabric of matter. That the universe is largely subject to discoverable laws is clear.

Spacetime because of its orderliness makes the occurrence, location and relationship of many events in it determinable and predictable, often precisely. Stars, planets and other celestial bodies keep closely to their appointed rounds, inspiring poetry, mysticism and religious fervor and belief. The speed of light in a vacuum is the same for all observers, and all parts of the universe are interrelated through spacetime, gravity and light and other electromagnetic radiation.

Particle physics is basically orderly, though the behavior of particles and radiation involves uncertainty, randomness and unpredictability, not due only to the inadequacy or observational and measuring devices. This disorder, however, appears to be a mechanism by which overall order is attained.

Life, both animal and plant, extremely variant externally, employs common basic ingredients and processes and has done so since its emergence.

Undoubtedly then the universe is cosmic on the whole, and also in its parts, though in it there is much physical violence, destruction and annihilation. The destruction and annihilation, however, are only of present forms of matter (including radiation) and always give birth to new forms of matter (including radiation). Energy is conserved. Destruction sometimes is a factor in future construction, and matter and radiation are converted at times into each other, as are mass and energy.

Giant red stars, in which heavy elements have been created (only in them can this be done), explode (only infrequently in a galaxy) in supernovae and spew their substance, including the heavy elements, into interstellar space, so that, when subsequently our sun and planets and others stars and their planets form out of interstellar gas and dust, they contain the heavy elements.

There is, admittedly, increasing entropy in the universe in which energy becomes unavailable in dead slag-stars, and eventually entropy will embrace the entire universe if the universe is infinite. But this ultimate happening is not inconsistent with its present cosmic character, or with its overall divine design if its cosmic character is divine design.

This fundamental question remains, however. Is this overall cosmic character of the physical universe evidence of divine design? In fact, the cosmos appears to be self-explanatory back to 10^{-43} seconds after the Big Bang began, the Planck time. That is, it seems possible in principle to explain all events subsequent to the Planck time without reference to anything other than the events themselves and to the physical constituents, forces, processes and laws of the universe. Given the incipient moment and its attributes, the cosmic development of the universe since then certainly does not in itself establish a superintellectual grand design, as contrasted with a mere "pouring forth from the blind lap of nature," in Hume's words, the entirety of events subsequent to the first moment. It is indeed plausible to maintain that the weaving of the fabric of matter and of radiation on the loom of spacetime has been self-explanatory and in a sense automatic since the Planck time. That is, as we have noted, chance and randomness have since then been utilized in, rather than being chaotically destructive of, the weaving process.

Science presently pleads ignorance of what was contained and what occurred and of what physical laws governed during the first bit of time. We know only that the Big Bang at its inception had a potentiality and capability for cosmic development, at least by chance if not by coding. We do not know, however, that it could not have become a chaos instead of a cosmos. In fact science finds instances in which, for all that we know, calamity could have wrecked cosmic development. An early instance, for example, is the survival of enough matter after matter-and-antimatter annihilation of each other to endow the universe with the material particles and bodies that now exist, including our own bodies.

This possible potential for cosmic development had by the Big Bang at its inception is consonant with the supposition that the universe is the design of God. However, it is also compatible with the supposition that the universe is the result of unknown natural forces, or of a non-intelligent supernatural agency (like Aristotle's impersonal first mover), or of multiple divinities.

An opponent of the design argument well might say that the fundamental weakness of the argument is thus apparent because the burden of proof rests on the adherent of the argument, he who urges a non-natural explanation. That one cannot say whether or not there is design in the physical universe fails to sustain this burden of proof. This inability honestly to call the cosmos a divine design is the inevitable outcome of our ignorance, perhaps never to be escaped, as to what occurred during the first moment of time.

On the other hand, a proponent of the design argument might deny that the burden rests on him to prove that the cosmos is of divine design. He might say that cosmic order, greatly prevalent as it is in the physical universe, at least raises a strong presumption of intellectual design and, thus, of a divine Designer, so that the burden of next proceeding, as lawyers say, rests on the opponent.

Is the debate between opponent and proponent then a draw? Certainly it is at least in the sense that finding evidence of design and failing to find evidence of design are ultimately matters of subjective opinion. Whether or not there is evidence of design is thus not a resolvable matter of empirical fact, although empirical observations obviously are relevant to the issue.

Still, the net effect of contemporary cosmology on the design argument has certainly not been to lessen its force. From an elegant economy of yarns the fabric of the universe has been woven into a vastness and complexity nearly beyond comprehension, and all but the insensitive must be moved beyond words by the dazzling display. The universe as revealed through contemporary cosmology—the universe as depicted in Part One—is, we think, more, much more, commanding of admiration and awe then as it was as viewed through Galileo's telescope. This effect may be psychological rather than logical, but it is not less real for that. Serious contemplation of the universe is indeed an almost mystical experience akin to that created by an artistic masterpiece, and this experience is heightened, not lowered, by the details of recent cosmology. To have these emotions is thus to feel nearness with something remotely analogous to a vast and creative intelligence, to a mind which is "proportioned," as Cleanthes said, "to the grandeur of the work which he has executed."

While evolutionary theory has for many strongly, if not overwhelmingly, discredited versions of the design argument that are predicated on the close fit of the worldly environment to human needs, characteristics and traits, those people who still find within the orderliness of the universe evidence of something resembling a divine Designer have nothing to fear from contemporary scientific cosmology, both in regard to the micro and the macro structure of the universe. While recent scientific discoveries and theories have little bearing on the ontological argument, they tend to provide even more evidence of cosmic "design," in a subjective sense, as we have explained here.

Notes

[1] The passage represents Cleanthes' view, not David Hume's. See David Hume: *Dialogues Concerning Natural Religion*, in Charles W. Hendel, Jr., Ed.: *Hume Selections*. New York, Charles Scribner's Sons, 1955, p. 302.

24

Cosmological Argument

Broadly speaking, any argument or proof that God exists or that he created and sustains the universe that is predicted somehow on the physical universe is a cosmological argument or proof. Within this broad definition a teleological is one kind of cosmological argument.

More narrowly, traditional cosmological proof of God is one based on causation (including motion caused by motion) in the universe or on contingency in the universe. The material (physical) universe is meant here and throughout this discussion.

The argument or proof of causation begins with inference from observation of the universe that every physical thing, event and motion in the universe has a physical cause and that every physical cause has another physical cause preceding it in time, so that there are recessions or chains of causation going back in time. Thus, every physical thing, event and motion is in a chain of causation.

An *a priori* premise of the argument is that the recessional chains of causation must begin; they can't go backward to infinity. Unless there is a First Cause (or First Mover) there could be no intermediate causes (or motions) and no present effects (or motions); and the universe would not be.

The recessional chains of causation (motions) can't begin within the material universe since everything in it has a cause precedent to it in time. The conclusion is that all chains of causation begin in something beyond and other than the material universe, i.e., in a nonphysical or immaterial First Cause or God.

The argument or proof on contingency begins with the inference from observation of the universe that every physical thing, event and motion in the universe is contingent on some other physical thing, event or motion in it. Consequently, there are chains of contingency of things, events and motions, and everything and every occurrence in the universe is in a chain of contingency.

An *a priori* premise of the argument is that the chains of contingency must begin in something not contingent; otherwise, it is argued, no contingent thing could exist at all since the chains of contingency could not start or be. The beginning can't be in the physical world because everything in it is contingent on something else. Therefore, the chains of contingency must begin in an immaterial self-necessary being that is called "God".

Let us now apply the cosmological argument or proof to the universe as we have portrayed the universe in Part One, being guided in that portrayal by modern scientific cosmology. In other words, we shall interpret the cosmological argument or proof in the light of the universe so portrayed.

The chains of causation regress in spacetime, rather than in time, to the Little Bomb that exploded in the Big Bang that is the expanding universe, or to whatever is the material incipiency of the Big Bang. The chains must begin. They can't begin in anything material because everything and every occurrence in the universe has a cause. The conclusion is that the chains of causation begin in what is immaterial, i.e. in a God who caused the Big Bang or the origin otherwise of the universe. This is one implication of the modern scientific view of the cosmos on the cosmological argument on causation.

The chains of contingency under the cosmological argument, as related to the universe as now depicted by science, lead into the interiority of matter and of radiation to quarks and leptons, of which the universe is made, and perhaps to a basic kind of particle of which quarks and leptons are two different manifestations; to the four fundamental interactions of particles and perhaps to a single fundamental interaction of which the four now known are manifestations; and perhaps to a unified field associated with a single interaction of a single kind of particles.

That is, for example, your body is contingent on the atoms comprising it, and they are contingent on the basic interactions of leptons and quarks, which are contingent perhaps on a basic interaction of a basic kind of particles.

It is requisite, according to the argument, that the chains of contingency must begin. They can't begin in the material near-unity or unity of interactions and particles because everything material is contingent. Therefore, they must begin in an immaterial noncontingent or self-necessary being, who is God. This is the outcome of the argument, as related to the modern scientific view of the interiority of matter and of radiation.

Proponents of the cosmological argument might also reasonably contend that the chains of material causation lead inward to the basic interactions of leptons and quarks or a basic interaction of a fundamental kind of particles. For example, they could contend that molecules are caused by the bonding of atoms and that atoms are caused by the interactions of particles. Likewise, they could contend that the chains of contingency lead to the Big Bang. For example, they could claim that the earth is contingent on the sun, which is contingent on the Milky Way, which is contingent on galactic formation out of the primeval radiation, which is contingent on the Big Bang and the Little Bomb.

It might not be agreed that modern physics and astronomy establish that everything in the universe is in a chain of causation and of contingency going down in spacetime or into the interiority of matter and of radiation; but that would be a repudiation of the argument and not a criticism of our interpretation of it with respect to modern scientific cosmology. The argument could be altered to conform to how science regards causation or contingency, and there still would be chains of material relationships, whatever they might be, ultimately to something nonmaterial, according to the argument. For example, if the mechanics of the subatomic involve only norms of random activity of particles that can be determined statistically, the norms can be shown or contended to lead back to a material finality in the Little Bomb, or to lead inward to or toward a unity of interactions and of particles.

So far, we have sought to illuminate the cosmological argument, and to interpret it in relation to the portrayal of the cosmos in Part One. Now let us look at the development and criticism of the argument or proof.

St. Thomas Aquinas

Aquinas' famous five ways to prove the existence of a God who created and sustains us and the universe are stated in his *Summa Theologica* (First Part, Q. 3, Article 3). The first three ways are cosmological arguments or versions of a cosmological argument, depending on how they are viewed.

His fifth way is a teleological argument to the effect that order in the universe indicates God's existence.

His fourth way is that the gradation of goodness, truth and nobility in beings requires that there is something that is best, truest and noblest, which is to all beings the cause of their being, goodness and every perfection. This fourth way has been generally ignored. Its assumption that cause of gradation is the maximum perfection makes it bear a vague resemblance to the first three ways. It also suggests the postulation of

God on human recognition of ethical standards, set forth in Kant's *Critique of Practical Reason*. We shall not further discuss the fourth way.

Motion

Aquinas' first way is the attempted proof of God's existence by necessary inference from the observed regression of motions. It is apparent that some things are in motion, Aquinas and before him Plato and Aristotle perceived. Aquinas regarded motion as not merely the movement of things with reference to the earth but also as including the transmutation of something from potentiality to actuality. Plato thought of motion as including growth and decay, composition and decomposition and movements of the mind. Aristotle likewise conceived motion broadly as including change and the actualization of the potential. Motion of anything in this broad sense, Plato, Aristotle and Aquinas realized, is caused by the motion of something else, so that there is a chain of causation of motion back until a first unmoved mover is reached.

To Plato the first unmoved mover is soul, endowed with intelligence, first moving always and the fountain and beginning of motion for all that moves other than soul itself (*Phaedrus*, 245). However, the creator, or God, put intelligence in the soul and put the soul in the world (*Timaeus*, 30). There are more than one soul, at least, not less than two, one the author of the good and the other of evil. The best soul takes care of the world and guides it on the good path. Soul is plural—of the souls of the sun, the stars, the months, the seasons and every excellence that is God's (*Laws*, Book X).

To Aristotle the first unmoved mover is immovable substance, necessary and eternal, which is actuality and separate from sensible things. The unmoved mover causes the first intermediate motion, which is the eternal circular motion of the "first heaven." It does so, not by passing on motion, but by being the object of desire and thought. Motion is passed on then from the heavens to the world of nature. It seems from our reading of Aristotle that the unmoved mover is thought thinking on itself or the good God, who always is in that good state in which we sometimes fortunately are. It is an eternal situation, not involving an origin of the universe, in which God is contemplating rather than active in relation to the universe (*Metaphysics*, Book XII, chapter 7).

Aquinas favored his first way to prove the existence of God and developed it much more than he did his other ways. In the first way he contended that whatever is moved must be moved by another, but that this cannot go on to infinity and that there must be a first mover, which everyone understands is God. Logically, Aquinas is wrong; the concept of infinite regression of motion being caused by other motions implies that there is no first mover within the meaning of the concept. However, the concept neither proves nor disproves that in fact the regression is infinite; nor does it either prove or disprove that in fact the regression terminates in a first mover.

Today we know that all motion is relative. Any frame of reference is moving with respect to an object or particle just as much as that object or particle is moving with respect to it. Furthermore, all frames of reference are moving relatively to each other, and there is no ultimate fixed and unmovable frame of reference in the universe, as for example, the very distantpast observable stars, which in Newtonian mechanics were so regarded. Nor is there any absolute time and space, as in Newtonian mechanics there was thought to be, to which either motion or being at rest can be related. It seems that all relative motions in the universe are within the regression of causation of physical things and occurrences down in spacetime to the explosion of the Little Bomb in the Big Bang or to other incipience of the material universe.

Leastwise, all motions began with the motions of particles with relation to each other at the beginning of the Big Bang, if truly the expanding universe and spacetime then began.

Causation

Aquinas's second way to prove God's existence is from the nature of efficient cause. In the world of physical sense, which today is called the "material universe" there is an order of efficient causes. Every cause is the effect of another cause preceding it in time. There must be a first efficient cause; otherwise there would be no intermediate causes and no effects. Accordingly, the regression of causation cannot be infinite. It must end in God, who is other than material, i.e., immaterial.

The secondary way in relation to our present view of the cosmos has been interpreted above.

Contingency

Aquinas's third way to prove God's existence is that not everything can be contingent. A being is contingent if it is not necessary for it to have existed. If everything is contingent, Aquinas said, "then at one time there was nothing in existence." Thus, since something cannot come from nothing, not everything is contingent. Accordingly, there must exist something the existence of which is necessary. But it is impossible "to go to infinity" in necessary things which have their necessity caused by another. "Therefore we cannot but admit the existence of some being having of itself its own necessity, and not receiving it from another . . . This all men speak of as God."

The argument of the third way is thus that of the second way, the impossibility of an infinite regression of contingency replacing the impossibility of an infinite regression of causation.

It was previously noted that proponents of the argument could contend either that the regression of contingency leads ultimately to the Big Bang or, alternatively, into the interiority of matter to the basic interaction or interactions of quarks and leptons or to an ultimate kind of particles. Let us therefore consider, is the Big Bang a "self-necessary" event? Presumably Aquinas would have answered the question negatively, and then proferred God as the ultimate reason why the Big Bang did happen. However, before 10^{-43} seconds after the Little Bomb exploded in the Big Bang what happened is unknown, so cosmology, as far as we can see, does not give reason for agreeing or disagreeing with Aquinas.

Do the basic interactions and kinds of particles exist by self-necessity? Again, presumably Aquinas would answer "no," they do not exist by self-necessity. Here, too, cosmology does not provide reason for agreeing or disagreeing with him.

Is it perhaps the case, however, that such concepts of the human mind as necessity (or self-necessity), contingency and explanation are, ironically, wholly inapplicable in the first place to the Big Bang, basic interactions or fundamental particles?

Resort to ontological argument

In a cosmological argument the inference is that from the regression of motions, causation or contingency a First Mover, First Cause or Self-necessary Being must be acknowledged to exist. To determine the properties in fact of the First Mover, First Cause or Self-necessary Being beyond its existence and immateriality, e.g., its supremacy, omnipotence, omniscience and goodness, one must then speculate about God, and endeavor to prove that he has these properties by considering what is implied in the conception of him. One must resort to such speculations because these properties cannot be determined by experience and observation of the material world. In short, the cosmological argument fails to prove the existence of God as a Supreme or Perfect Being, the Being greater than which nothing can be conceived. Thus, to prove the existence of that being, the cosmological argument is inadequate, and the ontological proof must, in effect, be called in.

Kant perceived this basic flaw in the cosmological argument, which he called the ontological argument in disguise. The cosmological argument, he said, appeals to experience, and "experience may perhaps lead us to the concept of absolute necessity, but is unable to demonstrate this necessity as belonging to any determinate thing (*Critique of Pure Reason*, A607, B635)." Recent cosmology, indeed, does not provide reason for disputing this insight.

Plurality and regression in deity

The five ways of Aquinas prove the existence of deity, insofar as they do so at all, in the plural as much as in the singular. That is, they prove deity, insofar as they do, without any distinction as to whether it is singular or plural. Aquinas would not have disputed this; and he believed on faith that the deity which he thought was proved to exist by his five ways is the God of the Trinitarian doctrine of the Church, in accordance with which distinction in God "is by the persons and not by the essence."

It is perhaps illogical to apply concepts of number, divisibility and person which pertain to the material universe and of material things, to an immaterial deity thought or believed to exist. If so, any objection to Aquinas' five ways, that they prove the existence of several gods as successfully as they prove a singular God, is meaningless. And, if so, it may also be meaningless to ask, as some do, "Well, then, who or what moved God to cause or move material things?", or "What caused or necessitated God?", or "Why must the regression of motions, causation or contingency stop with God?" We consider these last questions, that are critical of cosmological argument, below.

Copleston-Russell debate

In this century the causation and contingency cosmological argument or versions of it have been widely accepted by Catholic theologians and others. F. C. Copleston, in a radio debate with Bertrand Russell that has been widely anthologized, defends what seems to be a contemporary example of Aquinas's third way, as Paul Edwards has pointed out. Copleston holds that the universe is "intrinsically unintelligible" apart from the existence of God. This is because the universe consists of contingent events, events that need not have happened. Since they need not have happened, why they did happen needs explaining, if they are to be truly "intelligible." The explanation, however, cannot be predicated solely on other contingent events, for their existence, too, requires explanation. Thus, the explanation of contingent events, their intelligibility, can only be found in terms of a non-contingent being, a necessary being, a being which has "the reason for its existence within itself."

Bertrand Russell, Copleston's opponent in the debate, found Copleston's argument unsatisfactory, for essentially two reasons. First, Russell professed not to understand Copleston's references to a "necessary being." Echoing Hume and Kant, Russell maintained that it is never self-contradictory to say of a thing that it does not exist. In Russell's view, only certain propositions could be called "necessary," namely, those the denial of which are self-contradictions; to call a being "necessary" is to string words together in a way that Russell said that he could not understand. Copleston, on the other hand, thought that Russell was arbitrary in restricting application of the concept "necessary" to propositions.

Russell's second objection to Copleston's cosmological argument was, in effect, that Copleston dogmatically refused to countenance any explanation of events that failed to make reference to a necessary being. In Russell's opinion we have done all that can be done to explain an event if we state the cause of the event; but in Copleston's view an explanation of an event in terms of its cause does not fully explain why the event happened. No doubt, neither Russell nor Copleston believed himself to have been bested by the other.

Mortimer J. Adler

A contemporary cosmological argument similar to Aquinas's second way is expounded in Adler's *How to Think About God*.[1] He constructs his argument on four propositions that together persuade him "that God exists, either beyond a reasonable doubt or by a preponderance of reasons. . . ." These propositions[2] are as follows:

1. The existence of an effect requiring the concurrent existence and action of an efficient cause implies the existence and action of that cause.
2. The cosmos as a whole exists.
3. The existence of the cosmos as a whole is radically contingent, which is to say that, while not needing an efficient cause of its coming to be, since it is everlasting, it nevertheless does need an efficient cause of its continuing

existence, to preserve it in being and prevent it from being replaced by nothingness.

4. If the cosmos needs an efficient cause of its continuing existence to prevent its annihilation, that cause must be a supernatural being, supernatural in its action, and one the existence of which is uncaused: in other words, the supreme being, or God.

As can be seen, Adler's cosmological argument differs from Aquinas's second way in certain respects. For one thing, while Aquinas argued for an uncaused first cause, Adler argues for an uncaused sustaining cause, a cause that "preserves" the universe in being". (According to some commentators Aquinas was in fact arguing, in the second way, for an ultimate sustaining cause, too.) For another thing, while in his second way Aquinas addresses "the world of sensible things" taken individually, Adler is concerned with the cause of the physical universe, the world of sensible things, as a whole, i.e., taken collectively.

The first two of Adler's propositions seem indisputable. The third and fourth, however, would doubtlessly be questioned by some. The fourth proposition will call to mind Schopenhauer's famous criticism of the cosmological argument, to the effect that the law of universal causation is not a hired cab that we can dismiss when we reach our destination. If everything needs a cause of its continuing existence, the criticism implies, then so does God. But if we allow something—God—to be uncaused, as does Adler, then to be consistent we must extend the same priviledge to the cosmos.

Others would regard this criticism as weak. The question, they say, is: Has the reality of an immaterial God been proved by material evidence? You cannot logically argue that it has not been so proved on the grounds that further questions about God have not themselves been answered. Further, they say, a request for proof of who or what made or caused or sustains an immaterial God, whose existence is thought to be proved by a cosmological argument, assumes an illogical divisibility or plurality of the immaterial deity as though it too were material, or otherwise sureptitiously ascribes to it predicates of materiality. It also in effect asks for repetition of proof already made. Many, too, are interested in how the physical universe came to be and when this question is answered "by God," regard the new question, how did God come to be, as futile to contemplate.

Concerning Adler's key third proposition, Adler's reason for thinking that the cosmos is "radically contingent" is that it is only one of a plurality of possible universes that might have been, and "whatever can be otherwise than it is can also simply not be at all." Critics may argue, however, that, for all we know, the universe was originally coded to develop as it did and had to develop as it has. We don't have any justification, they may say, for accepting Adler's claim that the universe could be otherwise than it is.

Other critics will argue that, even granting that the universe might have been otherwise that it is, it doesn't follow from this concession that the continuing existence of the universe must be caused. Might not the continuing existence of the cosmos just simply be uncaused, these critics will ask? Still other critics will say that the continuation of the universe does not need an explanation beyond the physical explanation of each event in it. That the universe does not require a nonmaterial explanation of its continuation is developed independently by each author in Chapters 26 and 27.

The critics of cosmological arguments notwithstanding, it seems quite clearly intelligible to ask what gave rise to the universe. Indeed, the human mind seems virtually compelled to ask this question. As A. C. Ewing said, the possibility that the physical universe should just have happened seems too incredible to countenance. We shall consider the possibility of a happenstance universe later.

Adler thinks to conclude from the fact that the universe had a beginning that God caused it is to beg the question, whether or not God exists. However, given that God exists as Adler thinks he has proved by his cosmological argument, Adler prefers the assumption of a created cosmos to the assumption that "a possible cosmos has everlastingly existed."

Notes

[1]New York, Macmillan Publishing Company, Inc., 1980.
[2]*Ibid.*, pp. 136-137.

25

Justification of Belief

Have you, reader, a belief in God even though his existence cannot be proved by physical evidence or demonstrated by logical argument, or even though the weight of evidence of logical argument is strongly or convincingly against his existence? Do you have a similar belief in his creation and sustenance of the cosmos and in his endowment of human beings with immortal souls?

You may ask in reply, "What kind of a God do you mean?"

Our response is, "An impersonal God, a pantheistic God or a personal or living God. Take your choice. Do you believe in some kind of God on faith alone, that is, without or against logical argument? If so, you are a fideist."

"Know," "believe," "faith," and "trust" are ambiguous words, subject to vague and tricky usage. We use "know" to mean, as lawyers say, to know either of one's own knowledge or to know on hearsay, as specified, or as denoted by context. To know of one's own knowledge means to know by one's own sensory perception, and such knowledge as well as hearsay information can be erroneous. "Knowledge" also sometimes is used to mean the veracity of belief in what is deduced from what one knows of his own knowledge or on hearsay.

"Believe" we use to mean what one thinks, on his own knowledge or on hearsay, to be true; or what one thinks, on the basis of testimony or physical evidence or on either of these bases, to be true; or what one thinks to be true on faith, that is, without or against proof and logical argument.

By "trust" we mean confidence in knowledge or in belief or in that person, being, thing, concept or opinion that is thought or believed to exist or to be right.

Belief in God may be supported by postulational reasoning like Kant's in his *Critique of Practical Reason*. That is, belief may rest on experience, e.g., ethical or aesthetic, only understandable if God, or a personal God, is postulated or hypothesized to exist. Most theology and philosophy affirming the existence of God and of immortal life have been postulational reasoning since Kant demolished traditional theoretical proofs of the existence of God and of immortal life in the *Critique of Pure Reason.*

Belief in God, or in a personal God, or in immortality, based on postulational or practical reasoning, involves inference from effect to cause, just as the teleological argument does, and as the cosmological argument does except that that argument involves the *a priori* contention that the chains of causation begin with a First Cause and that the chains of contingency end with a Self-Necessity, which are something other than material or natural. Only the ontological argument seeks to prove that God exists without empirical evidence. Other arguments and a will to believe without sufficient evidence end with something other than what is material or natural. Then they stop or resort to some kind of ontological argument to prove that that something is God and that he exists or is real.

Fideists endeavor to explain God as a person or as having something like human personal attributes, such as purpose, power, consciousness and love, so that his acts manifested in the universe and in human persons have true reality and true value.

A person's belief in God based on his or her supposed personal encounters with God or on supposed revelation of God through that person's personal experience may be justified in that person's opinion, especially if others testify to similar encounters or revelations; but testimony of these encounters and revelations does not really justify anyone, even those having the encounters or revelations, in believing in God, since the encounters and revelations are illusory and easily explained by psychology and physiology, or well may be so, and since, moreover, testimony of the encounters or revelations may be deliberately false. This is not the kind of belief and trust with which this chapter is concerned.

Human passion for immortal life

Do you, reader, passionately want to live forever even though you know that everyone must bodily die? Do you desperately desire that you are an immortal soul that is your "I?" What is your I? Who knows that better than you, so why should it be explained to you what it is? Do you, to repeat, ardently hope that your I will never cease its being?

Do you, reader, emotionally crave the eternal existence of your soul, that is your I, even though your information and intelligence convince you that your mind, like the color of your hair and your liking of cherries, is the physical product of the evolution of the universe, of our galaxy, of the solar system and finally of life on earth? Are you, reader, imbued with this craving for immortality even though your information and intelligence explain wholly the phenomenon of your mind and the identity of it, your I, and your soul?

Do you, reader, feel that your soul, your I, is something that transcends and is different from your mind, be your mind regarded as intellect or as a combination of intellect and emotion, produced by your brain, nervous system and body; and is it this other-than-mental I, or soul, that you avidly want to be immortal, no matter what your information and intelligence tell you?

Philosophical theists, who are fideists, like Martin Gardner and Miguel de Unamuno y Jugo, emphatically claim that they have a thirst for personal immortality that is unquenchable even though what they know and think convinces them of the impossibility of proving the immortality of the human soul. These philosophical theists and fideists believe that most people have the same passionate desire for immortality that they themselves have. Not to have it they consider to be inexplicable and tragic.

We, the authors, however, have no great innate craving for immortality; and we believe that many people are like us in the matter. It certainly is possible, and indeed is most natural, to want to go on living unless life becomes unbearable. It could be pleasing if after bodily death one found her or his personal soul surviving intact, and somehow continuing to live as it had during one's bodily existence, or to find one's immortal soul, at some time after bodily death, reinstated in one's former body.

The immortality that these philosophical theists and fideists so ardently desire is a personal immortality, not one in which they will be embraced by, or embrace, God or nirvana, losing in the embrace all personal memory and all sense of self, individualism and identity. They want to continue to experience, after they physically die, all the happenings, pleasures and some pains, the good and some evil, and the free will of men and women of flesh, bone and blood: caress and chastisement by their physical and social environment; eating, drinking and sex; thought and feeling; intellectual, emotional and physical change and growth; love, friendship and society; solitude and reflection; kinship with, and dominion over, physical matter, flora and fauna; and contemplation and exploration of the physical universe or of whatever realm replaces it for them. If this vast variety of personal experience is impossible in a hereafter, they want an equivalence and depend on God somehow to provide it.

Because they passionately want this personal immortality, they "believe" that they and other humans have it, but they define "belief" in this context as the will or wish to believe. They consider that it is as reasonable to believe (will or wish to believe) in the immortality of the personal immaterial human soul as it is to believe in the reality of objects outside the mind, i.e., in the universe itself. We do not know and cannot prove that objects exist outside our minds. Our belief in their existence is merely our will or wish to believe that they exist.

Our strong inclination to believe in the universe outside the mind, they say, justifies our belief in it and is identical with that belief. Likewise, these philosophical theists and fideists argue, the deep desire that they and most of humanity have for immortality of the personal human soul justifies and is identical with their belief in it. Neither this immortality nor the reality of the universe can be proved or disproved by evidence or argument. Belief in either is as justified as belief in the other. Why not, then, believe or bet that the human personal soul is immortal, since that is what they desperately want to believe and since that belief gives them, not only immeasureable pleasure of anticipating fulfillment of their ineradicable longing for personal immortality but also gives them the pleasureable relief or assurance that eventually justice will be done for and among human beings, in the future, if not in this life, as will be more fully discussed below?

We, the authors, think, however, that there is a distinction between experience of the universe and experience of the supposed immortal human soul, of significance with respect to justification of belief in each. Our experience with the universe seemingly is introduced by stimulation of our sensory receptivity by something external to it. In regard to the supposed immortal human soul, however, our experience of it is not introduced by our sensory receptivity to it. Our "experience" of our souls is not nearly so direct and immediate as is our experience of the world of external objects. That this is so is true despite the fact that there are notorious philosophical difficulties in holding that we perceive external objects directly. We have representations, ideas or images of external objects; such is not the case with regard to the immortal soul. We communicate with others at length and in detail about the world outside the mind and about our experience of it. Such communication about the soul does not occur.

We, the authors, think that love of life and desire for its continuance are fully explainable as an evolutionary biological strategy for the preservation of the species (as, indeed, is the strong inclination to believe in the external world). Therefore, a desire for personal immortality is wholly a natural phenomenon, though we profess ourselves not to crave it beyond measure. Thus, a will or wish to believe in immortality predicated on desire for it, when made the basis for belief or identified with it, can properly be called a "wilfulness" to believe.

Martin Gardner, in *The Whys of a Philosophical Scrivener* writes:

> Perhaps this desire, this fear of falling into what Lord Dunsany once called the "unreverberate blackness of the abyss," is no more than an expression of genetic mechanisms for avoiding death. Or is it more?[1]

Subsequently, Gardner says nothing to show that the desire for immortality is anything more than a biological resort for preservation of bodily life. Instead, he says:

> If there is a soul capable of existing apart from that . . . lump of tissue inside every skull, it is as hidden from us as God is hidden.[2]

Faith, Gardner says, is absurd:

> Let us admit it. Let us concede everything! To a rational mind the world looks like a world without God. It looks like a world with no hope for another life.[3]

Yet Gardner chooses to believe in personal immortality. His choice he concedes, is a kind of madness, yet notwithstanding the "madness" of the belief, Gardner maintains that he, the believer, is not mad. Nor is he, of course. We shall subsequently further consider justification of his choice to believe in immortality and in God.

God posited on immortality

Theistic dogmas do not necessarily embrace human immortality, and conversely soul dogmas do not necessarily embrace God. Early Israelite religion displayed little, if any, concern with immortality. David Elton Trueblood has observed that argument about immortality play a small role in Jesus' thought, judging from the Gospels. Jesus, he observed, based his faith in immortality on a prior faith in God.[4]

On the other hand, some atheists, among them, J. M. E. McTaggart and C. J. Ducasse, have expressed belief in immortality, the former on metaphysical, and the latter on parapsychological, grounds. However, in Western religious thought beliefs in a personal God and in the immortality of the human soul, while more often than not both held, usually have been interdependent of each other.

Gardner and Unamuno base their belief (will or wish to believe) in a personal God on their own, and what they think is common, passionate desire for the immortality of the soul in its personal character. That is, they posit not only their belief in the immortal soul, but also their belief in a personal God, on their deeper hunger for immortality. Their belief in a personal God is secondary. Only through the agency of a personal God is the immortality of the personal soul possible or likely, they think.

Could you, reader, expect that an impersonal universe or an impersonal deity without something like your intellect and your feeling, even though responsible for your origin as part of the physical universe, would or could preserve you personally, with something like your intellect, feeling, memory and continuing identity, after your physical death and dissolution into dust, even after human kind ceases to exist on this planet and even after this planet and the Milky Way are no longer?

Unamuno especially, Gardner less emphatically, find their way to a personal God through his role as a provider of that personal immortality that they crave. This way to a personal God is perfectly clear to Unamuno. It suffices for Gardner emotionally, though he buttresses his confidence in it with the practical reasoning of Kant regarding morality as necessarily presupposing God, with Gardner's own view of the essence of Pascal's wager and, most of all, with James' elucidation of the necessity of emotional choice where proof and argument are inconclusive to the intellect.

Gardner and Unamuno understand Kant also to posit his belief in God fundamentally on a passionate want of the man, Kant, for personal survival after death, notwithstanding repudiation by the philosopher, Kant, of all proof and argument ever made, that human immortality and a personal God exist. Kant, writes Gardner, "may have thought he posited God to make sense of morality; actually he posited God because he needed God in order to live."[5]

Unamuno, in *The Tragic Sense of Life,* writes:

Whoever reads the *Critique of Practical Reason* carefully and without blinkers will see that, in strict fact, the existence of God is therein deduced from the immortality of the soul, and not the immortality of the soul from the existence of God. The categorical imperative leads us to a moral postulate which necessitates in its turn, in the telelogical or rather eschatological sense, the immortality of the soul, and in order to sustain this immortality God is introduced. All the rest is jugglery of the professional philosopher.[6]

Gardner further observes:

Kant argued that it was necessary to posit God to satisfy a universal desire for moral justice. Unamuno did not disagree. He simply saw more clearly than Kant, or perhaps more clearly than Kant was willing to admit, that the desire for moral justice flows from a deeper passion. For Unamuno, for all those who do not want to die, who do not want those whom they love to die, God is a necessary posit to escape from unbearable anguish.[7]

Unamuno thought it morally monstrous not to want personal immortality and not to want to believe in a personal God who has given personal immortality to oneself and to other human beings. However, he claimed that . . . "as a matter of fact, those who deny God deny Him because of their despair at not finding Him."[8]

To assert as Unamuno does, apparently without dissent by Gardner, that it is morally monstrous not to want personal immortality and a personal God who bestows it is an *argumentum ad hominem*. Why should an atheist want what he is convinced is impossible? Why should an agnostic who sees no possibility of a future life want it? Nor, certainly, do atheists and agnostics necessarily "abandon" out of "despair" what they deem to be a foolish and childish hope. They do not entertain the notion at all.

Unamuno's deep passionate desire for immortality and his belief (will to believe) in it and in a personal God because of the passion led him, though a like passion and belief well might not lead others, to extol social and economic strife, war and religious persecution, at least where "righteously" motivated. He wrote:

> My immediate first impulse is to protest against the inquisitor and to prefer the merchant who comes to offer me wares. But when my impressions are clarified by reflection, I begin to see that the inquisitor, when he acts from a right motive, treats me as a man, as an end in myself, and if he molests me it is from a charitable wish to save my soul. . . .
>
> Similarly, there is much more humanity in war than in peace. Non-resistance to evil implies resistance to good, and to take the offensive, leaving the defensive out of the question, is perhaps the divined thing in humanity. War is the school of fraternity and the bond of love; it is war that has brought people into touch with one another, by mutual aggression and collision, and has been the cause of their knowing and loving one another. Human love knows no purer embrace, or one more fruitful in its consequences than that between victor and vanquished on the battlefield. And even the purified hate that springs from war is frutiful. War is, in its strictest sense, the sanctification of homicide; Cain is redeemed as a leader of armies. And if Cain had not killed his brother Abel, perhaps he would have died by the hand of Abel. God revealed Himself above all in war; He began by being the God of battles; and one of the greatest services of the Cross is that, in the form of the sword-hilt, it protects the hand that wields the sword.[9]

Though Unamuno elsewhere in *The Tragic Sense of Life* warns of, and condemns, fanaticism in clinging tenaciously to tenets supposedly based on reason, his glorification of social and economic strife, war and religious persecution, where the goal is realization of what one wants God to want, certainly is a bigotry of the "heart"—of feeling—and of the worst imaginable sort. Obviously, an atheist or agnostic, viewing human life as a once happening for each of us, has no reason to devalue it as against its continuance or having another life after death, in appraisal of economic, political and religious controversy and in justification of oppression and killing of others in order to "save" them out of "love" for them.

Trueblood asserts, in contrast with Unamuno, that belief in immortality is "secondary to belief in God, both temporally and logically. It came late in the development of Hebrew faith, and it came late because it is strictly derivative."[10]

Trueblood's comment as to Jesus being little concerned with immortality is noted above. Trueblood also believes that immortality is often of less concern to the devout person than to the unbeliever, though he agrees with Unamuno that a personal God is necessary to human immortality.

An emotional choice

For many persons who think that God's existence, or a personal God's existence, cannot be proved by evidence or logic, that is, by science or *a priori* argument, it is important, nevertheless, that they believe or disbelieve in it or that they choose neither to believe nor disbelieve in it. The importance to them of making the choice may be in how it affects their view of the universe, in how it affects the way in which they live this life and in how it affects their expectancy of life after physical death. Other persons may be not much concerned with the effect of their choice on how they regard afterlife. Still others may be concerned only with how their choice affects their view of the universe; their ethical standard and valuation of life may be related to whether or not they believe in God or in a personal God; and they may think and feel that God, if he exists, will not punish them in a life after physical death, either for nonbelief or for disbelief in him in this life.

This choice for all persons who consider it important is for them what William James has called "a live option." An option, in order to be a live one in James' view, had to be plausible, important and forced. By "forced" he meant that the exercise of it could not be avoided. A choice between taking and not taking an umbrella to a ball game is not forced because one can avoid the option by not going to the ball game. But if he is asked to go to a ball game, his choice to accept or not to accept the invitation is forced; he cannot avoid making it.

James, Gardner and Unamuno think that if the existence of God is an issue that is important to one and if the issue cannot be resolved scientifically or logically, then he is faced with a live option to believe or disbelieve in God, which he must exercise emotionally only. They deny that he has a third choice: neither to believe nor disbelieve. This third choice is in effect a choice not to believe, they argue. They overlook that the third choice also is a choice not to disbelieve. Thus, they do not perceive that it is in fact a third choice, as it is.

James, Gardner and Unamuno emotionally choose to believe, meaning that they choose to will to believe, though they admit that to believe in this sense is not to know. Nevertheless, they believe more firmly in a personal God than they believe in the world or universe which they "know."

When these and other philosophical fideists equate belief with a will or wish to believe and admit that belief is not knowledge, they in effect confess to be agnostics, though they deny that agnosticism is a third alternative in emotional exercise of the option to believe or not believe in God or a personal God.

The live option, to be emotionally exercised, is to believe or not believe in a personal God, for James, Gardner and Unamuno, and also for Kant, Kierkegaard and Pascal, and for all fideists who emotionally desire a relationship with God as a person and who desire an afterlife as much like present life as possible. The God that they envision and feel for is one who thinks and loves and has attributes that make him a person or like a person. Only a personal God insures personal immortality. The choice between belief and disbelief in a nonpersonal deity or a deity who created and then abandoned the universe, though possibly of importance to others, is of no emotional importance to them.

A wager

Another fideistic approach to God, usually pursued to a personal God, is to wager that he exists, which is something very much like willing or wishing to believe in him and, therefore, believing in him. Blaise Pascal made this approach famous. Because one has far more to gain from belief than from disbelief, belief is more sensible. To wager is necessary because whether or not God exists cannot be determined by proof and logic.

Fideists continue to buttress their belief with the essence of the wager approach, doing so without reference to the rewards and punishments for belief and disbelief according to Pascal's seventeenth century Catholicism. There are still rewards, fideists like James and Gardner think, in satisfaction in the way one lives and in pleasureable anticipation of a future life, if one bets that a personal God exists. Gardner writes that he thinks "James would have liked the way Count Manuel, in James Branch Cabell's *Figures of Earth* formulates the wager," to-wit:

> "That may very well be, sir, but it is much more comfortable to live with than your opinion, and living is my occupation just now. Dying I shall attend to in due turn, and, of the two, my opinion is the more pleasant to live with. And thereafter, if your opinion be right, I shall never even know that my opinion was wrong: so I have everything to gain, in the way of pleasureable anticipations anyhow, and nothing whatever to lose, by clinging to the foolish fond old faith which my fathers had before me," said Manuel as sturdily as ever.[11]

The reply of one who wagers that God does not exist, to one who makes the contrary wager because of enhanced satisfaction with this life and pleasureable anticipation of the next, could be that his satisfaction with this life is greater if he is entirely on his own in living it without possibility of being swayed by the possibility of a future life, and that he thinks that, if most astonishingly there is a future life, he will enjoy it fully as much as he would if in this life he anticipated it. Also, he is certain that God, if God exists, would not in his future life punish him because in this life he believed neither in God nor in a future life.

God as essential to ethical life

Immanuel Kant thought that practically a belief in a personal God and in immortal life gave justification and meaningfulness to ethical living and to never-ceasing endeavor to improve the ethical quality of one's life; and he thought that only by belief in an immortal life bestowed on one by a personal God could one regard one's self as never-ceasingly endeavoring to improve one's self ethically. Therefore, one is justified in belief in a personal God and in personal immortality, though it is impossible by evidence or logical argument to demonstrate that God exists and that humans have immortal souls. Kant made this "leap of faith" as Kierkegaard called it, in *The Critique of Practical Reason*, after having demolished all traditional proofs of God's existence in the *Critique of Pure Reason*.

One can call Kant's practical belief in God and in immortal human life pure fideism or regard it as a moral argument for the existence of God.

It is more accurate, however, to regard it as belief for practical reasons. Likewise, Unamuno's belief because of passion for life, James' will to believe because one is faced with a live option and Pascal's belief on wager because one has much to gain and little to lose by it, are also belief for practical reasons.

Practical reasons for fideism have no significance for an atheist or agnostic whose ethics and asthetics are grounded in self, society, life and the universe, satisfy her or him, and are considered by her or him to be the same as they would be, or superior to what they would be, if they were grounded in belief in God and in human immortality. Some theists and fideists claim that agnostics and atheists unwittingly are beneficiaries of ethical standards of their culture, founded on the religion of their culture. This may be true, but the atheist or agnostic who adopts those standards may do so only because they are justified by his own view of himself, of humanity and of the universe. In any event, his ethics and aesthetics do not depend on his belief in God and in human immortality.

Questions of justice

Another practical reason sometimes assigned for belief in personal immortality and in a personal God, though his existence cannot be demonstrated to the intellect by science and logic, is the rectification in a future life of wrongs and injustice in this life. Another way, however, of regarding the problem of evil, whether one is theistic, deist, pantheistic, atheist or agnostic, is that its emergence is a concomitant of the evolution of life from matter, and most of us are glad enough to have life though it is beset with problems which we do, or should do, our best to solve and minimize.

If there is no free will, why should a personal God punish humans in a future life for wrongs done by them in this life? If there is free will by which some go astray, why should a personal God punish them when he endowed them with free will that made it possible for them to do wrong?

Still another practical reason for pure fideism, urged by Unamuno and Gardner, is the injustice of giving us, or of our having, this good life and then, though we desperately want it to continue forever, to take it from us, or for it to cease, at death. Believe, says Unamuno, that this most evil injustice will not be meted to, or befall, us. Accordingly, believe in a personal God and in personal survival, and live accordingly.

264 Justification of Belief

death without personal survival need not be viewed by an atheist or an agnostic, or even by a theist, as the slightest injustice if he regards reflective life, conscious of its consciousness and of the universe, as a most fortunate and marvelous evolutionary occurrence, whether or not it is through the grace of God. "Sufficient unto the day is the good thereof," he may say, and add "Thy will be done, if indeed Thou art."

He may say further to himself, and to God if God exists, "The emergence of human intelligence from matter may have been inevitable, but more likely it has been by chance insofar as physics reveals, though your hidden hand may have guided the process. Evil, including pain and injustice, necessarily have accompanied the happening, or have come along with the gift, if it is your gift. To some extent evil can be understood. Violence is necessarily incident to cosmic evolution. To be free in will is necessary to personality; or at least the consciousness of freedom of will, whether or not the freedom exists in fact, is necessary to the consciousness of personality. Freedom of will can be only at the risk of causing some wilfulness and disagreement, which lead to evil or to what some regard as evil. To the extent that evil is not understood, there is no sense in blaming blind nature for it; nor is there any sense in blaming you, God, for it, if you exist, since we cannot know your reasons, and it is vain to judge them by the standards by which we approve or disapprove our conduct.

"We do not see that good and evil in this life call for rectification in the next life or are a reason for believing in our surviving our human death. Nor do we perceive why we should despise and not be delighted with the happening or gift of life because it will end with our physical death. Far be it from us to lecture the universe on the morality of physics or to lecture you, God, if you exist, on divine conduct."

God as essential to reality

Another practical reason why some fideists believe in a personal God is the essentiality, as they see it, of God to reality or, what may be the same, the essentiality, as they see it, of God as consciousness of the universe to its meaningfulness or reality. The rationale of their belief is in effect a cosmological argument for the existence of a personal God based on the contingency of reality, or on the fact that there is human consciousness.

Hans Küng in his scholarly and comprehensive *Does God Exist? An Answer for Today* "prepares" his "solution" in "extensive discussions of the natural theology of Vatican I, on the dialectical theology of Barth and Bultmann and Kant's theology of moral postulates." He "briefly recapitulates" this solution.[12]

> If God is, he is the answer to the radical uncertainty of reality.
> The fact that God is can be assumed not strictly in virtue of proof or indication of pure reason (natural theology),
> not unconditionally in virtue of a moral postulate of practical reason (Kant),
> not exclusively in virtue of the biblical testimony (dialectical theology),
> but only in a confidence rooted in reality itself.
> This trusting commitment to an ultimate ground, support and meaning of reality— and not only the commitment to the Christian God—is itself rightly designated in general usage as "belief" in God, as "faith in God."

Humans have free will, Küng says, to have a fundamental trust in God as a "primal ground, primal support and primal goal" of reality or to have, instead, a fundamental trust in reality without God. To abstain from voting is to deny God.

> Denial of God implies an ultimately unjustified fundamental trust in reality. Atheism cannot suggest any condition for the possibility of uncertain reality. If someone denies God, he does not know why he ultimately trusts in reality.[13]

Belief in God, like fundamental trust, is

> a matter not only of human reason, but of the whole concrete living man . . . there is no logically conclusive proof for the reality of reality, neither is there one for the reality of God. The proof of God is no more logically conclusive than is love. The relationship of God is one of trust; but not irrational; there is a reflection on the reality of God emerging from human experience and calling for man's free decision.[14]

Küng in effect says that reality is understandable and truly real because of belief in God. He does not explain how God or belief in God makes uncertain reality certain. He does assert that one who has belief in God can "with good reason perceive in all disunions a unity, in all worthlessness a value, in all meaninglessness a meaning of the reality of the world and man."[15]

One can conjecture that why God as the necessary cornerstone of reality makes all reality, including God, truly real is that God has consciousness. Küng hints at this explanation in saying that security in trust and belief in God is not "simply an abstract security, in isolation from my fellow men, but always involves a concrete reference to the human 'thou.'"[16]

Küng does not regard God as a person as human beings are persons, but also he does not regard him as impersonal. In every affirmation of human qualities of God they must first be "negated and then raised to the level of the infinite." With regard to the use of the term "person" this means:

> God is not a person as a man is a person. The all-embracing and all-penetrating is never an object that man can view from a distance in order to make statements about it. . . . God transcends also the concept of person. God is more than person. . . .
> God is not neuter, not an "it," but a God of men. . . . He is spirit in creative freedom, the primordial identity of justice and love, one who faces me as embracing all interhuman personality. If, with the religious philosophers of the East, we want to call the absolutely last and absolutely first reality the "void" or "Absolute Nothingness," then we must also call it "being itself," which manifests itself with infinite understanding. It will be better to call the most real reality not personal or nonpersonal but—if we attach importance to the terminology—transpersonal or suprapersonal.[17]

Thus, the God who, in Küng's view, makes all conditionally-real reality truly real is a God who is transpersonal or suprapersonal. Presumably Küng thinks, though he does not explicitly say, that God has transpersonal or suprapersonal consciousness of the universe. Since, as Küng says, God "is not an infinite—and still less a finite— *alongside* or *above* the finite," but "is the infinite in all finite,"[18] it follows that one is justified in saying that the cosmos according to Küng, is imbued with the infinite transpersonal or suprapersonal mind of God. Thus, God explains and conditions reality for Küng.

"Faith" is defined by Paul Tillich as ultimate concern, and the ultimate concern of humanity, he thinks, is with the Ultimate, which is the "non-symbolic element in our image of God—namely . . . ultimate reality, being itself, ground of being, power of being." Our highest derivative concern from the ultimate concern is the image of God as "a highest being, a being with the characteristics of the highest perfection;" and this image is symbolical of the Absolute or the non-symbolic element of God. In "our relationship to" the

> ultimate we symbolize and must symbolize. We could not be in communication with God if he were only "ultimate being." And so in the symbolic form of speaking about him, we have both that which transcends infinitely our experience of ourselves as persons, and that which is so adequate to our being persons that we can say "Thou" to God, and can pray to him. And these two elements must be preserved. If we preserve only the element of the unconditional, then no relationship to God is possible. If we preserve only the element of the ego-thou relation-

ship, as it is called today, we lose the element of the divine—namely, the unconditional which transcends subject and object and all other polarities.[19]

On lower levels of symbolism of God (the absolute or being in itself) there are his attributes "taken from experienced qualities we have ourselves," such as love, mercy, omnipotence, omniscience, omnipresence; his acts such as creating the world, sending his son, fulfilling the world; he and his son having substance; incarnation; and sacraments.[20] These symbols, taken literally, embrace wholly and endlessly only absurdities. The truth of symbols "is their adequacy to the religious situation in which they are created, and their inadequacy to another situation is their untruth."[21]

Tillich predicates his understanding of faith as ultimate concern in an Ultimate Reality, which is being in itself, and is the unsymbolic in "God," on analysis of the human situation in relation to the world, which is essentially what Küng does.

Tillich also substantially agrees with Küng as to the personality or nonpersonality of God, in our opinion. Tillich wrote:

"Personal God" does not mean that God is person. It means that God is the ground of everything personal and that he carries within himself the ontological power of personality. He is not a person but he is not less than personal. It should not be forgotten that classical theology employed the term *persona* for the trinitarian hypostases, but not for God himself. God became "a person" only in the nineteenth century, in connection with the Kantian separation of nature ruled by physical law from personality ruled by moral law.[22]

Both Tillich and Küng think that God is not a person as a human being is a person, and they agree that God is not less than a human person. For Küng God embraces all interhuman personality. Tillich thinks that God or the Absolute contains the ontological power of human personality. What they say is substantially the same, and it is in accord with viewing human personality as having evolved from matter through natural law, or, in other words, from God or from the Ultimate through the evolution of the physical universe. God (according to Küng) or the Ultimate (according to Tillich) conditions reality, and, according to both, human personality is a part of reality.

Küng says no more as to the essence of God than that he is the answer to the radical uncertainty of reality and to human personality; and Tillich says no more as to the essence of the Absolute than that it is being in itself and absolute reality and the ontological source of human personality. What each says accords with our (the authors') view that human personality is a natural consequence, whether inevitably or by chance, of the Big Bang, and, beyond the Big Bang, of whatever it was, if anything, that caused the Big Bang. Küng and Tillich would have to doubt, one must think on the basis of their theology, that a person like a human person caused the Big Bang, which is the expanding universe.

Professor Trueblood regarded Tillich's view that God is not a person though he is the ultimate source of human personality (which is also Küng's view) as mystifying, especially in view of Tillich's making "freedom his main point of philosophical departure" and in view of Tillich's having said that "Man cannot be ultimately concerned about anything that is less than personal." Trueblood dismisses Tillich's distinction between God as "a person" and "not less than a person" as a mere quibble, and Trueblood agrees with William Temple, justly considered, in Trueblood's opinion, "the most distinguished theologian of our century," that "God is the explanation of the world because He is Person."

Trueblood writes:

> The central point is that, if God is not personal, in a literal sense, then God is not the ultimate explanation of that which most requires explanation. What baffles the materialist is the emergence of even the finite personality . . . in our fellows and . . . in ourselves. If God is only an impersonal force, then the stream has risen higher than its source, for we can at least be certain that personality appears in us.[23]

But Trueblood goes on to say:

> No one in his senses would think of interpreting the personal character of God as limited to the low level of personality illustrated in ourselves. Of course, God is more than we are, but He must be at least as much as we are.[24]

The above statements seem to be substantially in accord with Tillich's and Küng's view that God is not less than personal notwithstanding Trueblood's disclaimer.

Unamuno thought that he saw clearly that his craving for eternal life required the posit of a personal God, a consciousness of the universe, whose consciousness distinguishes and thereby creates reality from nothingness, and is essential to God's bestowing on human beings both conscious mortal and conscious immortal life. He wrote:

> We must needs believe in the other life, in the eternal life beyond the grave, and in an individual and personal life in which each one of us may feel his consciousness and feel that it is united, without being confounded, with all other consciousnesses in the Supreme Consciousness, in God; we must needs believe in that other life in order that we may live this life, and endure it, and give it meaning and finality.[25]

Also, Unamuno asks,

What would a universe be without any consciousness capable of reflecting and knowing it? What would objectified reason be without will and feeling? For us it would be equivalent to nothing—a thousand times more dreadful than nothing.[26]

For Unamuno it is God as supreme consciousness, in which we shall merge while retaining our personality, that gives finality to the universe and to ourselves. Thus, he agrees with Küng, Tillich and Trueblood insofar as they consider God or the Absolute as conditioning reality, i.e., making it truly real.

From what has been said, it is clear that the practical reason why some fideists believe in a God, or a personal God, is the meaninglessness of the universe in the absence of consciousness of it. The rationale of their belief is something like a cosmological argument for the existence of God based on the fact that there is a human consciousness. More accurately, however, the rationale for their belief is, as said, the practical reason that consciousness of the universe is essential to its comprehensibleness. That consciousness has emerged from matter does not prove the existence of a God, or of a personal God, but it does, they say, justify belief in him as the consciousness or as the source of consciousness of the universe. To believe in a personal or a suprapersonal or transpersonal God is the only way in which we can understand the intelligibleness, that is, the reality of the universe. Without this belief we are reduced to nihilism, believing in nothing.

This way of justifying belief without sufficient evidence or logical argument for a God's, or a personal God's, existence, is a further utilization of Kant's practical method. It goes beyond making ethics presumptively authoritative and practical to making the universe presumptively real and practical for intelligent and purposeful living, by the posit of a personal or suprapersonal or transpersonal God, as the consciousness, or the source of consciousness of the universe.

Justification on basis of consciousness

Suppose that we are not immortal, that in time all life ceases on earth and that there is nowhere else in the universe a consciousness of it, like human consciousness. That certainly was the state of the universe before consciousness like ours evolved from it, unless there is divine consciousness. It certainly will be the fate of the universe at some future time as well, unless there is divine consciousness.

How, asks these fideists, can the universe exist without consciousness of it? How is it distinguishable from nothing if there is not a distinguisher? What is reality other than something and consciousness of it? God equated with consciousness, in their view, makes the universe meaningful to us even though human or like consciousness at one time was not, and at some future time will not be. Therefore, it is argued in effect, belief in the unproved existence of God is practically justified. The argument obviously is remindful of the anthropic principle discussed in Chapter 19 and also of Berkeley's idealism.

The answer to justification of belief in this manner is that while the universe necessarily, if there is no conscious God, is meaningless before consciousness evolved in it, it becomes meaningful to consciousness when consciousness does emerge in it. Accordingly, the universe has the potentiality of becoming meaningful to consciousness evolving in it before consciousness does evolve in it, whether or not there is divine consciousness of it. After consciousness, other than divine if there is divine consciousness, ceases in the universe, it still at one time had consciousness of it, other than divine. Accordingly, the universe or reality ultimately is distinguishable to us from nothingness because of its potentiality for producing consciousness of it. Therefore, God, or a personal or suprapersonal or transpersonal God, need not be posited in order to make the universe meaningful to us.

Weight of evidence; probability; and belief

The forgoing discussion of belief avoids the weight of evidence as proving or disproving, or as affecting the probability or improvability of, the existence of God, or a personal God, of his creation and sustenance of the universe, and of his bestowal of human immortality. However, philosophical theists and fideists like Kant, Kierkegaard, James, Unamuno and Gardner hold staunchly to their belief, though they consider the weight of the evidence and of logical argument other than those practical reasons that they propound for their belief, to be overwhelmingly against the truth of their belief.

In cases at law juries, or judges trying a case without a jury, must render a verdict or finding according to the weight of the evidence if the case is a civil suit; and in a criminal trial the jury, or the judge if jury trial has been waived, must acquit the accused unless his guilt has been proved beyond a reasonable doubt. A verdict or finding must be rendered though the evidence lacks certainty, and often the evidence is more or less uncertain.

A similar situtation often exists in political elections, in determination of public or business policy and in other instances, where factual issues must be decided.

A decision must be made and one seeks to make it according to the weight of the relevant evidence. One considers not only the obvious bearing of evidence on involved issues, but also the bearing of implication, varying in clarity and significance, of the evidence on the issues. One considers even bare suggestions and hints in the evidence, especially their cumulative effect. The endeavor is to determine what probably is true and to ascertain the greatest probability. The same procedure in evaluating evidence is pursued preparatory to wagering.

For many people it is likewise as to belief or disbelief concerning God and immortality. On the other hand, strongly motivated believers like those we have been considering choose and will to believe though the weight, or even the overwhelming weight, of the evidence is against the truth of their belief. There never has been conclusive evidence and logic against the truth of their belief, but one suspects that, even if there were, they would steadfastly hold to it. Their will to believe is, from an intellectual perspective, only sheer wilfulness. They justify their belief as mandated by their hearts.

Modern cosmology and belief

The tremendous revolution and increase in this century in knowledge of matter and the cosmos can have no negative effect on the will to believe in God, or a personal God, in his creation and sustenance of the universe or in human immortality, of those who hold fast to their belief notwithstanding the weight or overwhelming or even conclusive weight of evidence and logical argument against the truth of that belief. Certainly, the new cosmology will not affect their belief if they regard the total evidence, including the new cosmology, as evenly divided on the issues involved in their belief.

On the other hand, the new physics and new cosmology present new facts and theories and raise new questions of possibly enormous importance to those who choose to govern their belief or disbelief as to God and immortality by their view of the weight of the evidence and of probability established by the evidence, much as though they were compelled to render a verdict in a law case or as though they were placing a heavy wager on the outcome of a game, an automobile or horse race or a political election. This is especially true of those who

suppress emotional drives stemming from parental and cultural influence, in choosing to believe or disbelieve or to do neither.

The new facts and theories presented, and questions raised, by the
new physics and new cosmology having possible relevancy and weight
as to belief or disbelief in God or immortality include, *inter alia*, the
origin and evolution of the universe in a Big Bang from a minute or even
dimensionless Little Bomb; the possible coming-to-be of that Little Bomb
out of nothing; the one-time compression in the Little Bomb of all matter
and radiation now in the universe; the unity of spacetime and its
commencement with the Big Bang; the denial of absolute time and of
absolute space; the possibility of the present universe being only an
expansionary state in an eternal alternation of Big Bangs and Big
Crunches; the expansive force in the Big Bang and the balance between
it and the implosive force of gravity; the weaving of matter and of
radiation on the expanding loom of spacetime; the emergence of life and
of the human intellect on this earth; the probable emergence of like life
and intellect at millions, if not billions, of other places in the universe;
and the resemblance of the cosmos to that which an intellectual
Architect would design for a purpose, though one cannot fathom that
purpose unless it is life and intelligence such as ours, perhaps a vain
conjecture.

Of no small importance as to the possible existence of God, or a
personal God, and as to the possibility of human immortality is the
insignificance of man and woman, despite their amazing reflective
intelligence, in the vast cosmos. Are God and immortality perhaps
posited by some on a mistaken view of human importance in the
cosmos?

What implications these and other staggering facts and theories
presented, and questions raised, by modern physics, astronomy and
cosmology have that may profoundly affect mental persuasion and
emotional belief, and traditional proofs and arguments concerning God
and immortality must be determined individually by each of us who are
interested in the matter. This book is one of only a few books pioneering
in the study of these implications and of their effect on religious thought
and justification of belief.

Notes

[1] New York, William Monroe and Company, Inc., 1983, p. 13.
[2] *Ibid.*, p. 214.
[3] *Ibid.*, p. 214
[4] *Philosophy of Religion.* New York, Harper and Brothers, 1967, p. 303.

5 Gardner, *op.cit.*, p. 216.
6 London, Macmillan and Co., Ltd., 1926, pp. 3–4.
7 Gardner, *op.cit.*, p. 217.
8 Unamuno, *op.cit.*, p. 164.
9 *Ibid.*, p. 278–279.
10 Trueblood, *op.cit.*, p. 304.
11 Quoted in Gardner, *op.cit.*, pp. 219–220.
12 Edward Quinn, Trans., Gardner City, New York, Doubleday and Company, Inc., 1980, pp. 569–570.
13 *Ibid.*, p. 571.
14 *Ibid.*, p. 574.
15 *Ibid.*, p. 572.
16 *Ibid.*
17 *Ibid.*, pp. 632–633.
18 *Ibid.*, p. 632.
19 "Religious Symbols and Our Knowledge of God," in William Rowe and William J. Wainwright, Eds: *The Philosophy of Religion: Selected Readings*. New York, Harcourt, Brau, and Jovanovich, Inc., 1973, p. 484–485.
20 *Ibid.*
21 *Ibid.*, p. 487.
22 *Systematic Theology*, vol 1. Chicago, University of Chicago Press, 1951, pp. 244–245.
23 Trueblood, *op.cit.*, p. 270.
24 *Ibid.*
25 Unamuno, *op.cit.*, p. 251
26 *Ibid.*, pp. 183–184.

26

What I Think

Brooke N. Moore

Scientific cosmology and the cosmological argument

Until recently traditional cosmological argumentation in support of God's existence as the creator and ultimate explanation of the universe has been widely rejected by naturalistic philosophers because they have implicitly subscribed to a steady-state-universe or oscillating-universe theory, or to some other theory according to which the universe has always existed. Each natural event, they have thought, can in principle be explained by reference to some earlier natural event, and thus there has seemed to them to be no need to invoke a non-natural entity in the explanation of the universe.

However, critics of the naturalistic philosophers have disagreed. Granted, these critics have said, granted the universe may always have existed and granted there may therefore not have been a first natural event, still, shouldn't we also seek an explanation for the entire class of such events? F. C. Copleston, in the radio debate with Bertrand Russell discussed in Chapter 24, argued that the explanation of the entire class of natural events must lie with God. For natural events are contingent and need not have happened. Thus, since they did happen, they require explanation—and an explanation for the entire class of such events must therefore make reference to a non-contingent being, a necessary being that has the reason for its existence within itself.

Russell was dissatisfied with Copleston's argument because he thought we have done all that can be done to explain an event if we state the cause of the event; to suppose that the universe as a whole must have its own explanation, Russell maintained, is mistakenly to assume that what holds for the parts must hold for the whole. Russell, I think, assumed that the universe just always was and that there was no earliest event; and, given this assumption, perhaps there is no clear meaning in asking for a single explanation of the class of all events. If every event were explained by reference to an earlier event, then every event would, after all, have been explained.

But now current scientific evidence and theory overwhelmingly indicate that the universe had an absolute beginning out of a singularity or compact minuteness in the Big Bang, and thus suggests that there was, perhaps, a first natural (i.e., physical or material) event. So naturalistic philosophers who, like myself, were accustomed to regard the universe as having existed forever, are forced to reconsider the cosmological argument. For, assuming that there was a first natural event, either that event is explicable or it is not, and, if it is, then it would certainly seem that the explanation must refer to some non-natural phenomenon, a phenomenon which, since non-natural, rightly would deserve the name, "God."

Further, it certainly is difficult to believe that the first natural event has no explanation. This event is, after all, or was, quite significant. Indeed, everything depends on its having happened. A special effort of the mind seems required to believe that an occurrence so important could merely have just happened, for no reason, fortuitously. The colossal size of the universe alone overwhelms us into belief that the event that led to this vast and complex conglomeration of matter and energy be explainable. The possibility that the physical universe should just have happened, as A. C. Ewing said, and as we noted in Chapter 24, seems too incredible to countenance.

In addition, to say that there is no explanation of the genesis of the universe, to say that it all arose through some random, uncaused, inexplicable occurrence, would not this be to deny that there is or could ever be a complete explanation of the cosmos? Certainly, we have always believed that a complete explanation of the universe could well be beyond the power of the finite mind to comprehend. But that there might be no explanation at all, this is a possibility that seems to undermine the value and purpose of human inquiry. If there is no complete explanation, then to what do all other explanations point? To what Final Answer do they make advance? Are the glorious accomplishments of human scientific curiosity and endeavor no more than mental amusements with perhaps some incidental utilitarian side benefits? For such they might seem to be, if there is no complete explanation of which they are a part.

But these considerations, while having much force psychologically, carry very little weight logically. Whether an event is regarded as important or signficant is one question; whether it is caused is another, and wholly unrelated, question, and the latter question cannot be answered by considering the impact the answer may have on our opinions about the value of scientific inquiry. It is therefore important to consider carefully whether there is a rational justification for the belief that the first natural event is explainable.

Inductive grounds for thinking that the first natural event is explainable

Our experience consists largely of witnessing occurrences for almost all of which explanations may be found. Accordingly, don't we therefore have compelling grounds for believing that all occurrences, including the very first occurrence, have explanations? To reason thusly from what holds for a sample of a class to what holds for another member of the class is to reason inductively, and the inductive reasoning in question, based as it is on such a large sample of occurrences, all of which have explanations, to the likelihood that another occurrence too has an explanation, would appear at first glance to be logically strong indeed.

Yet I do not think this inductive argument provides much justification for believing that there is an explanation for the first natural event. The difficulty in the argument becomes clear when we consider what must be involved in an explanation of an event.

There are many different kinds of things that people need explained, and many different reasons why they need explanations. For this reason, there are many different kinds of explanations. There are explanations of what something is like, how it works, what it means, what it might lead to, what good it is and so on. However, when it is asserted that everything has an explanation and that, therefore, the first event must have an explanation, it is safe to assume that the type of explanation in question is one that makes clear why a thing happened by reference to its causation.

Causal explanations are seemingly of two types, physical-causal explanations and psychological-causal explanations. Physical-causal explanations have two parts or components. One part, Part A, must make reference to certain earlier specific events, and the other part, Part B, must make reference to a law that governs those events.

For example, a puddle of water on the kitchen floor might be explained by saying simply that someone spilled water out of a glass (Part A). But implicit in this statement is Part B, a law to the effect that spilled things fall to the earth.

Both parts of the explanation are required for the explanation to succeed. If it were not a general law that unsupported things fall to the earth, then the puddle would not be explained by stating how the water became unsupported. Equally, citing a general law about the behavior of unsupported things would do nothing to explain the puddle unless we also gave information with respect to how the water became unsupported.

It is difficult to see how the first natural (i.e., physical, material) event could be given a physical-causal explanation, because the two requirements for physical causal explanations cannot be met. First, there are no earlier specific physical events. Second, because of this there are no applicable general laws that govern those earlier events. Therefore, the fact that all other natural events we have encountered have explanations of this sort does not provide inductive warrent for believing that the first natural event has an explanation of this sort, for the events we have experienced are fundamentally different from the first event: they, unlike it, are all preceded by earlier events that are subject to general laws.

So, if the first event has a causal explanation, it is not a physical-causal explanation, as is perhaps already obvious from the fact that the first event was first.

Quite commonly, we do explain physical events in psychological terms, as due to some agent's motives, desires, fears, inclinations, or other psychological states. Thus, for instance, we explain the bright lights that surround the house on the corner by saying that the owner is afraid of darkness or intruders. We explain a boy's selfish behavior with respect to his brother by reference, perhaps, to the deeper psychology of sibling rivalry. We also sometimes explain physical events by reference to some agent's reasons, as when we say that a man was killed because the killer reasoned he had nothing to lose, and much to gain, by killing him. It is true, we do not ordinarily say that a person's reasons caused his actions, but we do explain why a person did something by citing his reasons, and thus we may treat reason-explanations as a kind of psychological-causal explanation.

A difficulty in the view that there might be a psychological explanation of a first physical or natural event is that logically nothing whatsoever, psychological or otherwise, could possibly occur prior to the first event. This difficulty might be circumvented by waiving the requirement to which physical-causal explanations are subject and saying that a psychological explanation of an event need not make reference to earlier psychological factors but only to concurrent factors. We do say, for example, that one moved one's arm because one decided to, and deciding seems sometimes to occur contemporaneously with the physical activity so caused (though this view is controversial). The difficulty might also be circumvented by saying that psychological occurrences take place in non-physical "psychological" time, though I suspect that this distinction would, on scrutiny, turn out to be incoherent.

A further difficulty is that psychological-causal explanations might also seem to require reference to a general law that governs the nonphysical conditions that are said to cause the physical happening. (Such psychological laws are not deemed to hold as inexorably as physical laws; but still, unless it were in general true that fear of darkness and intruders would lead a person, under certain appropriate circumstances, to install bright lights around his house, then we would fail to explain the lights that surround the corner house by mentioning the owner's fears.) But in the case of the first event, the agent, God, by reference to whom this event, according to some, is to be nonphysically but causally explained, is only in a very dubious sense subject to any laws at all, physical or otherwise.

However, I shall put aside these two difficulties and consider directly the question whether we have any legitimate inductive grounds for believing that the first event has a psychological explanation. For it is my distinct impression that we do not.

Certainly much of our own physical activity is due to our psychological condition and to events within our minds. But all these activities consist in doing something to the existing physical environment. They consist in rearranging the extant matter and in utilizing existing energy. We have no experience of creating something physical out of thin air, let alone out of absolute nothingness; nor do we have any experience of rearranging the existing material stuff by processes that generate activity without utilizing some form of existing energy. Even psychokinesis (moving objects at a distance from one's body through telepathic powers not dependent on an intervening physical medium), if not a sham, rearranges the existing physical world.

The first event, however, is one in which something comes into existence from nothing, or, if the first event is construed as the first thing that happens to some already existing stuff, then it is one which involves an initial input of activity, and thus the activity itself has come into existence out of nothing. Even if the universe started as a "perfect vacuum," in which spacetime started to expand creating actual particles out of virtual particles, the commencement of expansion has come into existence out of nothing. The first event, as it involves creation of something out of nothing, whether the something is matter, activity, energy, "expansion" or anything else, is thus fundamentally unlike any event with which we have had experience.

Often these facts, that the first event must have been unlike any event we have experienced, and must have involved creation *ex nihilo*, are advanced as reasons for saying that the cause of the first event must therefore be immaterial (supernatural, divine, etc.). But we can infer that the cause of the first event is immaterial only if and only after we have good reason for thinking the first event is caused. Unless we have good reason for thinking the first event is caused, then we never reach the second step of the argument, which is that this cause must be immaterial. However, the fact that the first event is so very unlike any event with which we have experienced undercuts the first step in the argument; that is, it removes the grounds for believing that the first event is caused. Since the first event is unlike the other events in our sample class, we cannot reason inductively that, since they (the events in our sample class) are explainable causally with reference either to physical or psychological factors, the first event also must be explainable causally.

My conclusion is that there is not an inductive warrant based on our experience with events as always having explanations, for saying that the first event must have an explanation. Though we are profoundly disposed to feel that the first event must have an explanation, there is nothing behind this feeling than force of habit.

The argument from design

These reflections may serve equally well to rule out as unsound any latter-day version of the argument from design. In the design-argument, the existence of an intelligent creator of the universe is inferred from the fact that the universe exihibits all the characteristics of a well-thought-out design. Such reasoning is often construed as inductive: every item we have encountered that displays a certain high degree of complexity and order has been the handiwork of an intelligent creator; therefore .every such item without exception, including the universe itself, is the handiwork of an intelligent creator.

However, once again, the universe as a whole is importantly different from the things in the sample class (i.e., the things we have experienced). For they, the things in the sample class, all consist of rearrangements of existing matter and energy; whereas the universe itself, if it is the creation of an intelligent agent, is or involves a creation *ex nihilo*, as I explained before.

It might be objected, however, that the design argument should be viewed as analogical in character rather than as a simple inductive generalization. The two kinds of reasoning are, of course, very similar, so similar that it is controversial among philosophers as to whether they really constitute different types of argumentation. In a simple inductive generalization one reasons that because such-and-such holds true of a sample of a class, the same holds true for all members of the class. In analogical reasoning the principle is that things that are known to be similar in certain ways must also be similar in certain other ways.

The argument from design, construed as an analogical argument, would therefore be that the universe is similar to items of human contrivance in that it, as well as they, display an orderliness in complexity, a fitting-together of parts to whole so that the whole functions as it does, etc.; therefore it must also be similar to them in having been the creation of an intelligent mind.

But the argument from design construed in this way as an analogical argument still fails because of the important difference between the terms of the comparison. Even if the similarities between objects of human contrivance, on the one hand, and the universe on the other, were far clearer than they are and were not subject to the infamous and inconclusive debate to which they in fact have been subject, these similarities could not overcome the weakness in the argument that is due to the fact that the universe, unlike any of the things with which it is compared, if it is a creation, is a creation *ex nihilo*.

Deductive grounds for thinking that the first natural event is explainable

There are, then, no sound inductive reasons for assuming that the first natural event must have an explanation. There is certainly a powerful psychological disposition to believe that it must, but a first natural event would seem to be so fundamentally dissimilar to all other events with which we have had experience that these events cannot be viewed as lending much support to the doctrine that the first natural event too has an explanation.

Further, it certainly seems that there are no valid deductive arguments that support the notion that a first natural event must have an explanation. There is no self-contradiction in such statements as "the first natural event does not have an explanation" or "the first natural event was uncaused." Thus, there really cannot be any deductive demonstration of the falsity of such statements.

Is an explanation of the first event even possible?

To review briefly, current cosmological theory and evidence strongly point to an absolute origin of the universe in the Big Bang and thus, perhaps, to a first natural event, an event that presumably could not have any explanation except one that makes reference to some non-physical form of causation. It is difficult to think that an event of such importance might just simply be an unexplainable accident; nevertheless, there are no compelling reasons, either deductive or inductive, for believing that it was more than this.

Further, it is unclear that there even could be an explanation of the first natural event. Such an explanation, as we have seen, would have to be of a psychological variety: an explanation that refers to the first event as having been caused by the desires or psychological states of, presumably, God. It would, in essence, have to say that the first natural event occurred because God wanted it to occur, or wished and willed it to occur, etc.

But in terms of any reasonable criteria for the appraisal of explanations, this "explanation" seems to me rather to fail. That is to say, I have misgivings as to whether it could even be counted as a genuine explanation. An explanation must, I think, in some way illuminate or enlighten us relative to the thing explained. But the explanation of the first event as due to God's willing or wishing it to happen seems quite unilluminating to me. My understanding of the first event is not enhanced or enlarged, in any way I can see, by the explanation. Were I offered a more penetrating analysis of the psychological factors in play in God's creative act, then I might form a different opinion of the explanation. To refer to an earlier example, one could, presumably, go quite some way toward understanding and explaining the lights around the house in terms of the psychological mechanisms underlying the owner's fears; but any attempted analysis of God's psyche would be bizarre and idle speculation.

Further, the explanation can be plugged in unthinkingly as an explanation of any phenomenon whatsoever. Why do carbon and hydrogen interact as they do? Because God wants them to. Why can't light escape from a black hole? Because God desires that it be that way. The explanation applies equally well, in other words, to any and every physical occurrence, and, accordingly, serve to explain none.

The explanation also cannot be used to make predictions. Being informed that the boy hurt his brother because he was deeply envious of him would enable one to make certain projections about other things the boy might do or say, especially if this explanation were amplified. But learning that the first event occurred because God willed it to occur does not enable one to predict anything about any other event. An explanation must have some sort of predictive value, it would seem, if it is to have explained something.

Finally, and closely related to this last point, the explanation of the first event as due to God's desires cannot be verified, or refuted. This indeed is precisely because the explanation does not lead to any predictions. There is no state of affairs that we might watch for such that, if it happens, then it confirms the explanation and if it does not happen, then it places the explanation in doubt.

So, on the whole, I am inclined to think that the words, "the Big Bang occurred because God wanted it to," fail to explain the Big Bang. Certainly the words may have some other purpose in human discourse than to explain; they may, for instance, function as an expression of awe and admiration and bewilderment with regard to the Big Bang. They may be a kind of shorthand for saying that there is a guiding intelligence to the universe, though it is mostly unclear to me in what sense the universe might be thought to be "guided."

And if the Big Bang, viewed as the first natural event, cannot be explained by reference to the will or desires of God, then, as I have indicated, it cannot be explained at all.

Is God required to sustain the universe?

Events are popularly conceived as of two kinds, those that last or endure for some period of time, and those that are instantaneous and therefore do not. A drive from Toledo to Detroit is an event of the first kind; the arrival at the Detroit city limit is an event of the second kind. "Events," as we defined and used that term in Part One, refers to the dimensionless events of the second kind.

It is not necessary, or even possible, to make reference to a sustaining cause in the explanation of non-enduring events. Immediately as they happen they have happened, and there is nothing to be sustained. But events that are conceived as lasting invite curiosity as to what sustains them or keeps them lasting. At the time of this writing, for example, there has been a severe and prolonged drought in Africa. This is an enduring event, and why it continues is a matter of great concern to those affected. Likewise, since the existence of the universe can itself be viewed as an enduring event, one may wonder what sustains it, and thus be led to think of God.

However, any event that lasts over time is in fact sustained only by the instantaneous events that comprise it. Indeed, there seem to be no scientific or philosophical reasons for postulating enduring events in the first place. At any given instant the matter in the universe is arranged in one way; at any other instant the arrangement is different; what we think of as an enduring event is but some sequence of such changes or events that is of interest or importance to us.

Philosophers have argued, nevertheless, that, for there to be changes of any sort, whether these be atomic or subatomic interactions or changes involving larger objects, at least some things must persist from moment to moment. For if, at every instant, *every* item in the universe were entirely new, there would not be *a* universe but a new universe each instant; things would not *change*, they would be replaced. As Kant observed, you cannot suppose that some things change without supposing that some things are permanent.

But even assuming that *objects,* if not events, endure or last for some period of time, it does not seem necessary to suppose that they require anything to "sustain" them. If an object changes, it is reasonable to wonder what caused that change. If it changes again it is reasonable to wonder what caused that change, too. But if, in the between-time, it doesn't change there is not a question as to what sustains the object. The object remains as it is not because something is acting on it, but precisely because nothing is acting on it.

In sum, neither with respect to the origination of the universe nor with respect to its continuation does the call for an explanation have any meaning that I can understand.

Conclusion

In the next chapter, my father states his belief that the universe is self-sustaining; thus, we agree that God is not required to explain the continuation of the universe. However, his view on the origination of the universe, as it bears on the question of God's existence, is, I think, radically different from my own. My own view is that, if there has been an absolute beginning of the universe, that beginning just was, without explanation. In this sense the coming to be of the universe I regard as having been a matter of happenstance. However, when I say that the universe just happened, without explanation, I really am only saying something about a concept, and not about the universe. I am saying that the concept of explanation, in reference to the origination of the universe, has no intelligible application that I can see. For the reasons I have tried to present, those who seek an explanation of the first event, and those who "explain" the initial event as caused by God, do not use the concept of explanation in a way that I understand.

27

What I Think

Ralph J. Moore

I think that there is a slightly better than even chance that God exists and that he willed and caused the Little Bomb to be and to explode in the Big Bang, which is our expanding universe, of which we are a part. If I were on a jury impanelled to render a verdict as to whether God exists and did this, on the basis of evidence and argument as assembled in this book, and if the jury were instructed as in a civil case to render its verdict upon the preponderance of the evidence, I would find that there is a God who created the cosmos in this manner.

If, however, the jury were instructed, as in regard to a verdict of guilty in a criminal case, to find that God exists and was the cosmic creator only if this had been proved beyond a reasonable doubt, my verdict would be against the divine existence and divine cosmic creation. That is, I am not convinced beyond a reasonable doubt that God exists.

The verdict of a jury is always only conjecture upon evidence and argument, more or less approximating the truth as the case may be. The evidence always is merely hearsay to the jurors though it be eye-witness testimony. That is, jurors have only heard the evidence and have not themselves seen, heard, smelled, felt or otherwise sensually observed that to which the evidence relates except insofar as they have viewed exhibits or places; and the relevancy or weight of viewed exhibits and places depends upon what the jurors have heard. Consequently, jurors do not know, of their own knowledge (as lawyers say), that what they find to be true is actually true. After jurors make their finding, however, it is treated for legal purposes as though what they found is actually true; that is, that the defendant is either guilty or innocent of the offense charged or that either the allegations of the plaintiff or those of the defendant are true.

Likewise, on the basis of evidence and argument, there can be only conjecture, more or less true as the case may be, as to the existence of

God and his creation of the world. My personal conjecture in this regard is as I have stated. If I were to bet, I would bet that he exists and was the creator, but I would want almost even odds.

Most certainly, I think that the evidence shows beyond a reasonable doubt that the universe is self-sustaining and will run its course, without any divine intervention, whether or not God created it. Nor does he affect in even the slightest way the course of our lives or of any life in the universe, I am sure.

If God exists, he would not punish me for finding against his existence and his creation of the universe. Nor would he reward me for finding otherwise. Why should he punish or reward me for using the brain he has given me, to make my bet, whether I bet right or wrong? That brain tells me to mind it and not what others say or have said, in all my mental decisions, though it counsels me to give due weight in my mental decisions to what others know and think. It would be especially monstrous of God to throw me in hell for honestly betting that he does not exist and did not create the universe.

Blaise Pascal deemed it prudent to wager that God exists, though, he thought, God's incomprehensibility makes it impossible to know whether or not he does. Pascal reasoned that by betting and believing that God exists we may win his favor and that by not believing in him we may incur punishment by him. Nor have we anything to lose by betting and believing that he exists. This is a shabby basis for belief in God or for religion or morality, though it may be a popular one.

Why do I think that the preponderance of evidence and argument is that God exists and is the creator of the universe? I do so because the great consensus of scientific opinion, by which I am persuaded, is that the universe is the Big Bang from the Little Bomb, and because more likely than not there is not enough matter in the universe to cause it to stop expanding and to contract back into another dimensionless or almost dimensionless Little Bomb like that from which it erupted. It seems that the universe will go on expanding forever, though this is by no means certain. This want of certainty is one reason why the evidence only slightly predominates that there is a God who is the cosmic creator.

If in my lifetime it should be scientifically ascertained that there is enough matter and so enough self-gravitational force in the universe to stop its expansion and to cause its collapse, then I shall think that the preponderance of the evidence is against the existence of God. That is, the crucial fact determinative of the preponderance of the evidence on the issue of God's existence and his being the creator is the amount of matter in the universe, a fact that we do not now know, though it seems probable that there is insufficient matter to reverse cosmic expansion. This, however, is by no means certain.

Suppose, contrary to what seems true, that there is enough matter and density to reverse cosmic expansion. Then the universe under its self-gravitation eventually will begin to contract and will continue to do so until it plunges into a black hole and at the bottom of the black hole becomes a dimensionless or almost dimensionless Little Bomb like that from which the current Big Bang exploded. If this new Little Bomb has no dimension in space or time whatsoever, then space and time will no longer exist. Or, if this new Little Bomb has barely some dimension in space and time, then it can hardly be true that space and time began with the Big Bang, although it could be said that space and time begin anew with each successive Big Bang in an oscillating universe.

This new Little Bomb into which our immense current physical universe will have pulled itself by its self-gravity presumably then will explode into a new universe, just as that Little Bomb that exploded into this present physical universe did so, for the same unknown physical reason. Presumably, also, if this present physical universe thusly will be succeeded by another, it was also similarly preceded by another infinite succession of universes. Then, if all this be true, the oscillating-universe theory that there is an infinite succession of Big Bangs and Big Crunches is sound. This being the case, that is, if the universe in its oscillation has always existed and always will exist, the existence of God cannot be based on his creation of the physical universe.

I shall first discuss the preponderance of the evidence as to whether God exists and is the creator, if the physical universe began with the Little Bomb exploding in that Big Bang and if the explosion was not caused by anything material. I shall then discuss the preponderance of the evidence on the issue, if the universe is infinite and oscillates continually between a Big Bang and a Big Crunch.

If no material cause of the universe

It seems true on the basis of the great consensus of scientific opinion that the physical universe began with the Little Bomb exploding in the Big Bang; that matter, energy, time and space began with the inception of the Little Bomb; and that the Little Bomb and its explosion were not caused by anything physical or material. By "physical" and "material" I mean the same, and in the following discussion will use the word, "material." I shall also use "material" as including radiation and energy as well as matter and anti-matter.

The issue, if the material universe was not caused by anything material, is whether it was caused by anything immaterial or was uncaused and just happened. The preponderance of the evidence on the issue, thus defined, is that the material universe was caused by something immaterial, which I call God, and that it did not just happen or, in other words, emerge without cause from nothingness.

All physical evidence, including our experience, observation and the credible testimony of others as to the material universe, is that anything material has been caused by something else that is material. By "anything material" I mean any material thing or material event. The issue we are addressing now is what made the Little Bomb and its explosion occur and not what makes the Big Bang continue to be.

I do not mean to be technical in my use of the word "cause." By it I mean what appears to be the relationship between cause and effect in the popular mind, whether or not in philosophy or physics it is something else, such as what usually happens though we cannot prove it invariably happens.

To repeat, all material evidence is that material things and material events are caused by material things. I shall represent the causing thing as C, that caused as E, and the causal relationship between them as R. Symbolically, then, all material evidence is that C→R→E, meaning that any material thing or event is caused by something material.

If C is deleted in my symbolic representation of causation, I still have →R→E. I choose to put a question mark where C is deleted, so that ?→R→E. Eliminating C does not automatically eliminate R insofar as E is concerned. Supplying the question mark for C is my symbolic representation that all material evidence is that any material thing or material event, including the inception of the Little Bomb and its explosion in the Big Bang, has a causal relationship as the effect, and the question mark questions what the cause is. That is, every material thing or event, on the basis of all material evidence, must be caused, even though all material evidence is that every material thing or event has been caused, by something material. In other words, all the material evidence indicates the necessity of causation in itself, for any material thing or material event. Therefore, the universe must have been caused, the preponderance of the evidence signifies, by something immaterial (other than material) rather than be uncaused. My use of symbols is meant to represent, and not to prove this.

The following analogy may illustrate my argument. Suppose that there is a virgin birth of a man, there being conclusive evidence that fertilization of the egg occurred but was not caused by a sperm. Our past experience would induce us to look for some cause. If there were no evidence of any physical cause, we would continue to search for such evidence, perhaps in the direction of psychosomatic inducement of the fertilization through some not understood physiological capability. Sceptics would hardly look for a divine fertilization of the egg. Initially, I wouldn't. But the point that I wish to make is that all our experience would lead us to think that the birth somehow was caused rather than that it just happened and was uncaused. The preponderance of the physical evidence is that the birth was somehow caused rather than uncaused, even though all physical evidence is that human beings are produced only through the fertilization of a human egg by a human sperm.

Why should I look for a divine creator of a universe without material cause, if I would expect not to find a divine cause of a virgin birth? The answer is that despite that expectation, I would, indeed, look for an immaterial cause rather than assume that there was no cause for the pregnancy, given that there was no material cause for it.

I buttress my argument by the fact that a causal relationship, when it occurs, is something in itself and not nothing. It is supplementary to the causor, i.e., that which causes and usually is called the "cause." That is, a material thing continues to be a material thing though it does not cause another material thing or material event. It becomes a causor when there is a material causal relation with an effect. For example, a 100-mile-an-hour wind continues to be that though it does blow my tree down. If it blows my tree down, the wind is the causor, that is, the cause, the tree falling is the effect, and the causal relation is a material existent.

Why then should nothing be substituted for a causal relationship if the cause that always has been in the relationship is eliminated? Symbolically, if C is eliminated, why should R also be eliminated, so that E stands alone, uncaused? Thus, the preponderance of the evidence is that the universe had an immaterial origin, if it had no material origin, rather than that it was uncaused, just happening.

I realize that opponents of my argument may contend that it involves a nonsequitur: that from the fact that everything material has a *material* cause I have inferred that it has a cause, immaterial if a material cause is impossible. My reply has been that the unexcepted material causation of material things and material events has always involved causation as well as a cause. Thus, in the unprecedented instance, that of the Big Bang, where there is no material cause of material event, the preponderance of evidence, indeed "all" the evidence, is that it was still caused. Of the two alternatives, then, immaterial cause or no cause, all the material evidence is that there was an immaterial cause. However, I reduce "all" to "preponderance" because my reasoning involves admittedly some weakness in inferring causal relationship as a self-existent from our experience of material causation.

Accordingly, if I were on a jury to try the issue now in question, I would find that by a preponderance of the evidence the God-Creator exists. Or, if I were betting on the issue, I would bet that this is the case. I am calling the immaterial cause of the material universe, which I have inferred from the preponderance of the evidence, the "God-Creator." Whether or not we can rationally attribute to this God-Creator intelligence and other attributes, anthropomorphic and otherwise, I shall later discuss.

If the universe oscillates infinitely

In the event that science someday should determine that there is sufficient matter and density in the material universe eventually to turn the Big Bang into a Big Crunch, then it would seem that the material universe is an uncaused infinitely oscillating material universe, but that every material thing and material event in it are caused to occur by some other material thing or material event in it. That every material thing and event in it are caused to occur by something else in it that is material has always been true according to all material evidence, and inferentially would always be true in an infinite universe.

Obviously, the infinity of the material universe, if it is infinite, precludes an immaterial God as its cause, but it has been argued that its infinity would not preclude God as its cause of continuing to be. There is, however, neither any material evidence nor any immaterial evidence of an immaterial God. Nor is there any credible testimony of any such evidence. Nor can the existence of an immaterial God be demonstrated by any ontological argument.

Furthermore, the material universe, whether it is finite or infinite, strongly appears, on the basis of all evidence as viewed by modern science, to be wholly self-sustaining notwithstanding extensive uncertainty and unpredictability in the subatomic world. Even though the universe might have developed differently than it has, whether after its origin in the Big Bang if it thus originated, or during the course of its infinity if it is infinite, the cause of its continuance obviously is within itself.

An intellectual God

It is only by the slimmest margin that the preponderance of evidence favors a finding that the material universe was created by something immaterial, which I have called "God." The crucial fact is that the material universe appears to lack enough matter and density to have enough self-gravity eventually to stop expanding and to collapse back into a Little Bomb. This crucial fact, however, is by no means certain.

Is this God, this immaterial something that caused the Big Bang, something like human intelligence? The preponderance of the material evidence in this material universe favors an affirmative answer. To regard God as intelligent or as being possessed of something like human intelligence is to make him anthropomorphic, but it is also to make human beings God-like. That something like divine intelligence should after billions of years emerge from matter on this tiny and inconspicuous planet is amazing. Nevertheless, that matter divinely created contains the potentiality to produce intelligence is understandable. Our intelligence is an imprint of our maker, whom I wager exists for reasons I have stated.

Human intelligence has emerged from matter; and thought by the human brain, that is, mind, like the brain itself, is wholly material. The divine intelligence, on the other hand, is the cause, and not the effect of matter. It is wholly immaterial. I refer to the divine property resembling human intelligence as "divine intelligence" though it must differ in extent and nature from human intelligence.

I think that the immaterial creator is divine intelligence because of the resemblance of the material universe in its orderliness, in its whole and in its parts, to design in human artifacts. I accept the teleological argument as persuasive as to God's intelligence, if he exists as I wager that he does.

Moreover, the human experience is that by our intelligence chiefly, though aided and motivated by our emotional and other properties, we accomplish God-like feats in the manipulation and arrangement of our environment and of our society and ourselves, though some of these are evil in that they are either environmentally destructive or destructive of ourselves. Of course, whatever is environmentally destructive is also destructive of us, and vice versa. It is reasonable, furthermore, since human intelligence alone has made possible the vast creation of artifacts out of human environment, to infer from that that the divine immateriality possesses and used intelligence or something like it, infinitely greater than that of humanity, in causing the Little Bomb and its explosion in the Big Bang.

We enjoy what seems to us to be God's or nature's benevolence, despite sufferings. His favor, however, if it is his, is exceedingly indirect, coming to us through cosmic expansion and evolution from the Little Bomb. Beyond this, I cannot conjecture as to whether or not God, if he exists, is possessed of affections like those of human beings, or why he created this self-sustaining universe, if he did. Others may do so, I hope with justification.

My son's argument that the Big Bang or any origination of the universe *ex nihilo* is inexplicable is unassailable except that the slight weight of the evidence justifies my wager, I think, that the coming to be of the universe in this manner, is its creation by an intelligence whose benevolence is manifest.

28

Conclusion

We have stated what we think about God and about the origin and sustenance of the universe, relating what we think to our portrayal of the universe in Part One. Now we invite you, readers, to think about your own conclusions in these matters, relating what you think to your views of the universe.

Your views, undoubtedly, have been formed by your own lifelong experience, reading and thinking. We hope that what we have said has contributed in some appreciable measure to the mental picture that you have of the interiority of matter and of radiation and of the weaving of matter and radiation on the expanding loom of spacetime; and has contributed also to your thinking about God and about the origin and sustenance of the universe in relationship to that mental picture.

Our goal has been to follow the advice of Paul and Newton to look for God in his works. But in that quest we have also looked for an alternative to God; and, if there is an alternative, then we have been examining the works of that alternative.

Have we found anything conclusive, persuasive or helpful? One of us found reason for betting that there is a God. The other of us found reason for thinking that the universe just happened and has no explanation. We both are convinced that it is self-sustaining since its inception. Neither of us has any fear of punishment after death for honestly thinking as we do. We think that God, if he exists, most certainly is just and will not punish anyone for his or her honest thoughts about him. At the same time, we think it impossible to know the mind of God, if he exists. One of us thinks, however, that the Big Bang is reason for betting that God is intelligence or something like it in an infinitely high degree.

We know that your conclusions, beliefs and convictions about God and about the origin and sustenance of the universe, and about the impact of modern scientific cosmology on the traditional proofs of God's existence are affected, as ours probably are, not only respectively by what reason tells you and us but by how you and we feel. Indeed, some of you may will to believe in God, irrespective of proof or disproof of his existence.

We suggest to you that in your thinking and feeling you consider, in relation to traditional arguments that God exists and created and sustains the universe, or in your will to believe irrespective of proof, the following aspects of the cosmos as now portrayed by science.

In regard to the ontological argument

(1) The logical immunity of the argument to cosmology.

The argument is unaffected by the cosmos or changing scientific portrayal of it. The argument, however, has been logically refuted by Aquinas, Hume and Kant, rightfully we think. However, eminent philosophers still espouse it.

(2) The probability of life elsewhere.

The probability is of intelligent life in many, perhaps millions, of places in the universe and of belief in the ontological argument in these places, as windows through which God can be conclusively known in the mind's eye. This has nothing to do with the intrinsic validity of the argument, but might have extrinsic significance to some in that God has provided these windows through which he can be seen mentally, not only on earth, but elsewhere where vital intelligence flourishes.

(3) Finding God in the mind.

Is it not surprising, if the ontological argument is valid, that God should conclusively be found in the mind of a mammal on a planet that is less than a speck in the universe, when it is so difficult, at least for many, to find him otherwise in the entire immense range of his works, if he indeed exists? This, of course, logically has nothing to do with the intrinsic validity of the argument, but it has much to do with probability, however probability is understood. Is it not even more surprising that God should reveal himself in this mode, not only on earth, but in millions of places elsewhere, if he does? Of course, if you are a believer in him, it may not be at all surprising to you that he thus reveals himself on earth and elsewhere.

In regard to the teleological argument

_ (1) The repetition throughout the universe of patterns of intergalactic gaseous space, galaxies, nebulae, stars and stellar systems.

On the exterior of the fabric of matter and of radiation there appears a repetitions of patterns, remindful of repetition of patterns used by fabricators of fabrics and weavers of rugs. Today our astronomers are searching for repetition of the basic pattern of our solar system in other stellar systems. In planetary systems we find extensive repetition of satellite, geological and other patterns. On earth we observe a multiplicity of repetitions of patterns, including those of ourselves.

Discovery in this century of the vastness of the universe has not changed the repetitiveness of patterns of matter and of radiation throughout it.

The cause of this repetitiveness seemingly is implicit in the original stuff of the Big Bang, or in the original stuff with which the universe otherwise began, or in the stuff of an oscillating or steady-state universe if either of these is the true nature of total material reality. That is, the cause is the basic interaction or interactions of truly elementary particles, the kinds of which probably are no more than two and possibly only one.

A question for you, readers, then, is this: Is the original or basic stuff of the universe thus coded by something material that we don't understand; by something immaterial that we don't understand or that you perhaps think that you understand; or just by chance?

Is there any indication of purpose in the repetitiveness of macroscopic patterns throughout the universe? Is purpose evidenced otherwise?

(2) Similarity in evolution of galaxies and stars.

This similarity is related obviously to repetitiveness of macroscopic patterns, and the same may be said about it as has been said in regard to repetitiveness being evidence of a divine Creator.

(3) The nuclear furnaces in the cores of stars that emit heat, light and other electromagnetic radiation.

In the solar system the light and heat make life and intelligence on earth possible. Is there purpose in the mechanics, classic and quantum, coded into the stuff of the universe at its beginning?

(4) The Gaea hypothesis.

Does the seeming intent of earth's biosphere to preserve and foster itself denote purpose coded into the initial ingredients of the Little Bomb that exploded in the Big Bang? Is there also a cosmic biosphere perpetuating itself by seeding life in suitable places for it in the universe and thereby manifesting a divine purpose?

(5) Starlight and other electromagnetic radiation.

Are they intended, not only to illuminate the universe for living and intelligent creatures, but also to serve as a language by the interpretation of which, though spectroscopy or otherwise, intelligent beings can learn enormously about the universe for billions of lightyears into the distancepast, in addition to what they learn about it by observing it by eyesight and by optical, radio and other telescopy?

(6) The four interactions of leptons and quarks, by which the universe is made.

As said before, the process is probably manifestive of a near or actual unity of interaction of particles. Does the simplicity of the process in the weaving of the vast and complex fabric of matter and of radiation on the expanding loom of spacetime persuade or convince you that a divine Engineer of infinite intelligence probably or possibly coded the particles and devised the process? We are not persuaded or convinced, though on other grounds one of us bets that there is a God. If there is, that he is the Engineer is hardly questionable.

In regard to the cosmological argument
(1) The Big Bang.

Does the beginning of spacetime, matter, radiation and everything in the Little Bomb that exploded in the Big Bang, or possibly in a somewhat different process, persuade or convince you that possibly, probably or certainly an immaterial God created the universe, or that it was otherwise caused or that its origin is inexplicable and a happenstance? Do you agree with us that once instituted, the universe has been and will be self-sustaining as long as it endures?

Or are you disposed to think or believe that the universe always has been and will be, or that it renews itself perpetually in Big Bang and Big Crunch alternation? Or is it your view that God created and sustains the universe, whether or not it began in some fashion or is infinite in duration?

Or are you a believer because, like James, you will to believe or because, like Kant, you postulate God on human ethicalness, or because, like Unamuno and Gardner, you predicate your belief on your desire for immortality?

(2) The causation and contingency of everything in the material universe.

The cosmological argument asserts that everything in the universe is caused and contingent. Thus, there are regressions of cause and contingency back in time to the Big Bang and into the interiority of matter and of radiation to the basic interactions or interaction of leptons and quarks or of particles of only one kind, if leptons and quarks are different manifestations of that one kind of particles. Do you agree that beyond the Big Bang and beyond the unitary, or almost unitary, interaction of a few kinds or only one kind of particles the chains of causation or contingency must begin with an immateriality that must be

God, as he is conceived in the Christian, Mohammedan and Judeo tradition?

We, the authors, do not subscribe to the cosmological argument of Aquinas, although one of us bets, on ground he has explained, that there is a God.

In regard to justification of belief without proof

(1) The immunity of belief without proof to modern cosmology.

Attempted justifications of believing in God without proof of his existence do not assume any particular view as to the nature of the material universe. The changed picture of the cosmos afforded by recent science does not show these justifications to be invalid. Likewise it does not provide them with support.

(2) The immunity of belief without proof to philosophical argument.

Philosophy does not demonstrate the invalidity of attempted justifications of belief without proof. Yet it is not unreasonable to reject such attempted justifications, as we did in Chapter 25. Further, if it is justifiable to believe without proof, then it is also justifiable to believe, again without proof, in the falsity of what is believed in the first instance.

Final comment:

There are doubtless many other considerations in regard to the cosmos as depicted by modern science, in addition to those presented above and elsewhere in our book, that might govern you, readers, in your evaluation of the traditional arguments that God exist; in your beliefs about God and the origin and sustenance of the cosmos; in your own relationship to God, if he exists, and to the cosmos, which does exist; and in your entitlements, obligations and responsibilities in that relationship.

Bibliography

Books Treating Science Philosophically in Relation to Cosmology, Religion, Life and Humanity

Adler, Mortimer: *How to Think About God: A Guide for the 20th Century Pagan*. New York, Macmillan Publishing Co., Inc., 1980.

Barrow, John D., and Tipler, Frank J.: *The Anthropic Cosmological Principle*. Oxford, Clarendon Press; New York, Oxford University Press, 1986.

Billingham, John, Ed.: *Life in the Universe*. London, The MIT Press Cambridge, Mass., 1981.

Chaisson, Eric: *Cosmic Dawn: The Origins of Matter and Life*. Boston, Toronto, Little, Brown and Company, 1981.

Davies, Paul: *God and the New Physics*. New York, Simon and Schuster, 1983.

Davies, Paul: *The Edge of Infinity: Where the Universe Came From and How It Will End*. New York, Simon and Schuster, 1981.

Feinberg, Gerald, and Shapiro, Robert: *Life Beyond Earth: The Intelligent Earthling's Guide to Life in the Universe*. New York, William Morrow and Company, Inc., 1980.

Ferris, Timothy: *The Red Limit: The Search for the Edge of the Universe*. New York, Quill, 1983.

Gardner, Martin: *The Whys of a Philosophical Scrivener*. New York, William Morrow and Company, Inc., 1983.

Gribbin, John: *Genesis: The Origin of Man and the Universe*. New York, Delecorte Press/ Eleanor Friede, 1981.

Harrison, Edward R.: *Cosmology: The Science of the Universe*, Cambridge, London, New York, 1981.

Hoyle, Sir Fred, and Wickramasinghe, N.C.: *Evolution from Space, A Theory of Cosmic Creationism*. New York, Simon and Schuster, 1981.

Kolenda, Konstantin: *Cosmic Religion: An Autobiography of the Universe*. Prospect Heights, Illinois, Waveland Press, 1987.

Küng, Hans: *Does God Exist? An Answer for Today*. New York, Doubleday and Company, Inc., 1980.

Narlikar, Jayant: *Introduction to Cosmology*. Boston, Jones and Bartlett Publishers, Inc., 1983.

Rolston, Holmes, III: *Science and Religion: A Critical Survey*. New York, Random House, 1987.

Sagan, Carl: *Cosmos*. New York, Random House, 1980.

Sagan, Carl, and Shklovskii, L.S.: *Intelligent Life in the Universe*. San Francisco, London, Amsterdam, Holden-Day, Inc., 1966.

Seielstad, George A: *Cosmic Ecology: The View from the Outside In*. Berkeley, University of California Press, 1983.

Toulmin, Stephen: *The Return to Cosmology: Postmodern Science and the Theology of Nature*. Berkeley, University of California Press, 1982.

Wagoner, Robert V., and Goldsmith, Donald W.: *Cosmic Horizons: Understanding the Universe*. San Francisco, W.H. Freeman and Company, 1982.

Subject Index

Action at a distance, 62, 63, 77
Analogous argument as to God, 218, 219, 281
Andromeda, 93, 94, 124, 131–141, 147
 birth process, 166
 distance past of, 22, 132, 138
 Milky Way and, 94, 126, 131–141
Angular momentum
 black hole, of, 177
 electron orbital, 70, 71
 galactic, 181, 183
 particle spin, 85
Anthropic principle, 199–202, 236
Antimatter, 44, 45, 239, 240
 annihilation, particle and antiparticle, 44, 45, 61, 180
 antineutrinos, 80
 antiparticles, 44, 45, 61, 76
 antiquarks, 79
Asteroids, 167
Astronomical unit, 18, 169
Atoms, 65–73

Basic interactions and forces, 8, 47, 57–63, 76, 98
Belief in God, justification of, 8, 231, 253–273, 295
Big Bang, 9, 25–29, 63, 77, 91–96, 289, 290
 background radiation proof of, 27, 28, 133
 Biblical story of creation and, 29
 cosmological argument and, 244, 245, 248, 276, 289, 290
 expanding universe, as, 11, 25, 32, 91–96, 237
 explainable, whether or not, 276–284

Biosphere
 cosmic, 203–205
 terrestrial, see Gaea hypothesis
Black holes, 25, 173–191, 238
 galactic, see Galaxies
 Milky Way, in, see Milky Way
 radiation from or caused by, 178–181
 stellar, see Stars
Blue shift, 12, 13, 155
Brahman, 210
Brownian motion, 66
Buddhism, 212

Causation, 275–285, 290, 291
 cosmological argument, in, 243–251, 275–285, 290, 291
Classical mechanics, 49, 50, 238, 247
 astronomy and, ix, 1, 238
 subatomic and, 51
Comets, 167, 168, 171
Compacted stars, 148, 149, 162, 173–191
Complimentarity, 52, 53
Confucianism, 211
Consciousness, justification of belief on, 269–270
Contingency and necessity
 cosmological argument, in, 243–252
Copleston-Russell debate, 249, 250, 275, 276
Cosmic rays, 75, 76, 82–84
Cosmological argument as to God, 243–252, 264, 275–294, 298, 299
 ontological argument, resort to, 248, 249, 254
 scientific cosmology and, 243–245, 275–277

Vatican I, 265
Vishnu, 210

Wager as to God and creation, 256, 261,
   262, 287–294
 Pascal's, 261, 262, 288
War, strife and God, 259
White holes, 25, 173, 186, 187
White-dwarf stars, 148–152, 157–159, 162

World lines of things in spacetime, 34,
   35

X-ray
 background radiation in space, 115
 bursters, 182, 183
 pulsars, 189
 radiation generally, *see* Radiation

Year, galactic or cosmic, 134

Index of Names of Persons